How to Master
Change
in
Your Life

Praise for
How to Master Change in Your Life

"Mary Carroll Moore's personal experiences in surviving cancer, bankruptcy, and a host of other major life changes make her eminently capable to write on this topic. Her book presents many useful spiritual tools for anyone who wishes to move from victim to spiritual survivor."

> Harvey Diamond
> Author, *Fit for Life* and *You Can
> Prevent Breast Cancer!*

"A fine testament to the resilience of the human spirit."

> Gay Hendricks
> Author, *Conscious Loving* and
> *At the Speed of Life*

"Mary Carroll Moore took me gently by my heart and led me through her life of victories and defeats . . . to a self-assurance which can be found by anyone. For those of us who want to take our individual lives to a higher level of creativity and joy."

> Taylor Hay
> Author, *Synergetics, Your Whole Life
> Fitness Plan*

"More than just about dealing with change that is forced upon you, this book gently helps you recognize areas where you *need* to change for personal and spiritual growth. Very enlightening and inspiring exercises."

> Jane Nelsen, Ed.D., MFCC
> Author, *Understanding: Eliminating
> Stress and Finding Serenity in Life
> and Relationships*

"Your exercises and stories provide an inspirational and practical approach to the use of spirituality for enhancement of daily life."

> Michael Newton, Ph.D.
> Author, *Journey of Souls*

"Your personal experience on coping with, and surviving change, makes you an insightful expert on this topic."

> Leslie Myers, Soundworks Radio
> Bellingham, Washington

"We all face change every day and now thanks to you we know how to deal with it. Keep up the good work."

William J. Horan, "The Secrets of Success," Woodbury, New York

"Turns the difficult times we all experience from tragedy into opportunity. Would that we all had this grasp of being on a spiritual path."

Jim Burns, Editor, *Los Angeles Times* syndicate

"Practical help for facing difficult life changes. Uplifting, exciting, and just what I've been looking for!"

Lessandra MacHamer
Television producer

"Shows how to align and harmonize our work and spiritual lives, uncovering our unique and special purpose. What could be more important?"

Bryan Mattimore
Author, *99% Inspiration,* and contributing editor, *Success* magazine

"Spiritual techniques for meeting everyone's greatest challenge: change, today's increasingly rapid phenomenon."

Alan Caruba, Editor, *Bookviews*

"This book has the wisdom of a *Celestine Prophecy* or an *Ageless Body, Timeless Mind,* in down-to-earth language. Read it one chapter at a time, preferably with a journal and pen handy, and watch your own turning points evolve."

Lorraine Buell, *Monthly Aspectarian* Chicago

"An honest, courageous look at painful, fearful, joyful change."

The New Times, Seattle, Washington

"Insightful, humorous and charming, a must read."

Leading Edge Review

"Change is a fact of life. . . . How we approach change is an important key to our happiness, success and spiritual growth. . . . In Moore's opinion, if we listen to our spiritual wisdom, change is always beneficial."

Stepping Up, Minneapolis, Minnesota

How to Master
Change
in
Your Life

Sixty-seven Ways to Handle Life's Toughest Moments

Mary Carroll Moore

ECKANKAR
Minneapolis, MN

How to Master Change in Your Life:
Sixty-seven Ways to Handle Life's Toughest Moments

The terms ECKANKAR, ECK, EK, MAHANTA, SOUL TRAVEL, and VAIRAGI, among others, are trademarks of ECKANKAR, P.O. Box 27300, Minneapolis, MN 55427 U.S.A.

Printed in U.S.A.

Edited by Joan Klemp and Anthony Moore

Author photo by The Studio Central

I am grateful to those authors and publishers who graciously granted permission to use excerpts from their works. These include:

> *You Can Heal Your Life,* Louise L. Hay, © 1984, 1987, Hay House, Carlsbad, CA.

> *99% Inspiration,* © 1994, Bryan W. Mattimore, Published by AMACOM, a division of American Management Association. All rights reserved.

Acknowledgements are continued in the bibliography.

Library of Congress Cataloging-in-Publication Data

Moore, Mary Carroll.
    How to master change in your life : sixty-seven ways to handle life's toughest moments / Mary Carroll Moore.
        p. cm.
    Includes bibliographical references.
    ISBN 1-57043-123-X (perfect bound : alk. paper)
    1. Spiritual life. 2. Change (Psychology)—Religious aspects.
3. Eckankar (Organization) 4. Moore, Mary Carroll. I. Title.
BL624.M6627 1997
299'.93 — dc21   96-46476
                                                  CIP

♾ The paper used in this publication meets the minimum requirements of the American National Standard for Information Sciences—Permanence of Paper for Printed Library Materials, ANSI Z39.48-1984.

CONTENTS

Star? 🌀 *Exercise: Writing Your Contract with Yourself about a Change* • A New Road 🌀 *Ask Yourself: How Can I Bring More Meaning into My Everyday Changes?*

ACKNOWLEDGMENTS

Many wonderful people contributed to this book. Thanks to Joanie for detailed feedback and research; Beverly and Linda for urging me deeper into my story writing; Bryan and Fran for great end-of-chapter questions; Dick, Jeanne, and Mary Lou for video help; all the friends and coworkers who shared their stories and exercises; new and old friends who wrote me so many wonderful letters about how my earlier book, *Turning Points: How to Handle Change in Your Life,* inspired and motivated them; Turning Points workshop participants for their ideas and inspiration; Joan and Peter for welcome acceptance of new ideas; and Harold for inspiration and guidance.

Mostly, I thank my husband, Tony, for years of loving support during the ups and downs of living with a working writer, and for the practical help of title and revision ideas and editing.

I have changed the names of private individuals in many of my stories where requested to protect their privacy. If any of these names belong to any person, living or dead, it is pure coincidence.

INTRODUCTION

I once read that the Chinese character for *crisis* means two things: "peril" and "opportunity." When we meet crisis and change in our lives, we have an opportunity. We can look for the blessings and personal growth the change brings. We can move forward in awareness of ourselves, our life's purpose, and the interweaving of events. In this way, change can be a starting point for a new and better passage through life.

I wrote this book to help myself—and you—find that passage.

This book is more than about getting what you want. This book is about discovering more about who you *really* are, and then getting what you *truly* want. Not what someone else wants for you or even what you might "think" you want. But about getting what the highest, best, and most mysterious part of yourself wants. Call that part of yourself whatever you wish—consciousness, self, Soul—it doesn't matter. What matters is that this real you confronts the challenges of life and wants the best out of life. A state of balance, order, and beauty that surpasses day-to-day pain and pleasure. This kind of poise, this happiness, is real.

All sincere philosophies, all religions, all paths point to this goal, this kind of excellence.

My own search for this excellence has led me through many adventures. By the time I reached thirty-nine, I'd experienced cancer, bankruptcy and business failure, marriage, divorce, and remarriage. Each change was hard, but it never failed to open a door in my life. I learned that within each change is its unique solution, the path we can travel to become stronger, closer to who we really are, closer to the person we want to become. Closer to that excellence.

This personal journey led me to redefine spirituality. Spirituality is not reserved for saints and clergy. It's not locked away in churches. It's right here, in our lives, every day. In my own religion, Eckankar, I've learned that this everyday spirituality underlies everything I do. Seeing it at work in my life has taught me to value the small changes as well as the big ones.

My personal journey has led me to become an ordained minister in Eckankar, yet I feel no less a part of everyday experiences. Rather, it's brought me closer to people. Their stories fill these pages. Each story shows me how we all have at least two things in common: we all have our own purpose for living, and no one is exempt from change.

In this book I'll introduce you to universal tools to make your journey easier. You can use these tools regardless of your viewpoint on life, whether you are agnostic, atheist, Christian, Jew, Muslim, or Hindu. If you want to live your life with more creativity, less fear, more joy, these tools are for you. These stories will echo your own.

Where are we going? Why? What does change teach us? What does happiness—inner happiness—have to do with change, survival, and the journey to find ourselves?

Turn the page. You'll find out.

1

From Panic to Power

Begin to See Order and Beauty within Change

A turning point is life's way of giving you a chance to move ahead spiritually, though you must reach for the gift yourself.

—Harold Klemp

1. FROM PANIC TO POWER

When I was nineteen I took a trip across the U.S. by myself. I drove a little VW bug I'd named Bessie.

It was my first car, bought after working all summer in a natural foods restaurant in Baltimore. The excitement of the trip was not knowing ahead of time which route I would take. I only knew I wanted to get to Texas to meet a friend the following week.

One afternoon I was driving through the rolling terrain of the Ozark foothills when the road emptied onto a lake. This was a surprise.

Across the lake I could see the pinpoint of highway continue. But how was I to get across?

I waited on the shore for about fifteen minutes. When cars behind me started lining up, I realized there was probably a ferry that operated on the lake and carried cars to the far side.

The ferry did arrive. I watched the other drivers move onto the railless platform. Part of me was afraid to drive my little car onto that ferry. What if a wind came up, and the lake turned choppy? I imagined one dip of the boat and the whole load of cars sliding off the edge.

But I needed to cross, and there was no other road. So I found a spot toward the middle, in back of a Cadillac from Missouri. As the ferry's engines began to grind, the boat slid back into the wide expanse of water.

I stayed in the car, still gripping the steering wheel, even though it was hot and the scant breeze through the open window barely touched the car's steamy interior. Noticing how the ferry moved so evenly across the lake reassured me.

Finally I opened the car door and stepped out to stretch, breathe deeply of the pine-scented air, and chat with other drivers who were also emerging from their cars.

People wish to be settled: only as far as they are unsettled is there any hope for them.

—Ralph Waldo Emerson

As the ferry moved past one of the lake's small islands, a panorama opened up before us. It was close to sunset, and the hills were turning purple. The sky was a deepening blue, almost indigo, with pine trees silhouetted against it.

I felt I was being touched by pure beauty, almost more than I could bear. I knew that moment was a turning point in my life.

The metaphors were obvious: coming to a significant crossroads at sunset—the ending of one cycle and the beginning of another. A road ending. Crossing unfamiliar territory to take up another. Fears surfacing as I cling to the familiar for a while until I am reassured that my passage was safe. Then I step out to breathe deeply.

Thinking back, I'm pretty sure there were road signs announcing the ferry dock ahead, but I never noticed. If I had paid attention to the signs, I would have been better prepared for the change.

There are many such crossroads in life. We make decisions every day, big and little. Some decisions lead us down one road and away from another. And we confront changes every day, big and little. They, too, will lead us down different paths. These significant and sometimes irreversible moments in our lives are what I call turning points.

Many of us have difficulty navigating these turning points. We may close our eyes in fear of the change. We may make the change too late. We may say, "I don't want to get off the road I've been traveling!" and grip the familiar even tighter.

But there is a way to become a coworker with change. Working in partnership with the ebb and flow of life, working from the highest viewpoint, the spiritual viewpoint, we can learn to see the hidden blessings in the major, and even the smallest, changes in our lives. We can begin to see the warnings of impending change and prepare for it. We can learn to flow with our turning points rather than struggle against them.

After all, there is one constant in life: change. We cannot escape change. It is inevitable.

To have success with change means smoother travel through major life shifts—birth, death, marriage, divorce. We can develop the spiritual skills required to move more easily through life's challenges.

The process is slow, sometimes the learning curve is steep. But it always takes us to the core of who we are and what we want from our lives. The following story is an example of how such a challenge—again, one in my work life—provided the chance I needed to move toward a new way of being.

If you don't live it, it won't come out of your horn.

—Charlie Parker, American jazz musician

Toward a New Way of Being

With the economy at a low point several years ago, there was no way I wanted to leave my comfortable job. But I had been experiencing a vague restlessness, anxiety, and health problems at work.

It was the first job I had held for longer than a few years. I loved my work, editing and compiling books for several authors, but suddenly I was feeling unhappy about Monday mornings and couldn't wait for weekends. I am the type of person who likes a lot of variety, and my tasks had provided the stimulation and interest I craved. Until now.

Work is love made visible.

—Kahlil Gibran

I also began to develop numbness and pain in my right arm which severely limited my time on the computer. My productivity was falling fast.

A change was needed. In the past, my first guess would have been: Time to move on. But what if I couldn't find as good a job? The economy was tough, and many friends had been looking for work for months. My freelance writing business, while healthy, was not bringing in enough to replace my salary. My husband and I had just bought a bigger house with a bigger mortgage. Besides, my work was valued and leaving could put the office in a very tight spot. All this spoke against leaving, but what else could life be trying to tell me?

My job is the only possible candidate for change, I thought. *My marriage, writing career, and other areas of my life are all in great shape.*

One night after a very frustrating day at work, with such discomfort in my right arm that computer time was limited to fifteen-minute stretches, I asked my husband if he thought I should leave my job. It seemed the only logical choice. He looked at me for a long moment then said, "It does seem you're ready to change something. But what if life is telling you to change yourself rather than your job?"

What did he mean, change myself? The idea both confused and scared me. But his startling question pushed me into a personal spiritual journey that changed my basic beliefs about change—as it literally changed my life.

CHANGING BASIC BELIEFS ABOUT CHANGE

In *Plain and Simple,* her wonderful book about living with the Amish, artist Sue Bender writes, "Perhaps each of us has a starved place, and each of us knows deep down what we need to fill that place. To find the courage to trust and honor the search, to follow the voice that tells us what we need to do, even when it doesn't seem to make sense, is a worthy pursuit."

Like Bender, I was seeking a way to change my life. I was following a voice that told me, "This isn't working anymore. You need to change something."

While I held to the way I had handled my life for so many years, I knew I needed to find that faint trail, to find the "voice that tells us what we need to do," and learn a new way of being.

You may have faced decisions like this. They usually feel big and frightening. This one felt bigger to me than just how I handled my job every day. It felt like a crossroads for my whole life, a major fork in the road, a turning point. It involved the kind of decisions whose consequences would take me down one road and away from another.

My husband's comment hinted that there was a

What is the use of running when we are not on the right road?

—German proverb

deeper belief system causing my pain and unhappiness. I needed to examine it carefully. I needed to find what aspect in my beliefs about work had led me to this crossroads.

But I hadn't a clue where to start.

So I did what I usually do when I'm clueless: I sat down, closed my eyes, and became still inside. Perhaps life would give me something to start with.

Lightly, a conversation with another woman on the editing team passed across my mind. Earlier that day we had been talking about a book I was working on; I had told her about my arm and how it was delaying delivery of the chapters. "What a relief," she had laughed. "I was having trouble keeping up with you!"

Always a speedy worker, I had a tendency to plan way ahead and fairly rush through my days. My belief for years had been: Faster equals better. The more quickly I could produce what was asked of me, the more efficient I felt. I often did several things at once, priding myself on my ability to juggle many tasks and still have a good output level. I was becoming quietly exhausted by this pace; deep down, though, I didn't know how else to do it.

Perhaps my pattern of rushing had been a benefit for a long time but had grown to be an obstacle: something that was not only causing me physical discomfort but was holding me back in other ways.

I decided to keep an eye out for more clues and insights about the situation. One came the very next day.

CHANGE YOUR FOCUS, CHANGE YOUR LIFE

I had arranged to spend my lunch hour shopping with two friends from the office. The drive took about twenty minutes, so we talked about work on the way. One woman chatted about how she was so glad to have me as a role model.

"What for?" I asked.

"Learning how to slow down," she said. I had told her nothing of the recent thoughts about slowing my pace that had emerged the night before.

She added that she used to feel like a machine at work, always busy producing. Now she saw how she was able to serve in her job in other ways, by just being there for people and taking the time to relax and pace herself better.

"You know, I've always valued that quality in you," she said, turning around in her seat to look at me. She saw me as calm, cool, and collected, managing my work well even in the midst of deadlines and occasional office panics. I rarely showed my own panic. But I felt far removed from the serenity she was talking about.

Even so, the timing of her comment was incredible. Life was definitely trying to tell me something.

An even more direct sign came the next morning. I had made an appointment with an acupuncturist about my arm, since the other avenues of medical doctors and chiropractors had not helped the pain and numbness. The first thing the acupuncturist asked when he looked at me was: "Have you been pushing too hard?"

OK, I thought, *enough is enough. I get the message.*

Life was trying so hard to tell me what I needed to change. With very blatant signals, life was telling me: *You don't need to quit your job, you need to change your approach to life.*

But if I slow down, I wondered, *will I still be a*

valued person? Will people respect my abilities? How do I begin?

First Step: Ask for Help

That night before I went to sleep, I wrote in my journal. I have kept a journal for many years, recording my dreams and experiences, and I often write down my goals and questions for life. "I know I need to change my pace," I wrote. "I know I am hurting myself by the speed at which I'm living. But I don't know how to navigate this turning point. Please help me tonight in my dreams."

Healing is a matter of time, but it is sometimes also a matter of opportunity.

—Hippocrates

Although I remember many of my dreams, the next morning I woke up with only a vague recall of three phrases. They kept drifting across my attention during the day. I knew they were the keys to making this important change.

The first was: Do everything with careful attention to detail. As soon as I began to pay attention to the small details and not to finishing each task as fast as I could, I realized I was slowing down. It was a natural thing. The second was: Enjoy the process, rather than the result. I realized I had been so result-focused, I had lost my enjoyment of my work. No wonder I was unhappy. The third was the most simple: When you find yourself feeling pushed or tense, breathe deeply.

Guidance

When I began to work on this book, my purpose was to show others how to approach turning points with a new attitude. Right away, life had given me a chance to practice what I was writing about. And it was offering guidance on how to navigate a turning point.

Ever since I was a child, I have believed that a force greater than myself helped me through each change. And I knew it would help me with the turning point I was facing now. Life, the universe, the higher power, God—whatever you call this force—acts for each person's higher good, and I believed this force was always my friend, no matter what I was going through. And like a good friend, it would only bring me what I needed to grow spiritually, what I needed to take the next step.

As I worked over the next two years, learning to slow down and pace myself better, I received even more guidance, signs that showed how life works with us, especially during times of change.

Every day, in every way, I am getting better and better.

—Émile Coué

OPPORTUNITY KNOCKS

Like crossing a strange lake on a ferry, I am often confronted with something I need to traverse in order to grow. An opportunity to become more of who I truly am.

Turning points often give me this kind of spiritual opportunity. They are a way to cross to the next road that awaits me, to take the next step in my personal spiritual growth. And each turning point is always preceded by signs that alert me to the coming change and gently prepare me.

Life is a series of these cycles of change, from childhood into old age. It's a natural journey we all undertake. But certain people are able to flow with this process, these cycles of growth and change, and make decisions and choose what to do. They realize that change is a part of life that must be embraced.

Rather than being victimized by change, they see the options in life and are intrigued by the opportunities of turning points.

So what brings this healthy acceptance of change and the natural integration of it into your life?

I recently led a workshop on turning points at a local university. To give everyone a quick experience with change and their reaction to it, I asked each participant to pick a different seat in the room and move to it.

Will you, won't you, will you, won't you, will you join the dance?

—Lewis Carroll

It's a fairly unusual teaching tool, and I was prepared for a lot of grumbling. I had waited until about ten minutes into the session, when everyone was comfortable, books and papers spread out around them. I waited until they had settled in, chatting with the people at their table.

The change was annoying for most—unexplained and unreasonable. I watched silently as most people moved. Some didn't.

After they resettled, I asked the group to tell me what the change was like. What were their reactions?

"I was upset; I'd just picked the best seat in the room. No way I wanted to move."

"Why is she doing this?"

"I liked where I was. It's inconvenient."

"Maybe this'll be interesting, exciting, an adventure."

The answers ran the gamut, from feeling a victim, to slightly uneasy, to positively exhilarated. And that's how change is for most of us: upsetting, inconvenient, sometimes exciting.

I asked each participant to rate his or her response to change on a scale of 1 to 10, with 1 being "Change really bothers me" and 10 being "I handle change gracefully." Most participants gave themselves a score of 2 or 3. And they wanted to do better. They saw their current attitude toward change — and where they would like it to be.

In order to bring the benefits of turning points into our lives, we have to be able to see ourselves as cocreators of change rather than victims of it.

A couple came up to me after the workshop and told me that the moving seats exercise was very powerful for them. At first, the husband confided, he had planned to sit with his wife for the workshop because she was shy and he didn't know how she'd do in a group of strangers. By having to change seats she was put in the position of meeting others, and she opened up much more during the three hours than she would have otherwise. He, on the other hand, was free to pay attention to his own needs during the workshop rather than caring for hers. For both of them, it had been a huge success. And it all began with the discomfort of imposed change.

VICTIM OF CHANGE?

Unlike change that is imposed upon us by outside forces, we do better with changes we choose ourselves. This is because we feel more in control of the timing and pace of the change. But still there is risk involved. Especially for those who feel they are the victims of change.

Victims are immobilized by a dragging-the-feet kind of fear. They cannot see any possible future beyond the present one. They cannot take the action needed to envision, much less take a step toward, what they

Adversity is the first path to Truth.

—Lord Byron

*We must take
charge of our
own lives; each
one of us must
act to restore the
balance.*

—Duane Elgin

want. An attitude of helplessness is the victim's calling card: Life is out to get me. This attitude leaks through cheerful facades and determined attempts to succeed. It is a core belief that many people grow up with. It holds them back.

Change always surprises and distresses the victim.

There's a payoff for being the victim. You get to complain. I know because I've done my share. I've lain facedown and let life run right over me, all the time whining, "It's not fair." But after a while, that kind of scene gets pretty old. Not only does it hurt, playing the victim keeps you from looking around and seeing the turning points life is giving you. It blinds you to new opportunities.

In the victim role, there is often an unconscious (or very out-in-the-open) wish to move on. But the fear is too strong—you want life or someone else to make the decision for you. Mostly so you won't have to be responsible if something backfires.

Two close friends experienced this recently with jobs they hated but were afraid to leave. They both knew management was tightening its belt, and unless they showed more enthusiasm for their jobs, they would be laid off. One began searching for a new job; the other just complained over the phone at night to her girlfriends about how tough the job market was. Not long after, they were each laid off. Guess who landed on her feet? And who's still struggling to stand up?

A friend gave me the antivictim exercise on page 15. It's remarkable in its simplicity. It helps bring gratitude and an attitude of looking for the blessings within each change.

Exercise: To Stop Being a Victim

When Sharon was little, she used to enjoy the comic strips that showed a drawing of mixed-up objects. A caption would ask the reader: What's wrong with this picture? You were supposed to find all the out-of-place items in the drawing.

When things start changing in her life now and she starts getting uncomfortable with the unfamiliar territory, Sharon asks, "What's right with this picture?"

Look at a change in your life, and write down all the things that are blessings in disguise.

When you get tired of the victim game, you take the first step toward mastery of change.

FOUR STAGES OF MASTERING CHANGE

My friend Joan is a great example of someone who has worked hard to be a cocreator with change in her life despite recent rocks in the path. In her journey these past two years she's uncovered four major stages of change. When she was able to traverse each of them, the change became a blessing, fear was much reduced, and she felt mastery again.

Two years ago Joan was heading up one of the biggest projects she'd ever managed at a large corporation where she worked. She had been promoted a number of times during her twelve years there, and she had a reputation as one of the best project managers in the company.

It was a high time in her life: career, friendships,

If a man will begin with certainties, he shall end in doubts; but if he will be content to begin with doubts, he shall end in certainties.

—Francis Bacon

volunteer work, and her love relationship seemed very good indeed.

In December of that year, Joan got two severe bouts of what she thought was flu; they came two weeks apart. But she didn't get better after the second illness, only worse. Doctors started a barrage of tests for lupus, MS, tuberculosis, HIV, thyroid imbalance, Lyme disease, and more, but no answers came. Raging fevers began, then constant sore throats, swollen glands, migraine headaches, and extreme fatigue plagued her days. By March Joan was having a hard time with decisions, holding information in memory, relationships, and work in general. Her project team and bosses kept saying, "Stay, stay. Half of you is better than anyone else." But she was just getting sicker.

In May of that year, Joan left work on a month's leave to try to regain her health. It was then that the first clue came: a new doctor finally diagnosed her illness as chronic fatigue syndrome or chronic fatigue immune dysfunction syndrome (CFIDS). She had all the major symptoms as laid out by the Center for Disease Control in Atlanta. Now she had a diagnosis but there was no known treatment—except rest.

By the end of October, she knew she'd have to quit her job. Her staff was in tears after she handed in her resignation.

Earlier that year Joan had purchased a home in another state with her significant other, and now she moved there.

One year later, Joan was even sicker. And things looked grim: no way to work, living in a new place far away from family and friends she'd known all her life, with almost no money.

For the first few months, I could hear the desperation in her voice every time she called me. She had slowly found good doctors to help her function, but they kept telling her one thing: "You're never going to get better if you keep fighting this!"

Joan knew that the road to healing would indeed come through acceptance, but as she sat alone in the beautiful log home she now owned, she realized she didn't have a clue as to how to do it. How do you accept something as painful as this? No one could tell her.

That's when she got a draft of my earlier book, *Turning Points*. And by working with the exercises, came upon the four stages which began her healing.

He knows not his own strength that hath not met adversity.

—Ben Jonson

STAGE ONE:
FACE THE CHANGE AND INVESTIGATE IT

The four stages of change seem to be universal, yet most people never see them. They never get past the fear and the feeling of being victimized by change.

The first stage usually occurs in the midst of the change or right after the initial upheaval has passed. Suddenly you are in a new place—either physically or metaphorically. You want to know the answer to two questions: (1) What happened? and (2) Why?

The task here is to face the change and to investigate it as fully as you can. You slowly gain an understanding of what has occurred.

Joan used the Turning Points exercise on page 55 to explore these questions. She wrote the word *acceptance* in the center of a page in her journal, then free-associated—what did that word mean to her? She wrote all her thoughts, feelings, and ideas about acceptance, the key to her healing.

As she did the exercise, she realized she had lost her feeling of self-control, her proud sense of independence. For the first time in her life her enormous will and finely tuned intelligence were worth nothing. She felt she had lost her identity, and that hurt! Her illness had left her without the resources she had leaned on all her life. But the exercise also revealed words like *willingness, serenity,* and *blessing.* Joan discovered that facing her change directly through this exercise had allowed her to let go of two tremendous fears: What was she going to do? and How was she going to cope? Hope came peeking through the exercise and surprised her. She saw that within the despair were reserves of strength she had forgotten.

In creating, the only hard thing's to begin;/A grass blade's no easier to make than an oak.

—James Russell Lowell

STAGE TWO:
ACCEPT THE CHANGE

At the beginning of a change, there is a tendency to fight responsibility for the change. To imagine that we had nothing to do with it, that any negatives were someone else's fault. And on really bad days, when all the changes we have wrought feel like big mistakes, we refuse to see the spiritual purpose behind them.

Then, taking a big sigh, we move into the second stage, accepting our part in what has happened.

Joan said the question that characterized this stage was What is there to learn here? This was a monumental shift from victim consciousness to being a student of change. There was something to be understood and learned.

The most important exercise in this book for stage two is the Fear Room exercise on page 76. This exercise can be a daily practice during the acceptance stage.

Most people don't realize the amount of fear lurking amongst the changes, and it can take diligent inner work to remove those fears. Joan kept doing this exercise, removing fear—and anger and grief—from her inner room. She kept washing the windows of her consciousness to "keep the fear from escalating into terror and paralyzing" her as it had initially.

STAGE THREE:
SEE THE BIG PICTURE, AND TAKE ACTION

Once the obstacles of fear, anger, and grief that surround the change are lessened, we can begin to work with stage three.

The envisioning exercise on page 167 is an important key in stage three. "One brave day," Joan said, "I began to trust that there was a way out. I had never allowed myself to do something like this exercise but here I was, envisioning great blessings during one of the lowest ebbs of my life. Once I was able to list the qualities I wanted to bring into my life, the specifics flowed onto the page."

For me envisioning implies that the qualities do not need to be made up; you're just seeing what's already available but perhaps has yet to manifest in your life.

It creates a bigger picture, bigger than your fear. Now you can form your new future. And you can begin to take action toward that future.

By making choices, we learn to profit from our mistakes.

—Alexandra Stoddard

STAGE FOUR:
INTEGRATE THE CHANGE

A famous actor was interviewed following an accident that left him in a wheelchair. Instead of complaining about his terrible misfortune, the actor surprised both interviewer and audience by talking about the blessings in the change. How much he had learned, and the internal adjustments he had made. He had truly integrated the change into his life.

Stage four brings awareness of the blessings within the change. We ask ourselves, How am I learning from this turning point? How am I better because of it? A difficult thing to consider earlier in the process, at this stage Joan began to see how there was order and beauty in her universe. It gave her internal compass a true north again.

"I used to love Scout camp," she told me recently. "The troop leaders would take us into the woods, and we had only our compasses and a set of compass-point directions. We'd be on our own to find our way back to camp.

"The first thing you had to do was find north on the compass or all the other directions would be useless. I did it every time.

"Now that I know where my true north is, I'm having fun again being an explorer, turning point by turning point."

Why We Fear Change

Do we ever get rid of the fear? Maybe not. Fear is often a constant companion, even for those skilled in recognizing turning points. But courage, the antidote to fear, can be constant too.

"Courage is resistance to fear, mastery of fear—not absence of fear," Mark Twain once said. Courage walks hand in hand with stepping into new areas of living. It comes when we begin to use our creative resources to face and make changes.

Change is frightening because it takes us into the

unfamiliar. Change asks us to take a leap of faith; often when we have no idea of what's ahead, we're asked to move forward. Our self-confidence is sorely tested. Will we survive no matter what happens to us?

We tremble at the thought of reaching outside our comfort zone, what we're familiar with. We tremble at taking the risk of venturing into the unknown.

A friend dreamed of working full-time in the world of food but had a secure position as a computer programmer. As she assisted me with the cooking classes I teach part-time at a local school, she'd often talk about how much she loved creating and testing recipes, trying new foods, and working with people in the food world. But jobs that would give her all that were scarce.

How could she ever have the job of her dreams? Could she overcome her self-doubt and fear? Was she creative enough to make such a drastic change?

She wondered, *Will I fail?* Failure was something that rarely happened in the secure environment of her present life. But she realized her present security was beginning to feel like a prison because she had outgrown it. She knew she needed to pursue her dream, and she decided to take the challenge. So she started looking for work in this new field.

Within a few months, she was asked to assist a cookbook author, testing recipes in a beautiful and well-equipped kitchen. She quit her computer job and was soon working full-time in the world of food. The last time I spoke with her, she was the private cook for two film stars who were making a movie in her city.

When I asked her how she had managed to make the leap, she said that it took courage and persistence, mostly persistence. The dream was so strong inside her

Talent develops in quiet places, character in the full current of human life.

—Johann Wolfgang von Goethe

that, despite her fears, she had held on to her dream of what she wanted. Have you ever had a dream that propelled you way beyond what you thought you could do, despite all odds and obstacles? This is what she described.

Dream the impossible dream.

—Joe Darion

Her ability to dream a dream of what she really wanted—and hold a strong, yet flexible vision of the qualities of that dream—brought her through her turning point and changed her life.

The following exercise is a way for you to learn how to hold on to your dream and create a strong vision of what you want.

Exercise: To Dream Your Dream

To develop a strong vision, try this exercise. Take a minute, and imagine your next step: a dream job, friendship, love relationship, or house —whatever you feel would bring you more of what you want in life.

Close your eyes, and get a good feeling, image, or sense of it. Take five minutes, and write or draw everything you can about this image. Especially important: include the *qualities* the image brings, how it makes you feel.

After you finish the exercise, put the paper away for six months. In six months look at what you wrote; you may be surprised at what has happened with your dream.

Each time I have tried this exercise, I have been amazed at what this kind of dreaming can achieve. Others have had success with it too.

Never at ease with five-year plans or other kinds of business goal-setting, a reader of *Turning Points* tried this exercise. One June morning she wrote the qualities she'd like in her life on a white piece of paper, sealed it in an envelope, and put it away for six months in the back of her journal. She was reviewing her goals the next January and remembered the envelope.

"My heart opened," she told me, "when I read the qualities I had envisioned last year. It was like reading a page from my own book of life, a gift because it confirmed that I was still on the right track. Things I wrote back then had already started manifesting in my life."

WHY ARE THEY SO LUCKY?

About a year ago, when my freelance writing career was in one of its slumps, I would find myself being very envious whenever another writer got a good review or an award. Each month as I read their notices in the journal of a professional writing association I belong to, I'd grumble to myself, *Why do they get ahead when I never seem to? Why are they so lucky?*

One morning, I was feeling particularly low because the journal's editors had failed to include a mention of a new achievement I'd sent them—one of my few that year. I was feeling jealous, left out, and mad. Reading *The Artist's Way* by Julia Cameron, I came across an exercise called the Jealousy Map. The author instructs you to draw three columns on a piece of paper. One column would be titled "Who," the next "Why," and the third "Action or Antidote."

In the "Who" column I was to list anyone I envied for their achievements, career or otherwise. I listed famous authors who wrote award-winning books, a couple of friends who were talented and productive, family members, and business associates.

In the "Why" column, I wrote after each name the reason I was jealous of this person. The reasons sounded silly, but I kept at it. I remember writing "She has blond hair" and "He writes better poems than I do."

The third column listed any action or antidote I could take to counteract the jealousy. I thought this column would be blank. Amazingly, many things came to mind. I listed a host of activities I could begin, phone calls I could make, classes to attend that would help me achieve what I wanted.

The exercise worked: I no longer felt like a victim.

And as a bonus, phone calls I made after doing the exercise led to two very large and very unexpected writing contracts.

Change for Change's Sake

We've talked about the victim's fear of change, and how it shows up as dragging our feet whenever change lurks on the horizon. There's another kind of fear of change that is equally common. It manifests as changing simply for the sake of change.

People who change for change's sake have no trouble dreaming the dream. They can dream many dreams. But change is so intoxicating that they rarely stick with a dream long enough to see it manifest. Changing for the sake of change is a paradox: it actually avoids any real or lasting growth. And by making erratic changes you never settle into a commitment to work things out.

There is lots of movement but also the feeling that you are getting nowhere. You may be cheating yourself out of the growth and experience that comes with commitment.

This lack of commitment to real change can also influence our ability to take risks—and what kind.

Ralph Keyes, in *Chancing It,* describes two types of risk-takers. Level I risk-takers like outwardly challenging activities such as starting their own businesses, performing in public, taking up skydiving or other thrill sports. Someone comfortable with outwardly challenging activities may be the change-for-change's-sake type of person, quite nervous when it comes to making more meaningful changes. Turning points for these people would likely involve settling down and creating something lasting. Level II risk-takers are rarely as inclined toward the dramatic. They take risks that present, as Keyes says, "more danger to the spirit than to the body," such as getting married, starting a family, or slowly building a long-term career.

For either type of person, true, beneficial change is usually a lengthy process rather than one sudden movement. It works in harmony with life, with other people for the most part, with your goals for yourself.

It takes you somewhere. Often it involves a spiritual element, such as a higher realization about yourself. And it usually involves facing a fear.

We make our own magic.

—Sherry Suib Cohen

Exercise:
What Would You Change If You Could?

List ten things in your life you'd like to change or you feel need changing. Be as descriptive as you can. When you finish, put the paper away. We'll work on one of these changes in the next chapter.

DO IT DESPITE THE FEAR

My friend Lori is a tall blond woman in her thirties who carries herself with confidence and poise. She works as a computer analyst while pursuing a modeling career. She told me a moving story about the pain of facing herself on a very difficult front: overcoming an eating disorder.

When she was about fifteen, Lori began having an uncontrollable urge to overeat. She spent most of her teenage years in the kitchen. She'd bake large batches of sugar cookies for the family, then eat them all herself. It began four years after her mother and father divorced and Lori moved in with her father and his new wife. She gained forty pounds that year.

When Lori was twenty she joined the Navy. The eating disorder got worse: at one sitting she'd eat a dozen donuts, packages of cookies, a take-out dinner for two, entire boxes of chocolates (bought with gift cards as if they were for someone else).

She began running for fitness. But she was not losing weight, and food was still constantly on her mind. Where would she have her next meal? How soon would her roommate leave so she could go to the store for cookies or visit a fast-food drive-through? It wasn't until her late twenties that Lori saw this as a real problem. Her food addiction was something she could no longer control. And that made it worse.

She'd say she'd never do it again, and the next day she was eating even more. "I felt weak and stupid," Lori told me, "but I'd always make up a story in my mind that would convince me to go to the store and buy more food."

The turning point came when Lori met a man she

In nature there are neither rewards nor punishments—there are consequences.

—Robert G. Ingersoll

was very attracted to who "represented the perfect life to me. He had money, good looks, stability, and a great sense of humor. I thought he was attracted to me too. But when he decided it would be better if we were just friends, I was devastated." The pain and heartache that shook her to the core also shook loose her dependence on food. "The intensity of the pain made me look further because it wouldn't go away—and I couldn't solve it with food," Lori remembers. "The pain was so great I could barely breathe. I'd be driving down the road and have to pull over because I was crying so hard."

During those months, Lori searched for a way to face the change that was unfolding inside her. Her life was at its lowest ebb when a friend finally suggested Lori try Overeaters Anonymous.

At the first meeting, Lori learned something that changed the course of her life. What she learned was to choose not to eat your trigger foods for one day. Then choose not to do it for the next day. But always work one day at a time. Surrender the rest; don't worry about the future.

"I had always thought that I had to get over the compulsion to overeat before the compulsion would go away," Lori said. "This was backward. I only had to choose not to eat in that moment."

The future did take care of itself. Within a month, Lori noticed the driving urge to overeat had gradually disappeared.

"Once the compulsion was gone, I could begin to figure out what I really wanted," she said. "I could look at what was happening in my life." Not long after, Lori moved out of her father's house, took a dream trip to Europe, got into a healthy relationship, and found a

The truth . . . makes free those who have loved it.

—George Santayana

great job. But the biggest change was that she could pursue a long-held dream to become a model.

"I feel like a completely different person now. It was very hard to face the change I needed to make, so life set up something very painful and traumatic to shake me out of my paralysis," Lori said. "Changes like this feel as if someone were pushing you off a cliff to your death, but you land in a pillow of comfort."

There are several stages between the arrival of a big change like Lori experienced and the integration stage where we begin settling in to the new life our change created. Although Lori effectively faced her life at its lowest ebb and moved through the steps to overcome her problem, it took time. Pain motivated her but was eventually replaced by joy and hope. And much less fear.

In *Ask the Master,* Book 2, author Harold Klemp writes, "Each life cycle has a growth and fulfillment stage. We switch back and forth between them. The growth phase begins with a restless feeling that urges us into a new and greater opportunity, but fear holds us back. Finally, this need for growth outweighs the fear."

At that point we begin to consider accepting the spiritual opportunity of the turning point.

We begin looking at how to take the necessary steps and face the risks we must take in order to grow. Fulfillment comes as we allow the new skills to become part of ourselves, as we "master the new routines and plunge into the options of our unexplored life," as Klemp says.

Life always brings you to the first step to make such a change. In the next chapter, we'll find out why some changes are successful and others aren't.

Ask Yourself:
How Do You Feel about Change?

Write your answers to the following questions. They may help you understand your present relationship to change.

1. When is change most scary for you?
2. When is change the most exciting?
3. Are the most important changes for you often the scariest? Why might this be?
4. Do you seek out the advice of friends or relatives when considering making an important change in your life?
5. What would it take for you to be more comfortable with change?

2

Creating Successful Changes

*Become a Creative Force
in Your Own Life*

*We can tap into a part of ourselves—an
inner reservoir of knowledge, quite subterranean,
quite hidden—that holds all our answers.*

—Marsha Sinetar

2. CREATING SUCCESSFUL CHANGES

Most of us, when turning points hit unexpectedly, ask, "Why me?" Or "Why now, just when things are getting so good?"

Focused only on what's happening in our smaller world, we wonder at life's imperfect timing. If we were able to look from a higher viewpoint—one that stretched far forward and back in time—we could see the threads connecting this turning point with the next. Having gained an overview, we would be able to see the ferry coming around the bend.

How do we get this higher viewpoint that lets us move through change with mastery and grace?

By learning to be a creative force in our lives. By creating change that resonates with what we really want. Change that assists us to become better people, closer to the natural beauty and harmony of life. This is what I call *spiritually successful change.*

WHO ARE YOU REALLY?

Many modern and ancient writings speak of Soul, the eternal being that never dies. It's the spark of creativity, of divine light; It is you. If you imagine God

Beautiful dreamer, wake unto me, / Starlight and dewdrop are waiting for thee.

—Stephen Collins Foster

33

as an infinite mirror, and a piece of that mirror shattered into billions and billions of pieces, then each piece is Soul, a shining reflection of God, a spark of God.

Some people think of God as the Father or Mother of the universe and all beings. God to me is the greater power, an infinite ocean of love and mercy from which flows the creative force that holds the universe together and brings a sense of beauty to my life. You might think of God in another way—as energy, order, or purpose.

As a spiritual being, as Soul, you naturally have the higher viewpoint that you need to create spiritually successful change. But everyday hardships and challenges dampen the enthusiasm and ability to work from this higher viewpoint, so you settle for much less.

There is no duty we so much underrate as the duty of being happy.

—Robert Louis Stevenson

Thus, our first step in mastering change in our lives is to regain the inner confidence that as Soul, a unique spiritual being, we are cocreators with life, and with God, in the small and major changes in our lives. Our purpose in life is to become more aware of being in this creative, joyful state. And each change life brings us is custom-designed to teach us how to be more aware of who and what we really are.

Maybe you've experienced times when things just seemed to fall into place. You were able to view events from a higher level, be more loving and serene, trusting that everything would work out the way it was supposed to. And it worked! The puzzle pieces fitted perfectly, and life made complete sense.

As Soul, you have an innate ability to experience change like this most—if not all—of the time. You can move serenely from one experience to the next, without fear or judgment.

Sound impossible? Keep reading.

In my life, when I am able to maintain this higher viewpoint, my turning points are much, much smoother. I am able to weather change better. And from this viewpoint as Soul, I am sure that all that happens to me is for my own good, that there is order and beauty in the universe. It is then that I feel close to God's plan for my life, that I am operating in harmony with the movement of the universe.

This builds upon itself. The more I maintain this Soul viewpoint, the more open I am to guidance from God as to how to maintain it. It's a never-ending circle.

If I operate consciously within that order and `beauty, if I carefully attend to the guidance, I keep the higher viewpoint. Each day shows me how God's guidance and care are stronger in my life. I realize I am indeed Soul, beloved by the Divine.

Soul wears the physical body, the emotions, the memory, and the mind like the coats we wear in winter for protection. Soul is a refined being, and It needs protection in the harsh worlds It exists in.

The key to mastering change is to be able to work from the light, high consciousness of Soul—who you truly are — even while wearing these protective layers.

I developed the exercise on the next page to help me whenever I feel weighed down by life and its expectations and I need to regain the clarity of Soul, this higher viewpoint.

Have you ever truly experienced yourself as Soul? Take a few minutes now and try the exercise.

We carry with us the wonders we seek without us.

—Sir Thomas Browne

Exercise:
Who Are You Really?

Close your eyes and imagine yourself standing in a hallway by a green door. Beside the door is a coatrack. You notice you are wearing a heavy overcoat. Since it is hot and the coat weighs on your shoulders, you decide to take it off. You do so and hang it on the coatrack.

Immediately the door before you swings open. You walk through.

The scene is replayed four more times. Each time you find yourself in front of a door and a coatrack. Each time you are wearing a coat.

The first door was green, and the coat was heavy. It symbolized the physical level and the dense physical body. The second door is pink; your coat is slightly lighter. This symbolizes the emotional level and the emotions. The third door is orange, the coat lighter still, symbolizing the level of cause and effect and the body of past memories and seed ideas. The fourth door is a deep blue; the coat is thick but not heavy. It symbolizes the mind and your thoughts.

When you have removed the last coat and walked through the last door, you find yourself in a brightly lit room.

The light is pale golden yellow.

You have no coat on your shoulders to weigh you down. You feel light and free. This is you, Soul.

I am larger, better than I thought, I I did not know I held so much goodness.

—Walt Whitman

How practical is this higher viewpoint? Does it work with everyday things, like challenges at work, career moves, settling into a new job?

Yes, indeed.

In the following two stories, you'll see how two people learned that this higher viewpoint was very effective during times of great change in their careers.

CREATIVE FORCES IN YOUR LIFE

Jack was given a new job in February, an assistant role to train him for a future directorship in his company. If all went well, at year's end he'd be offered the higher-paying job.

He'd never been in a management position in this type of company, and he wondered how to make the transition smoothly.

His boss was wise. Knowing that time would take care of Jack's concerns, she decided to give him an unusual assignment to help him learn on the job. "Do three things," she told him. "First, do your daily work. Then listen to people you work with and learn from them. Finally, I want you to write a proposal describing the director's job; it's due in December." And there wasn't much more than that.

So Jack began.

Over the months from spring to fall, Jack did exactly those three things. Each day he dealt with the work that presented itself, managing to keep ahead of the piles of paper that went with the job. He practiced listening to comments and suggestions from coworkers, and over the months was amazed at the wisdom of others who'd been with the company longer. Finally, he diligently put together a proposal, based on what he was learning from

Here is what is truly amazing about life. Things change.

—Elizabeth Glaser

the everyday work, on what the director's job would be.

Year's end came. Jack was given the director's job, and it was surprisingly easy for him to handle his new duties.

He realized that the months of work in the assistant role had been excellent on-the-job training. But best of all, he saw how he had created his new role. The new job fit him to a T. His daily tasks as director were astonishingly similar to what he had written in his proposal. Even though the department was going through major upheavals at the time, his work was moving forward smoothly and steadily. Others in the office thought this was a miracle.

This experience changed Jack's ideas about change. "It's nice that you can sometimes go through change painlessly," he told me. "This experience taught me that I had to accept that I was deserving of change without suffering. And I was."

Jack's move up in his career was what I call a spiritually successful change. It assisted him spiritually as well as practically. It not only led him to a higher position in his company, the months of preparation built his confidence. He knew he could handle the promotion because he had written the book on it. He also learned spiritually from the exercise: that change, which used to be a painful part of life for him, could be a pain-free, joyous learning experience from this higher viewpoint.

Imagine you are being offered a beautiful next step in your life—something you truly desire. It could be the home or relationship of your dreams, a job that would fully use your talents and creativity, a chance to excel at a sport or athletic pursuit. Then try the exercise on the next page.

To be a spiritual being . . . means to employ the highest force of creativity that is possible among people.

—Harold Klemp

Exercise:
Write a Life Proposal

1. Write a one-page proposal, as you would for a business, describing the role you'd take on if this next step became real.

2. Write the daily responsibilities you'd have in this position, the expectations of others around you, the achievements you would bring about in your life, the inner skills you'd need to develop in order to fulfill this role (confidence? a better sense of timing? more love?).

To resist change is to work against the flow of life rather than surrender to and trust it.

—Susan Taylor

This is a very powerful exercise for seeing yourself as the cocreator of your life, rather than its victim. Doing this exercise regularly can help you set your feet on the road to great spiritual discoveries.

SPIRITUALLY SUCCESSFUL CHANGE

Jack's job change was a spiritually successful change. It marked a major turning point in his work and personal life.

Life constantly brings us chances for this kind of enriching change. God is on our side to make us better people, and one way God works is through changes.

How can we make our changes more spiritually successful? By following the four stages of mastering change detailed in chapter 1.

In Jack's apprenticeship for the director's job, he was exploring and investigating the change by listening to coworkers' suggestions and ideas. He was accepting the change by writing about it as if he'd already assumed the role. He took action each time he handled a daily task. He integrated the change when he moved up to his new job at year's end. Each was a small step forward. This is why the training method Jack's boss devised worked so well.

Let's face the music and dance.

—Irving Berlin

Taking small steps is a proven way to master change. Small steps—rather than dramatic leaps—are the smoothest way to make steady progress.

I was recently interviewed on a local edition of the National Public Radio show *All Things Considered*. It was New Year's Eve, and the host was interviewing celebrities and myself (as the "change expert") on making New Year's resolutions. I was being asked to comment on how these famous folk could achieve their goals.

From big goals (winning the next election) to smaller ones (making a new policy work), the same answer kept surfacing. "Take it one small step at a time," I told the host.

When we were listening to a national basketball coach speak about winning more games, the host turned to me. "I guess that would mean practice dribbling?" he asked. "A first step to winning," I laughed.

If you'd like to explore more spiritually successful change in your own life, try the following exercise. It helped me greatly after a car accident left me with a stiff neck and a need to rest a lot. While I grumbled over the unexpected inconvenience, I knew there was a hidden benefit, a first step toward improving a neglected area of my life.

Exercise:
A Dialogue with Change

Imagine your current change is a person you can speak with. Close your eyes, and ask your change:

- How are you helping me?
- What positive gifts are you bringing me?
- What spiritual skills are you giving me?
- What new spiritual levels are you leading me toward in my life?

In your journal, write the answers you receive from your change.

Now write your response to these answers. Do you believe them? Ask the change to elaborate, if you like.

All the rivers run into the sea; yet the sea is not full.

—Ecclesiastes 1:7

Throughout this exercise, write as fast as you comfortably can. Do not think too much about the exercise. It may seem silly, but it can open you to new understanding of yourself. You may get surprising answers.

Repeat this exercise at any stage of a change.

When I asked my car accident what gift it was bringing me, the answer was very surprising: "To get you to slow down."

GETTING UNSTUCK

Did you ever feel that a change came just when you needed to move ahead?

I often think of a turning point as God giving me

a spiritual wake-up call. It's not always a pleasant feeling to be stirred from a deep sleep. I often prefer my dreams to reality. But the new job, the unexpected change in health, the move to a new house might be just the ticket for helping me grow and become more of who I really am.

I can best illustrate this with a story about my writing career, how a change came when I had begun to feel stuck and stagnant, and how the change unfolded me beyond my wildest dreams. Maybe you'll see something of your own life in my story.

In 1989 I had been a published magazine writer for twelve years. My work was good, I was happy to be paid for the articles I submitted, but my heart wasn't in it anymore. It had become formulaic, almost drudgery. My writing career no longer held a challenge for me. It was as if I were in a stable but unsatisfying marriage, where the spark had long been missing. Perhaps this kind of stuck feeling has happened to you.

The restlessness in me and the lack of spark in my work must have been communicating itself to my editors too, because I wasn't getting any new work, just maintaining the regular assignments I'd done for years.

I didn't want to divorce the magazines I wrote for, chuck it all, and find a different career. I wanted, with growing intensity, to move forward, to become a better writer. I wanted to be interested and inspired. I wanted other people to be inspired by my writing too. Then I could sell to bigger, better paying markets.

But, as with most changes, I couldn't see all of this in the beginning. There was only that nagging feeling of "something's not right." I had no tangible clues as to what needed to be changed.

By divine grace, we come further along the path, closer to the realization that we are looking for, more able to face the world that we have created for ourselves.

—Harold Klemp

WORK AS CREATIVITY

Eventually the nagging feeling got strong enough, and one day in late spring I wrote a goal in my dream journal. I imagined myself writing for publications all over the U.S. and Canada. I saw my writing as clear and interesting, uplifting the reader's everyday life. It was also honest writing, courageous, reaching into who I really was, allowing more of my heart to come out and touch the reader. I felt this would fulfill my spiritual purpose as a writer.

But what did I need to do to get there? Take a writing class? Join a group of published writers who met regularly to talk about their writing?

Stumped, I decided to begin seeing my writing from the highest viewpoint I could muster. What would make me happiest as a writer? Five years from now, where would I like to be in my writing career?

As I wrote my goals, using the To Dream Your Dream exercise from chapter 1, I asked life to bring me any opportunity I might be ready for, since I really didn't know which direction to pursue.

In this theatre of . . . life it is reserved only for God and angels to be lookers on.

—Francis Bacon

SYNCHRONICITY

Synchronicity involves unexplained patterns of seeming coincidences. Carl Jung wrote about synchronicity and recounted many examples of amazing "coincidences" in his life.

Unbeknownst to me, my goal set in motion a series of such events that involved many people. I was to receive three phone calls that would change my career and my life. They were all unexpected, yet I realized later that I had set them into motion myself through writing down my goals.

Three weeks after I wrote those goals, an old friend called. Carol had coauthored *Laurel's Kitchen,* a very popular natural-foods cookbook, one of the first of its type. Riding on the popularity of this homey style of cooking, she began writing a weekly column on food and health. She then sold the column to newspapers around the country. Thirty papers had picked it up; the column was successful enough to pay her well for eleven years.

She called me one day in the early summer and casually asked if I would be interested in taking over her column. She was about to retire from weekly deadlines.

Hitch your wagon to a star.

—Ralph Waldo Emerson

Fear and excitement fought for equal time as I struggled to absorb the idea. I knew absolutely nothing about writing newspaper columns. I had only written full-length feature articles for small magazines, a very different ball game. But before I refused the offer, I wanted to check it out in contemplation.

Have you ever received a phone call that changed your life? I felt Carol's call was the turning point I had been waiting for in my writing career. But I wasn't sure.

How Does the Change Fit You?

As an experiment, I closed my eyes and tried imagining myself as a published columnist. I tried to view the situation from the highest level I could imagine. How did it fit the dreams I had written in my journal? Was I happy, fulfilled, challenged?

I let the concept of taking on the column float gently around me. I felt peaceful, happy, yet on the cutting edge of my present abilities. I wondered if this turning point would lead my writing into totally new areas.

I wondered how this decision would affect my future writing career. It would certainly stretch every skill I had.

As I did this little exercise, I also felt a stillness that was familiar. I had encountered it before at major turning points in my life.

So much fear lurked in the shadows though! If I gave in to the fear, I would probably never grow to be the writer I wanted to become. But if I could move beyond any discomfort and fear, I just might. A slogan on a billboard I had passed suddenly flashed into my mind: *I don't feel my age if I focus on my dreams.* Could I keep that focus? When I managed to, the fear looked smaller and the risks were something I could handle.

So I said yes, putting all the certainty I felt from that high vision into my voice. "When do I start?"

"Probably September," she said. "I'll write the editors and introduce you, then you'll have to call them and sell them the idea yourself."

Ugh! I thought. I'd always hated selling myself on the phone. The fear rose again, but I pushed it away. Overriding it was that feeling of certainty: This was the right decision. I reasoned I had until September — almost four months — to learn the newspaper-writing game. I would take it a step at a time!

Of course, the money also lured me. Carol had made money from this once-a-week, thousand-word effort. Maybe writing a column would be my ticket to fame and fortune.

A month later, I was having trouble keeping my high vision and remembering what this change was really all about — wanting to become a better writer. It was an awful lot of work! The learning curve had never

It is not easy to be a pioneer — but oh, it is fascinating.

—Elizabeth
Blackwell

seemed so steep.

Has it ever seemed that life pushed you into deep water just to see if you could swim? That was exactly how I felt. The effort of pulling together my first column wore me out. I had read every book detailing the art of newspaper columns that I could lay my hands on. I had pumped friends for information. I had studied the food sections of major newspapers.

Comparing my writing to the published columnists', I didn't feel I had much hope for a warm reception when I began calling the editors on Carol's list. But the first editor said yes. I silently whooped with joy. Until her next words: "We'd like to see four sample columns by the end of the month."

Four! I had spent a month writing just one!

The next few weeks I worked harder at my writing than I ever had before, cajoling editor friends to give me feedback, rewriting draft after draft of the four sample columns. Finally I had them ready—and the editor liked them! But that was only one editor. To make it worse, the newspaper business slumped terribly that year. The editors I contacted complained about lack of money, lack of advertising, and lack of space for columns like mine.

From Carol's thirty newspapers, I landed only four contracts in all.

I began to wonder if my viewpoint when making the decision had been that high after all. What if it was a big mistake?

All interesting voyages involve hardships and hurdles.

—Alexandra Stoddard

ON-THE-JOB LEARNING

Learning on the job is rarely easy for me. And I stumbled often that first year. I made plenty of mistakes, sent the wrong files to my editors, got letters full of questions from readers when I inadvertently left out an ingredient and a recipe didn't work. So many times it left me discouraged. But I didn't quit.

I worried constantly, battling with self-doubt each time I wrote a column. Was my writing good enough so the editors would keep me on?

By the end of that year, two of the four newspapers had canceled, but two hung on and continued to buy my weekly column, earning me a few hundred dollars a month. When I counted up the hours I spent putting each column together, developing and testing the recipes, and sending it to the two papers, I often wondered why I continued. Was I improving my writing enough to make this mountain of work worthwhile?

I was too busy to know that answer, so I just kept on producing those columns.

And each time I did my short exercise and looked at the situation from my original goal of becoming a better writer, I got reassurance. I hadn't a clue why. From the everyday viewpoint, things looked dicey.

But I was about to receive the second amazing phone call.

One day, in the midst of my worst self-doubt, an editor from a magazine I'd written for since the seventies called me. She had noticed that the style and quality of my articles had changed in the past year. What had I done differently—taken a crash course? My writing was tighter, cleaner. I said more in fewer words. I made fewer spelling errors. In short, she said, I had become one of their best writers. Would I be willing to take on a monthly column?

This was the first tangible sign that I was traveling

Whether the change is one you have chosen or one you wish would go away, the transition forces you to leave the known and step into the new and unknown territory.

—Sabina A. Spencer and John D. Adams

the right path, that my vision had been correct. My crash-and-burn apprenticeship in the field of journalism had taught me more than I realized. I had grown enough to warrant the trust of this editor.

I gratefully accepted the assignment for the monthly column.

My relief was profound! Life had sent me a sign that, yes, I was improving as a writer. Yes, the immense amount of work—for pennies—was paying off.

I decided to hold on to my dream a while longer.

Embracing the Turning Point

Obviously, the story isn't over yet, but I want to take a break here to recap.

I was beginning to learn how to work with greater levels of change. I was seeing how my desire to become a better writer had brought me to this turning point of writing a weekly column. I saw how I had created this change in my life from the higher viewpoint of Soul. It was spiritually motivated and was affecting me on more levels than just my career. I was having to face fears about myself, about my abilities. I was being stretched way beyond my comfort zone.

From a spiritual viewpoint, everything was working great. As Soul, I had no fear of the change, no doubt that I was doing the right thing. The fear of trying something new—like the column—rarely causes Soul to flinch. This is because Soul lives in the present moment—and in the present I knew this was the right direction.

I was coming to understand that, as Soul, I lived only to grow and expand into greater awareness. That each change was custom-designed to teach me this.

And challenges were only natural. Turning points were to be embraced.

This was a spiritually successful change!

I looked back and saw how I had envisioned success in my writing career. I wasn't sure how I would get there, though. I had naively imagined instant fame, my name in fifty newspapers across the country overnight. But life knew better. Life had known that first I needed a crash course in journalism. And life arranged for me to get this training on the job.

PURSUE YOUR PASSION

By the sixth year—with over three hundred published columns under my belt—meeting the weekly deadline had become a graceful routine. Topics came easily, I had gotten much better at crafting anecdotes to illustrate ideas. My proofreading and editing skills were sharp.

Financially, however, the column was barely pulling its weight. I often talked with writing friends about the idea of dropping it and concentrating on the better-paying world of magazine writing. After all, I reasoned, I had learned the lesson of my crash course in journalism.

It was after such a conversation that the third amazing phone call came. The final turning point of this story.

One afternoon I got a call from the food editor of the *Los Angeles Times* syndicate. I had written him four years earlier about becoming a syndicated columnist. Although I knew it was nearly impossible to enter those hallowed ranks—especially as a beginner—I sent him a proposal and samples of my current columns. Digging through stacks of old proposals he had come across mine.

A columnist on their staff had just canceled, and he

thought my topic of healthy eating would be perfect to start the following month!

Could I provide them with a column every two weeks?

I carefully asked how many papers the syndicate serviced. "Eighty-six and growing each week," the editor told me proudly.

Three years later, with many newspapers regularly publishing my bimonthly column, my editor asked me to make my national column available weekly.

As I look back on the six years of apprenticeship, I am so grateful for the time it took! Impatient then; grateful now. I had a chance to really test my wings before taking off to the national syndicate. I am also grateful for the higher viewpoint when I needed reassurance. It said, "Hang in there," even when my doubts had argued fiercely.

And God sent encouragement in the three phone calls—to keep producing the column even when only two papers wanted it. Whenever I reached a low point in my enthusiasm, a letter would come from a happy reader, a friend would call to ask me to teach a writing class on column-writing, my editors would leave encouraging messages on my answering machine or give me an unexpected raise, or I'd read an old column and marvel at how my writing had improved.

Spiritually successful change affects the entire person.

And so it often takes time to manifest fully in a person's life. It moves in a series of major and minor steps forward, as it did for me and as it did for Jack in the earlier story. You have to keep your dream strong, your enthusiasm bright.

If the concept of God has any validity or any use, it can only be to make us larger, freer, and more loving.

—James Baldwin

Exercise:
What Is Spiritually Successful Change?

Close your eyes and relax. Gently go back in your memory to a time when you made a change that affected you on many levels and propelled you forward in your life in an unexpectedly positive way. The change may have been hard for you, but looking back, you can see the results were truly beneficial on many levels.

Now open your eyes. List in your journal the qualities of that change.

Maybe you'd write: "More confidence in my abilities," "It got me unstuck—and I hadn't even realized I was stuck," "It led to that book contract or that gallery show years later," or whatever comes to mind for you.

Include how you felt after the change. What had changed about you?

Why was this a spiritually successful change?

DEFINE WHAT YOU WANT

My friend Dave used to work as a consultant for a company that taught people how to set goals and create action plans. He recently attended a goal-setting meeting and was surprised to hear so many of the people there, achievement-oriented adults like himself, complain that they never reached their real goals in life.

They actually didn't know how to start.

After telling me this, Dave said, "From my years of working with people and helping them set goals, I learned that the reason so many people don't achieve their goals is because they never truly define them."

The first step to define a goal or bring about a change in your life? Face it. Look at it, and investigate it. If it came true in your life, what would it feel like? I did this with my column. Even though on one level, I had accepted Carol's offer to take over her weekly column because I wanted to make money, I also wanted to become a better writer.

Being true to your priorities requires setting goals.

—Jeff
Davidson

Those who experience spiritually successful change knowingly or unknowingly face the change and define their goal. This is stage one of the four stages we explored in chapter 1. Facing the change is a step that can't be skipped. Each time you go through these stages, starting with facing the change, the results allow you to master the change.

You have to look at what you truly desire from a change before you can master it.

Facing the change involves making a road map for yourself. Most changes start with a nebulous feeling of "This isn't working anymore," as it did for me in my search to become a better writer. It's common not to have a road map at this stage. I didn't know exactly what to do to make the change. But that's not really the problem at this point. As we face the change and explore what we want, we begin to create the map we will follow through the remaining stages of the change.

Two exercises have helped me tremendously in facing major and minor changes. The first one (on the next page) allows me to see what might be behind "This isn't working anymore." I used the exercise to get a clear focus on what I wanted next.

To prepare for this exercise, find a quiet place to

sit and relax. You may have a favorite piece of music or healing image to help you let go inwardly and relax. Or do a short visualization exercise where you imagine being in a safe place that you love. Let go of your expectations about the change you're facing. I often say to God, "Thy will be done."

Exercise:
Facing the Change

1. Close your eyes, and ask life, God, or you spiritual guide, "What is the most important change I need to make right now? Is there something that is no longer working in my life?"

2. Relax, and let an image or an answer come to you. Remember to be open to unexpected ones.

3. Open your eyes, and turn to a clean page in your journal. Write about what you experienced. Write about what you really need to be happy and satisfied in the broadest sense.

Truth is the most valuable thing we have.

—Mark Twain

There is no right or wrong answer to this exercise. Try it as many times as you like. I have used it in many areas of my life that needed a significant change: an unsteady relationship with a friend or loved one, my finances, my job, where I lived. I usually targeted the area that gave me the most dissatisfaction, the strongest feeling of "This isn't working."

If you're stumped, try asking yourself these questions: *What's behind my dissatisfaction? What do I really want in my life?*

When I first did the exercise many years ago, I

focused on a stagnant job I was unhappy with. I thought it was because I wasn't making enough money. Then I thought it was my controlling boss. Each time I did the exercise, like peeling an onion, another layer sloughed off and a new realization came to me. Finally I saw that I was unhappy from years of pushing aside a dream of having my own business. That was what I really wanted to do.

It was a great relief to finally pinpoint what would make me happy. Not long after, I quit my job and started a business venture.

Often the feeling of "Something isn't working anymore" comes from ignoring a goal or aspiration. Uncovering the basic problem will reveal that goal. It's a vital first step, and it saved me a lot of wasted time. Otherwise, I might have just quit my job and moved to another, equally unhappy position, not realizing that my main problem or dissatisfaction was again being overlooked.

You can do anything when you find the heart for it, and the courage.

—Dan Millman

TURNING POINTS EXERCISE

My second exercise for facing the change is on the next page. It's popular in my Turning Points workshops. I use it on every change I face, and it helps me find out just how to take the next step.

A favorite writing book I discovered many years ago is Gabriele Rico's *Writing the Natural Way*. In it, she gives an exercise she calls clustering. It appears in many other books under different names and applied to different objectives, but for our purposes this exercise is about turning points and how to explore them. A woman in one of my workshops named it Exploring the Galaxies.

It goes like this: Start with an area you want to explore, summed up in a word or phrase. I started with the phrase "start my own business." My friend Joan from chapter 1 used the word *acceptance*. Write your word or phrase in the center of your page, then begin to free-associate and write down other words, images, sounds, places, people's names, and so on that come to mind when you think of this area. The steps are below.

Exercise:
Turning Points

1. In the center of a clean sheet of paper, write the word or phrase that describes your turning point. This is the seed idea.

2. Begin to free-associate, writing new words or phrases around that seed word or phrase, drawing strands from the center to link the new words you write.

3. Allow yourself to expand the first ring of words or phrases into a second or third, by drawing strands to connect them.

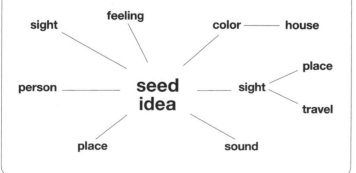

Here's how my Turning Points exercise looked.

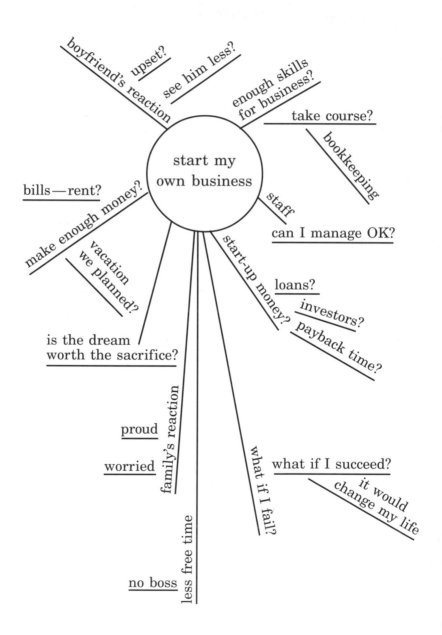

The exercise brought together many more details that had been simmering in my mind. Just as Joan had discovered in chapter 1, the exercise was able to pinpoint fears and doubts as well as important questions. By facing them, I stopped worrying unconsciously.

It worked a lot better than the lists I had made over the years. Only half of these issues emerged in linear sequence.

Try this exercise to face a change, especially one you feel overwhelmed by or stuck in. When fear of making a mistake paralyzes you and you can't see which way to go, the exercise can help you break free.

If any one area of the diagram intrigues you during the exercise, take a new sheet of paper and begin another, using that word or phrase as the seed idea. I did this to explore my resources for skill development.

The two exercises we just covered allow you to investigate your change in more detail. They allow you to get a better idea of what is actually happening in your life. Facing the change is the first step to mastery of change.

In the next chapter we'll explore how the timing of your change is important.

We should be ready for all issues, not daring to die but daring to live.

—Henry David Thoreau

Ask Yourself:
What's the Real Problem?

Write answers to the following questions. They may help you through the first stage of spiritually successful change—facing it.

1. What do you like most about yourself? Least?

2. If you could change three things about your life, past or present, what would they be?

3. If you could change one thing about yourself, what would it be? How hard would it actually be to start changing this one thing?

4. What talent do you have that other people admire? Is there some way to use this special talent for yourself to help you make this change?

5. As a way to help you face the change, imagine yourself in the future looking back at your life now. Would you regret not making this change?

3

Creative Change, Creative People

Learn to Move with Life's Natural Rhythm

As we recognize our oneness with all there is, we sense what is possible when we concentrate our energy on any one desired result.

—Ruth Ross, Ph.D.

3. CREATIVE CHANGE, CREATIVE PEOPLE

ot long ago, I was contacted by a large publisher of cookbooks. They asked me to help revise one of their best-selling low-fat cookbooks. Besides writing a food column, I had also been a restaurant chef for a number of years which gave me a strong background in recipe development. The publisher asked me to create forty-seven original recipes for their new book.

I had done this before. It was a challenging but fun job.

I was about to say yes when the editor added, "The book's on a tight deadline. We'll need all forty-seven recipes by October 1." This was a mere six weeks away! Then she dropped another bomb: I was to prepare samples of the recipes and present the dishes to a panel of food editors for judging. The editors would decide if the recipes were good enough. If not, I would have to redo them and still keep to the six-week timeline.

Was this even possible? With my current workload, I had estimated that it would take three months to create and test forty-seven new recipes.

Despite my misgivings, I had a strong hunch to do

We begin the process of transforming all those things we usually consider stumbling blocks into the stepping stones they really are.

—Rick Fields

the project. So, not really knowing how I'd manage it, I accepted the job.

After our meeting, I sat down by myself to recalculate my timeline. How would I ever fit this amount of work into six weeks? Normally it often takes three or four tries to perfect a new recipe. First I write what's called a paper recipe — a formula based on an idea. Then I shop for ingredients and prepare it once. Usually it will need adjustments: the cooking time is too long, the cake batter is too wet, the vegetables dry out. So it's back to the drawing board. I make notes, purchase new ingredients, and test again. Two or three tries later, the recipe works. The whole process can take many hours.

With their timeline and my already-packed schedule, there was no way I could spend more than a few hours on each of the forty-seven recipes. No way to rework each one three or four times. Each recipe would have to come out perfect the first try.

And what if the panel hated the dishes? How would I fit in retesting as well?

Well, I decided, *if life has given me this challenge, there must be a way to do it.* My hunch was still strong: It would somehow work. And I would learn a lot in the process about how to be more creative in my work!

A New York radio host once interviewed me on his show, "The Secrets of Success." At one point we talked about hunches and nudges. I said I used them constantly in my writing and other work. "That's interesting," the host commented. "Almost every CEO I've interviewed this month has spoken about gut feelings and hunches, how they are vital to his or her work. No one in business used to talk about this stuff, but it's quite common now."

As your commitment to life deepens, you learn to look at everything that has happened as having meaning, and see its importance in bringing you to where you are now.

—Sabina A. Spencer and John D. Adams

As I began work on the recipes, I made a deal with God. Each hunch or nudge I got, I would follow. If I had an intuitive feeling to try a certain spice or combine ingredients a certain way, I would faithfully follow it, even if it seemed silly. Here was a real-life business dilemma. Would my hunches prove accurate?

My job would be to pay attention to my hunches, which I knew were God's guidance. In this way, God would show me how to meet my impossible deadline.

The first morning I wrote out five paper recipes, then shopped. By afternoon I was in the kitchen. The first dish was a pasta entrée with vegetables. *Should I roast the vegetables first, steam them, or sauté them?* I wondered. Immediately the answer came: "Sauté them." *In oil or broth?* "Combine the two, use more broth," said the inner guidance. Later, I got: "Add a teaspoon of peanut butter to the sauce." And so this expert inner cook guided me through preparing a low-fat pasta dish with a creamy peanut sauce—very delicious.

At first it felt awkward following inner nudges in cooking—an area in which I had always been practical and professional. But, to my surprise, the nudges were very strong.

It sounds like a fairy tale, but the guidance continued through the entire batch of recipes. Each recipe worked—and it worked the first time I tested it! I retested each to make sure, and they all worked! This was truly unheard of.

Four weeks later I called the cookbook company and told them I was ready to present my results to the taste panel. They told me to come in the next morning at 11:00.

When I arrived early to heat my dishes and garnish them for the panel, another recipe developer was just

In our natural state of well-being, we will listen to our inner wisdom, and it will not lead us astray.

—Jane Nelsen, Ed.D.

finishing up. I cringed for her, as I heard the editors verbally destroy her dishes. "This won't work at all," I heard one say. "Why did you use asparagus here? Our readers can't afford that as an everyday ingredient," another scolded. These women were very direct and very critical. *Just doing their job,* I told myself. But I knew I'd be up next. The other recipe developer was visibly shrinking under all that criticism. How tall would I be when I left that room later?

How do I manage this? I begged God. "Follow the inner nudges," came that quiet voice inside.

I looked at my seven reheated recipes. *Which should I present first?* I wondered. The inner nudge came, "The pasta with peanut sauce." And next? "The Chinese soup." Each recipe found its place in the order—an order I never would have dreamed up myself.

But it worked! The editors' stern looks turned to surprise, then delight as they tasted the first dish.

"This is wonderful!" one of them exclaimed.

I said a thankful prayer.

The story ends on a positive note. All forty-seven recipes were accepted by the taste panel—each on the first try! Not one needed to be redone. I finished the project a week ahead of the impossible deadline. And the cookbook company called me again later that year to do another project for them.

This experience amazed and delighted me. It showed me two things: (1) even with great creative challenges we have tremendous guidance available to us, very practical guidance. And (2) if we listen to this guidance we automatically begin to move in concert with life's natural rhythm.

The pace may not be what I expect. It could be slower,

or as I found with the recipe development, much faster. But if I work in harmony with it, great fortune comes!

THE RHYTHM OF LIFE

Is this rhythm seen in other aspects of life too? Are there tides or cycles of learning that we can work with? And how do we become aware of them?

I've found these rhythms in relationships, jobs, family, even money. For the past two years I have charted my family's monthly income and expenses on a graph. Each summer, the income from my freelance business dipped alarmingly. In the spring and fall it would rise again. When I saw this pattern repeat again the next year, I knew I was seeing the ebb and flow of work in my particular field. In the fall and winter, most books are launched, so writers are busier. Summer is a fairly slow time, as books are in production for September release. Understanding the cycle eased my worry. Each time the cycle repeated, I knew it was part of the normal rhythm of my life.

In an insightful interview in the February 1996 *New Woman* magazine, best-selling romance writer Judith Krantz spoke about her forty-two-year marriage. "Inside my marriage are vast, fairly incomprehensible tides," she said. "The only thing that's absolutely certain is that the tides will always change."

Like school, there are study days when we are busy learning. I call these learning zones. There are also times when we catch up with what we learned, absorb and process it, and grow; these are our comfort zones. There are periods of great activity, then quiet pauses.

Refusing to move in accord with these natural rhythms can create problems. Or, as I learned,

There is a tide in the affairs of men, / Which, taken at the flood, leads on to fortune.

—William Shakespeare

following hunches and flowing with natural rhythms can bring unexpected benefits.

What's our goal in mastering change? To learn to use this natural rhythm as it works within our own lives.

LEARNING HOW TO SLOW DOWN

"When we find and live the rhythm within," writes author Jennifer James, "we are at peace." But it's not easy to (1) recognize that we're out of sync with life and (2) adjust our inner rhythm.

Why?

We become comfortable. Even living at an unnaturally fast pace, outside of the rhythm of life, can become familiar. Believe it or not, years of doing it the hard way make it tough to change to an easier way. And we may not believe that we can relax into life's arms that much or that the natural rhythm will work for us. I certainly didn't — which made learning to slow down a tough challenge.

Nature never makes haste; her systems revolve at an even pace.

—Henry David Thoreau

I had years of training in moving fast. From the high tension of restaurant work—both as a chef and manager—I had learned to do several things at once. In computer language, this is called multitasking. I could cook two omelets, stir-fry vegetables, and garnish plates, all at the same time—without anything burning. When I left restaurant work, I translated this "skill" to my home and writing life. I'd wash the dishes while heating water for tea while talking on the phone. I'd watch TV while sewing. Or brush my teeth as I searched for clothes in the closet.

It became a kind of game. I did a lot of simultaneous activities just to see if I could keep all the balls in the air. And I usually could. But it was not the natural rhythm of my life. It began to wear me out. I was wound so tight, watching and fearing one of those balls would drop, that I fatigued easily. I got more unhappy. I was never content with what I had because there was never enough of anything—time, money, love.

I realized one day that I was never living in the present moment. My mind was always focused on the next activity to add to those I was already juggling.

That day I tried a new technique: I began to do one thing at a time, very carefully, completely focused. Life became a contemplative exercise. How carefully could I wash this dish, sew that outfit? Brushing the dog was a religious experience when done with great care—and the dog loved it!

I remember being interviewed for a Chicago magazine around this time, and we discussed my struggle with slowing down, how fast equals best in the urban work ethic—something taught by our bosses and pumped up by the media—buy the faster car, the quicker plane flight, the fax and modem for your commute to work. My work background had taught me that too, I agreed.

But life had brought me a turning point to let me change this ingrained belief: my painful arm had caused me to look at my premise of how I was working.

"If you had ignored the message and just kept working at the same pace, what might have happened?" the interviewer wondered.

"I saw down the road," I told her, "that it was possible I might not be a writer, because my arm pain would have developed into a permanent problem. And since writing is one of the loves of my life, it was very frightening to me to think I could lose that vehicle for self-expression."

When it hits you where it hurts, you know you need

to make some kind of change.

When we're in the middle of a major turning point, it's sometimes hard to break with past training and see the gift in the change. One day I made a list of the benefits of living at a slower pace:

The operative word in "take time to smell the roses" is take.

—Adair Lara

1. Slowing down makes me restful inside and gathers my strength.
2. If I slow down and pace myself, I will have more energy for whatever life asks me to do.
3. Slowing down fills the well of creativity. I get great ideas when I am not rushing through my days.
4. Slowing down is more peaceful. My family likes it when I am more peaceful.
5. I am more graceful when I move slower.
6. I feel more of the natural abundance of life; there is less scarcity in my thinking when I slow down.
7. Slowing helps me focus on the moment.

Exercise:
To Recognize Benefits in a Change

Take ten minutes and make your own list of seven gifts a current change is bringing to you.

HOW SUCCESSFUL ARE YOU WITH CHANGE?

Here are two keys to moving through life's cycles with grace: (1) become aware of the natural rhythm of life, and (2) begin trusting the way life teaches us. It might teach through hunches, as I experienced with the cookbook project. Trusting the way life teaches us is essential to mastering change.

A friend had a significant dream that showed her more about this.

In the dream, she was moving into a new home provided by her church. Her boss had arranged for some of her old furniture to be moved, plus he had sent over new furniture. When my friend and her husband arrived at the new house, she was amazed but concerned.

"I'll have to work for God the rest of my life to pay for all of this," she said to her husband.

"But look," he said, "it's coming from the sky." Sure enough, the new furniture was falling out of the sky and landing softly inside the home. "Let's see the shipping slips," she argued. "Maybe there is something we don't need."

"Accept it all," her husband said softly. "What we don't need now, we'll store."

My friend was profoundly moved by this dream. It seemed to be saying to her, through the voice of her husband: *Accept the gifts life brings to you.* A benevolent force was telling her that she was completely taken care of if she would surrender and relax.

In the past, my friend had at times wondered if life was truly on her side. The dream brought her added reassurance that life was here to help her, not hinder her. "It's not that we won't have hardships," she added after telling me the dream. "But hardships don't have to be the point of life."

Such understanding grows as you develop trust in the rhythm of life, in yourself, and in God.

The inclination to goodness is imprinted deeply in the nature of man.

—Francis Bacon

CREATIVE PEOPLE, CREATIVE CHALLENGES

When I worked for the cookbook publisher, I noticed a great shift in my attitude. The job had been difficult, but I viewed it as creative challenge. And that made the turning point easier.

People who work easily with their turning points usually view changes as creative challenges, rather than unwelcome stress or disasters. They ask themselves first: *How can I make the best of this? How can I discover something new? What is the gift within this experience?* Many of these people have a basic belief: life, or God, is looking out for them.

They don't shirk responsibility, but they do believe wholeheartedly that life brings blessings rather than curses. They have a steady faith in life's process—that it continually evolves for good rather than bad.

To this kind of person, change can bring the excitement of discovery rather than dismay. If there's a gift within the experience, a creative person finds it.

"Creative people are often more able to live with tension, including constant change. The excitement of discovery outweighs anxiety over turning one's world upside-down," commented Dr. Wayne Myers of Cornell University Medical Center in a 1989 article in *SELF* magazine.

How do they do this? They remove the obstacle of fear.

Fear is born in the mind, and people who view change as a creative challenge reduce the fear by distracting the mind. They give it a puzzle to solve—a puzzle such as how to make the change work. Intent on solving the puzzle, the mind has little chance to become frozen and immobilized by fear.

Why is the mind so afraid of change? Because change gradually moves us away from the familiar. Even pain is familiar, and sometimes we talk ourselves into believing it is better because we at least know it.

This attitude is common; unfortunately it allows fear to grow unhampered and become our main block to mastering change.

It's natural to be afraid. Once we're propelled out of familiar, comfortable areas, our learning may intensify. Creative people acknowledge this fear and take up the challenge despite the fear.

With each challenge, the creative person sees more and more how life monitors and directs the pace of learning, much as a conductor conducts an orchestra.

PUSHING THE ENVELOPE

Some people drag their feet when faced with change. Others itch to move on, wondering why life is taking so much time to manifest the change.

They may push the envelope.

I experienced this when one of my books was published recently. I wanted a lot of publicity all at once, certain I could handle it. So I begged the publisher to hire a publicist to help promote my book via radio and TV. We placed ads in national media publications, and the publicist took calls from producers who wanted to set up interviews.

Before I knew it, I was scheduled for five different shows in one week!

I had had some experience with radio and TV interviews, but it had been years before. And now I was talking about spiritual topics, not cooking or nutrition.

My first show was an AM station in New Orleans, a five-minute phone interview during commuter drive time. The host barraged me with fast questions, and I hardly had time to formulate my answers before we were off the air. "Mastering change?" I heard him say

Your ability to deal effectively with the challenges in your life is greatly enhanced by your awareness and belief that you're not alone.

—Susan Pilgrim, Ph.D.

skeptically to his audience as I ended my interview. "Sounds tough to me." I knew I hadn't been a roaring success on that program.

Over the next two months, I logged phone and studio interviews on thirty-five stations. Each time, I got better. My answers got shorter, I spoke more from my own experience rather than trying to be the "change expert" as they had pegged me, and hosts began to stay on the line after my interview to tell me how great it had been. The learning curve was getting less and less difficult to master.

I learned that when the natural rhythm slows down, it's often to give us a chance to catch up. To adjust to the new rules. To learn the ropes.

Moving too fast through such a learning period is not advised. If you push the pace, you may find yourself in tense situations of learning on the run. With my interviews, one a week would have been easier to learn from—rather than one a day! I got a lot of experience all at once, and it was very uncomfortable and almost made me stop my book publicity altogether.

TECHNIQUE TO DISTRACT THE MIND

Fear often promotes the pushing. We fear that our life will slow down too much, perhaps. One man I spoke with had a useful technique that eased the mind's fear and helped him relax into the natural rhythm of his turning points.

He regularly charted his personal growth in a journal. Over the years he had noted how his life worked in a predictable pattern. Growth opportunities came at certain intervals, usually just when he was outgrowing some present circumstance—an inner belief or attitude, a relationship, living quarters, a job.

When a turning point hit, instead of panicking he took time to read through his journal entries for the past two to four months and highlight with a yellow marker anything that seemed to foreshadow the change.

He'd look for restlessness or upsetting experiences, anything unusual in his waking experiences or sleeping dreams—signs that might have been nudging him to look more closely at his life. Using this information he was able to prove to himself that advance warning always came before a turning point and gave clues as to the direction to take and choices to make.

Once he was paying attention, valuable insights began to come in dreams, daily experiences, and his daily contemplation periods.

Keeping a journal is a valuable tool I highly recommend (and will discuss more in the next chapter). Start one today. Practice writing a page or two each morning, describing your feelings, thoughts, and ideas from the day before. Write down your dreams if you remember them. When change comes, ask yourself, Have I noticed anything in the months leading up to this turning point? Any pattern found may encourage you to begin keeping notes more regularly to help predict and flow more easily with the next turning point.

Your writing will allow you to take the time to reconnect with the source of your inner knowing.

—Joyce Chapman, M.A.

REMOVING THE OBSTACLE OF FEAR

A key step to mastering change is removing any inner obstacles to making the change. As we talked about in chapters 1 and 2, fear is the most common block to change. Other emotions may hinder change as well, like anger, grief, or sadness at the loss of something familiar. But from surveys done with participants in my

Turning Points workshops, fear is the biggest.

In chapter 1, I told the story of my friend Joan who left her high-paying job when she found out she had CFIDS. Fear was Joan's biggest obstacle in the year that followed her move. She told me she did the Fear Room exercise on page 76 over and over during that time.

Whenever participants in Turning Points workshops try this exercise, the results are amazing; I am awed by the power each of us has to break through our own limitations.

One woman explained how she was in the process of an uneasy, sometimes bitter divorce. Why wasn't she able to move on? When she did the Fear Room exercise, in her imagination she saw a soupy fog that represented her fear. She imagined vacuuming it out, and when it cleared her ex-husband was standing in the center of the room. He had been hard enough to let go of as it was—was she holding on to him in some unconscious way too? she wondered. She tried everything she could think of to get him out of the inner room. Finally she ran over to one of the windows, opened it, and waited. To her surprise, her ex-husband walked right over and climbed out the window. Intense relief came over her, as she watched him go. She realized she had at last taken control of her inner state.

Other workshop participants have visualized different symbols for fear. One man saw a giant cage in the middle of the inner room. This represented his locked-up feelings.

One woman said she saw a wave; she felt overwhelmed by her life, and the wave was huge. It gave her a clue as to her inner state—she had been too busy to notice anything but a vague uneasiness whenever she tried to move forward.

My favorite response came from Catherine, a woman who had been in a car accident that left her with severe head injuries. At the end of the exercise, when I asked the group their reaction, Catherine very bluntly told me she hated visualization exercises and wasn't even going to do this one. But something inside her said to try it once—that her strong reaction might be a clue that something needed to be looked at. She decided to adapt the exercise to her own style, her own preferences. So she closed her eyes and imagined the fog-filled room, all the while saying to herself, *This is stupid, really. I won't get anything out of it.*

When we had finished the exercise, Catherine's face was lit up, glowing. I asked her what had happened.

She said, "When I went inside, I asked *What does this room mean to me?* And a sentence kept repeating over and over, *It's too much, it's too much, it's too big.* Then I allowed the cleaning out, the vacuuming, to happen. And in a second I began to hear, *You have everything you need; you have everything you need.* I noticed when the voice was saying *It's too much* that the room was very dark. But as soon as I heard *You have everything you need,* there was so much light. Then I went over and opened the shades on the windows, and there was an incredible flood of light into the room."

I asked the group to add one piece to the exercise: imagine that in your pocket there is a special gift to help you through this change. Reach into your pocket, and pull out the gift. Place it in the center of the newly cleaned room.

Catherine told us, "When I reached into my pocket,

Minds are like parachutes. They only function when they are open.

—Sir James Dewar

I drew out a thin, flat rock, like the kind we used to skip across a stream when we were little. It was a perfect skipping stone. And I knew this was my gift: To learn to move through this change lightly, like a stone skipping across the water." She knew this would help her get more focused.

Try the Fear Room exercise as your next step to mastering change.

Exercise: The Fear Room

Close your eyes, and breathe deeply for a few moments to relax any tension inside.

Imagine you're looking through a window into a small room. It's dark inside and filled with fog, a fog so dense that it's hard for you to make out the shapes of any objects.

Behind you is a large truck. A machine is being unloaded by some burly men. They wheel the machine up to a hole in the outside wall of the room and attach a long tube, like a vacuum-cleaner hose. One of them flicks a switch, and you watch as all the fog is slowly sucked out of the room.

Then the men unhook the machine, load it back onto the truck, and drive off.

Walk into the room, and look around. The fog is completely gone. There's a pleasant fragrance in the air and a light, pleasing sound you can barely hear.

Go to each of the five large windows in the room, and open the shades, allowing sunshine to flood in. Look around the room. What is left?

The room symbolizes the inner bodies—the emotions, the mind—that are filled with fear. Sometimes when I am facing a turning point that frightens me, I do this exercise several times a week. Each time I try it, the inner room is filled with the fog of fear. But I find that when I clean out the inner fog, my heart feels lighter.

BENEFITS OF LESS FEAR

So many people live with fear all the time, they hardly even notice it until its grip is gone. A new lightness comes over them; you can see it in their faces. Where actions and decisions used to be guided by fear ("What will other people think?" "What if I fail?" "Do I really have the strength to try this new step?"), the fear is replaced by love.

Mary Lou, an actress in New York City, told me her experience with the Fear Room exercise.

"I'd just left my job as a preschool music teacher and had decided I wanted to become a full-time actress. But I had a lot of fear about stepping out into this new reality. During my last week of teaching, my husband brought home a copy of your earlier book, *Turning Points*. I took one look at the title and thought, *Wow, that's what's happening to me! I'm not just taking the next logical step in my career, I'm actually changing in some fundamental way.*

"So I began reading the book, especially the sections on the fear of change and how to let go of this fear.

"I tried the Fear Room exercise. In my imagination I walked into the room, lifted the five window shades,

Strong and content I travel the open road.

— Walt Whitman

and allowed the sunlight to come into the room. A really uplifting experience! What it created in me was more confidence in myself and freedom to express myself—which were exactly the qualities I needed as I was moving into a professional acting career."

Mary Lou uses the Fear Room exercise when she auditions; the audition waiting room is often full of everyone's fear, she says, but she feels much calmer and more confident now. Maybe it's just coincidence, but I wasn't surprised when Mary Lou recently got her first acting job in a television series.

No time like the present.

— Mary Manley

Present Moment, Wonderful Moment

Once we loosen the grip of fear or other inner blocks to change, we can be more comfortable with living in the present moment. There's less reason to rush through our days. We experience less self-imposed stress.

Deepak Chopra, M.D., world-recognized authority on holistic health, says that stress is not so much about present problems: "Instead we feel anxiety because we anticipate pain in the future, or we feel depression, guilt or sorrow because we brood on pain from the past. Freeing yourself of past and future relieves you of stress. . . . it also makes you better able to get things done."

The concept of living in the moment is basic to our survival. I began learning this long ago, but it didn't really hit home until my friend Suzanne told me this story.

She had fallen in love with Bill, who lived in another city. Bill was planning to move to be with Suzanne, but there were several loose ends to tie up with his business. Not sure if a crucial business transaction would go through, Suzanne worried on the phone with Bill about their future. Would they ever be together? Would she have to quit her job and move to be with him? Around and around the conversation went.

Bill finally was silent for a moment, then he said, "Remember, things are OK right now. We're happy now." Suzanne was struck by the simplicity of this statement. In essence, if they could keep their focus on the present moment, their lives were happy.

Living in the moment means that you do the best you can to take care of future circumstances then place the greater part of your attention right here and now. Once you have done everything you can, you don't need to worry about losing your job, your spouse, your home. You've done everything you can.

Once you have prepared as best you can, you don't need to let your mind stew about what you will do tomorrow. You've done everything you can.

Living in the moment means being aware of your power in the present.

—Jeff Davidson

BENEFITS OF LIVING IN THE MOMENT

If you ignore the present moment, you are missing out on most of the joy in life.

You are also doomed to miss most of the hunches, or messages from life, the guidance that will show you what to do to move to the next level. If your focus remains in the past, what you've done up till now, or in the future, what you will be doing next, that's a very limited perspective. Especially when you realize things only happen in the present.

Joe Bailey, author of *The Serenity Principle,* said, "We are never really *in* the future; we only *think* we are.

In fact, we are always in the present, whether our thoughts are of the future or the past."

Living in the moment also means letting go of the past. In his book *Breathing Space,* Jeff Davidson asks: "What are you waiting for before you're willing to fully engage in life, in this day?" Most people have a list of times others have "done them wrong." They carry the list around like the heavy overcoat mentioned in the exercise in chapter 2. And it weighs a lot. Worse, it keeps them from paying any attention to turning points in the present.

Unable to focus on the present, they often make the same mistakes over and over again.

Those who can live in the present are able to do all they can do about the past and are content to let it be in the past. They resolve the things they can and let go of the things they can't. They do everything they agree to do and trust that that is good enough.

I practice living in the moment by monitoring worries and negative thoughts, since they are the troublemakers that steal my attention. When I have my attention on this process and a negative thought comes up, I find it helpful to write it down, along with possible resolutions. When it is out of my mind and on paper, it can dissipate more quickly, as in the exercise on page 81, adapted from "Write It Down!" in *The Spiritual Exercises of ECK* by Harold Klemp.

Some participants in my Turning Points workshops who were initially very reluctant to write down any negative thoughts—for fear they would come true—later commented on how healing this exercise was for them. It's a useful step in healing the past to bring these worrisome thoughts into the light, which can

The payoff in life is greatest for the purpose-centered person.

—David K. Reynolds

shine on them and put them in proper perspective. It allows you to see how small most worries really are and how easily action can be taken to resolve them.

Exercise:
On Dissipating Worry

To dissipate worry and regain focus in the moment, write a letter (that you never send) to someone you trust. Describe your worry, problem, or negative thought in the first few sentences.

Then keep writing anything that comes to mind. Often you will get at least one small action that you can take to resolve the issue.

If we have our own why of life, we shall get along with almost any how.

—Friedrich Wilhelm Nietzsche

As you take this action, you find that it frees you up to focus more attention on the present moment again.

TEACHING STORIES

As you work with inner blocks to change, you may begin noticing something peculiar: Many of your past and present changes revolve around one or two life themes.

Life themes are big lessons we struggle with, over and over again, until a major turning point comes along that allows us to move up another step on the ladder that is our life. When we recognize and creatively work with our life themes, we can begin to master change.

A woman in one of my workshops gave me a great example. She had been working on an exercise where she listed twelve major turning points in her life. Then she wrote for ten minutes about one of them, without censoring or editing herself.

When she had written one page, she put the writing away overnight.

She reread it in the morning and discovered an important insight about herself. Throughout the turning point she had written about, she was being gently led in a search for an important quality: inner freedom, or what she called "spiritual freedom." A sense of being who she really was, without limits. With a great deal of excitement, she read over the other turning points on her list and saw that nine out of twelve had themes of spiritual freedom.

A primary life theme was emerging for her. And she could now see it reflected in most every major change she'd experienced since she was a child.

The woman attended a worship service that Sunday and was surprised to find the discussion topic was childhood experiences the group most valued. Several people talked about spiritual freedom, and some of them carried it a step further to talk about the responsibility that comes with freedom.

The woman was excited to see a common thread running through her life experiences, binding them together. A master plan was certainly in effect. Seeing this larger plan helped her to become more aware of the guidance she was receiving. She now knew a primary theme of her life from a spiritual perspective: to find spiritual freedom and learn how to become responsible with it.

Try the exercise on page 83, then read the following three stories for more examples of life themes and how recognizing them can help us master change.

Exercise:
Finding Your Life Themes

1. List twelve major turning points in your life.

2. Write for ten minutes about one of them, without censoring or editing yourself.

3. Put the writing away overnight.

4. The second and third day, write about another two turning points for ten minutes each.

5. When you have written three pieces, re-read them and highlight any similar themes.

LIFE THEME: LEARNING GRACE

A life theme of my own emerged when I was using the exercise. I realized that most of my turning points in the past five years had been about learning to move through life with more grace.

Robert Redford wrote about grace as a theme for his 1993 movie on fly-fishing, *A River Runs Through It,* in an article for *Vogue:* "Grace was . . . a tool by which you carved your way to salvation. . . . As Norman McLean says, 'Trout as well as eternal salvation comes by grace, and grace comes by art, and art does not come easy.'" Grace for me became a way to realize more about God and God's plan for my life. And it did not come easily. The first time I began to be aware of grace as a theme in my life had to do with the first flower garden I planted.

To teach us, life uses the things we love. Gardening

By grace I mean an inner harmony, essentially spiritual, which can be translated into outward harmony.

—Anne Morrow Lindbergh

would prove to be a turning point to teach me a valuable spiritual lesson.

As you read this story, perhaps you'll see something in your own life that appears simple, such as learning to be a better gardener, that is turning you toward a higher good.

Nature herself takes on most gardeners to teach them a hard lesson in humility. Just when you think you have a handle on the seasons, the weather, and what you can expect to grow where, you are reminded how little control a gardener may have. Experience and skill are not worth much in the face of a freeze in April or a hailstorm in July.

My gardening experiences started soon after I moved to Minnesota and bought my first house.

It was a time of uncertainty in my life as well as a time of hope and new beginnings. I had recently been through a difficult divorce and sudden move from California to Minnesota. I had struggled to make the marriage work but it was tied to a failing business and both went down together. The whole process felt very ungraceful to me, and many people were hurt — which saddened me even more. Often, I thought about how I might have done it more smoothly, with less trauma to myself and others. I felt wilted, like a dried-out fern I had once bought on sale in a nursery.

But here I was, in a land of four definite seasons. My new life was slowly being built around a new relationship and a new job. I longed for my own home and a place to plant a garden. That dream came true when I found a home for sale that was small enough and priced right.

The only drawback was the yard.

The house had been unsold for months because of

that yard. Although the interior sported new wallpaper, flooring, and carpets—even a few new windows—the outside was scraggly, with patches of decaying plant life, bare soil, and occasional tufts of grass. The previous owners had kept several large dogs chained in the back, and the dogs, probably bored out of their minds all day, had amused themselves by digging. Being a writer, I felt I had a well-developed imagination. But even for me it was a stretch to imagine a garden emerging out of that desert of a yard.

During that first month in the new house, the weather was rainy and miserable, but I made plans to achieve grace and beauty in this new landscape—somehow.

By luck, I met a landscaper who gave me a good price on building a long line of raised flower beds in a sunny corner. Another dug up the withered old bushes and a few tree stumps that lined the yard. With my dwindling savings I bought some tiny juniper bushes, northern azalea, and plenty of spring flowering bulbs.

Most of the techniques of northern gardening were new to me. My father and grandmothers had all been wonderful gardeners, but in temperate and southern climates. Here in the north there were strict rules— plants did not survive below-zero temperatures unless they were "winter hardy." Luckily, everyone on my block gardened. I began to question two gardening neighbors to find out what flowers would grow in the new beds.

The first year I planted everything I could afford that was on sale at the local nursery. In an effort to cover the bare spots, I packed tiny perennial seedlings into every inch of space. But learning grace also means having a view toward future growth and allowing for it.

Shall I tell you what knowledge is? It is to know both what one knows and what one does not know.

—Confucius

The first summer the flower beds looked lush and inviting. But by the third summer the lushness had grown into a jungle, with the stronger plants cheerfully growing and suffocating the tiny ones.

I realized I had been shortsighted. It was expansion time. Evenings and weekends throughout that third summer found me outside digging another large bed alongside the first one and transplanting fifty plants from the original bed. They grew and grew and grew—by the next summer I had to build a third bed to accommodate all the growth.

By then I was learning to space the plants well apart to allow for their growth and beauty for many seasons to come.

Gardening gives one back a sense of proportion about everything except itself.

—May Sarton

Ironically, that was the year my new husband and I decided to sell that house and move farther out of the city. I had to say good-bye to all my flower beds—which was hard—but I soon started another garden at our new home. And I got to keep the lessons I had learned.

In our new house, I encountered new lessons about grace and gardening. The previous owners had terraced beds in the private backyard but had not planted much in them. The first spring, as I mused over those open spaces, part of me wanted to run out and buy as many plants as the car could carry.

The other part, the wiser part, remembered all that transplanting and digging.

Looking back, I can see this gardening experience was a metaphor for my life at that time. As I built my garden with hardy Minnesota prairie plants, I became stronger myself. The lessons I had learned with each flower bed were parallel to the lessons I was learning in emotional strength: (1) plant your dreams with a view toward the future, and (2) allow plenty of room for growth.

* * *

Poet Richard Hugo wrote about the struggle of learning, in reference to writers, which I found quite apropos to my lessons of grace and flower gardening: "Actually, the hard work you do on one poem is put in on all poems. The hard work on the first poem is responsible for the sudden ease of the second. If you just sit around waiting for the easy ones, nothing will come."

We will reach turning point after turning point as we practice building skills wherever we are weakest. The dried-out fern had been replaced with a prairie wildflower, one that could withstand more of the harsh winters of life.

A friend shared an exercise she uses to recognize the themes of the turning points in her life. This exercise helps her cultivate a feeling of gratitude for the lessons and experiences given to her. It also helps her get an overview of her particular lessons. Like when we stand on a mountaintop and survey the valley below, an overview allows us to see our problems and experiences as manageable rather than monstrous. The three parts of this exercise let us transform any traces of victimhood into a real thankfulness for what we *do* have.

Each time I try it, I am amazed at how it lifts me out of feeling sorry for myself, especially when I am caught in a repeating lesson. It often stops the repetition, allows me to learn what I need to learn, and lets me move on. A very refreshing experience! Try it whenever you feel stuck and yearn for a new perspective.

Find a quiet place to be alone for fifteen or twenty minutes before you begin. You'll need your journal and pen.

When conflict arises in our personal life, we can . . . accept the troubles as strengtheners from the Holy Spirit.

—Harold Klemp

Exercise:
Gratitude and Trust

1. Write down all the negative feelings you may have about yourself and your abilities, in all the areas you can think of. Imagine you are just letting all the negativity in your life flow out on the paper. Try not to censor yourself— no one but you will see this page. When you run out of things to write, take a clean sheet of paper.

2. Now write down all the gifts you have received from life. You can start small at first; include even things you may take for granted like your ability to breathe, run, eat, or to smile at someone else. Move on to bigger items that enhance your life.

3. Take a third page. Write down what you hope to learn from life. You can divide the page into different areas, such as work or career, family, spirituality, finances, creativity, etc.

4. To carry this exercise one step further, get a colored highlighting marker. Highlight any parallels you see between the three sections you wrote—the negatives, the things you are grateful for, and the things you wish to learn.

How often have you lamented about what you didn't want? Did it ever bring you what you really wanted?

—Louise L. Hay

These parallels may be your life themes and may help you locate turning points that need looking at. Look for signs of life themes emerging in any turning points that come to you in the next six months.

LIFE THEME: OPENING THE HEART

A friend told me the following story about a man with a life theme of learning how to share his heart with others.

Jim was intelligent and insightful, but he had a reluctance to get involved in other people's lives. This had given him freedom for many years, but now he was older—and feeling lonely. The isolating wall he had so carefully built was hindering his next step—allowing his heart to open. Jim's story shows how he found this important life theme in his turning points.

Jim's turning point was more subtle than many of the more dramatic physical challenges that many of us face, but a change of heart can be just as hard to face.

Jim worked in an engineering plant in Dallas, Texas. Every morning he saw the same group of people get off the bus at his stop, and after a few weeks he realized these people worked in a sheltered workshop down the street. The workshop employed the mentally disabled.

One member of the group was a large woman with short red hair who appeared to have Down's syndrome. She was always terrified to cross the street. She would stand with her shoulders hunched, fear on her face, until one of her friends would take her arm. The friend would lead the red-haired woman across the street to safety. Jim often watched this process, worrying that the small group wouldn't make it across. Traffic rushed by; the street was very busy, with three lanes in each direction.

One day Jim reached his office about forty-five minutes later than usual and saw a woman, obviously very upset, walking toward the lobby.

She seemed familiar, but Jim was late and didn't want to get involved with someone else's problems. So he went through the lobby and down the hall to his office. In the time it took him to walk through the building, Jim realized that the woman in the lobby was the red-haired woman who had such trouble crossing the street. Shamed by his own indifference, Jim raced back to the lobby to see if he could offer his services, however belatedly. But the receptionist had already called the woman's supervisor, and he was coming to escort her.

Jim gave himself a C- for the episode. He hadn't been able to overcome his emotional inertia in time to reach out and help a fellow Soul in distress. He felt he had not made the most of that learning experience.

But opportunity always knocks again with our life themes.

Two months later, Jim was again late for work. As he rounded the corner from the parking lot, he caught sight of the red-haired woman. This time it looked as if she was in real trouble. She had tried to cross the busy six-lane street alone, but the task proved too much for her.

She stood frozen on the median, panic-stricken and hysterical.

As fast as his legs could carry him, Jim reached the woman. She grabbed his arm. "Let me help you across," he said.

"Do you know how to cross this street?" the woman asked nervously.

"Yes," Jim said, "I cross it every day, sometimes two or three times." The woman looked reassured.

When the traffic cleared, the pair walked across the street, calmly reaching the other side, although the woman never let go her iron grip on Jim's arm. The woman thanked Jim, her confidence restored, and they parted.

Jim saw the woman one more time after that—she was crossing the street alone and reached the other side safely, all by herself. He realized in challenging his own fear of getting involved with others, he may have helped make the world a better place for that woman.

LIFE THEME: OPTIONS TO ANGER

Reviewing our past is an easy way to learn to recognize the themes running through our turning points. A friend told me about a turning point that was very difficult, since it forced her to alter a fundamental part of her behavior. It also brought out a major life theme for her.

Looking back on all that happened, she realized how much happier she is now because of the change.

Margaret's story could be that of any one of us. It had to do with her temper, her best defense against the world. Raised in a crowded city that was known for its high crime rate, Margaret had always felt proud of her ability to protect herself under any circumstances. With her quick tongue, she could lash out scathingly at any potential attacker, whether it was a clerk trying to cheat her in the supermarket or someone harassing her on the subway.

In her late thirties Margaret and her husband moved to a small town in the Midwest, where Margaret got her present job working as the office manager in a small law firm. After about six months on the job, her boss called her in one afternoon. He explained that several of the lawyers were taking offense at her quick temper and found her extremely hard to work with.

You're traveling toward home— to the life you want, you choose, and you aim for.

—Mark Bryan and Julia Cameron

Margaret was sincerely surprised and quite hurt by her boss's comments. Growing up where anger was a convenient and popular weapon against crowded conditions, she thought little of her quickness to strike back when she felt taken advantage of. How did other people survive without this kind of defense?

Since she loved her job, she swallowed the retorts she wanted to toss at her boss and promised to try harder to keep a lid on her temper around the office.

This was her turning point—as she realized later. Life was asking her to change.

Margaret began an earnest search among her friends to find people she considered good survivalists but who didn't use anger indiscriminately. One woman in her church study group seemed a perfect example, and Margaret vowed to get to know her better. Surprisingly Jeannine called her up the following weekend to go to a show at the art museum. Jeannine was quite understanding when Margaret explained her situation.

The man who makes no mistakes does not usually make anything.

—William Connor Magee

"I feel like this is an important step for me," said Margaret, "but I'm very scared about changing my ways and letting go of anger. It's the best defense I know, and I don't believe I have any other tools to protect myself."

"Maybe your situation has changed," Jeannine offered. "I used to live in a big city. I taught at an inner-city school, and I felt anger was the best defense against the bullies there. But when I moved here, I realized anger was a tool I no longer needed.

"In fact," she added, "it stood in my way."

"But how did you let go of it?" Margaret asked.

"First I asked God for help in whatever way I could understand. My husband was a big help to me in this because he is very sensitive to anger; sometimes it even makes him sick. So I had to curb my instincts to lash out at him or the kids I work with whenever I felt threatened. I tried to go off by myself and cool down. I also had good friends to talk to. This showed me how to replace the anger in my life with love."

Margaret felt that the meeting with her boss and the conversation with Jeannine opened a new door. She didn't know it at the time, but she was preparing inwardly for a big change.

There is something in us mortals that is immortal.

—Elie Wiesel

Life had placed the crossroads before her as a test to see what she would do. Her willingness to learn another way of being, to put anger aside, softened her heart.

The following year Margaret got the confirmation she needed about the changes she had allowed to happen.

She was asked to give a short presentation at a church conference about spiritual lessons and spoke very humbly and simply of the changes she had encountered that year. A woman she had known before came up to her in the hallway after the talk. The woman had tears in her eyes.

"I can't believe how much you've changed. How have you managed to become such a loving person in so little time? When I knew you back in the city, you had such a hard edge," the woman told Margaret.

Margaret realized that her theme of using anger had served her for many years but she had grown to the point where she needed new tools. She now watches for opportunities to use love instead of anger in situations.

Reading the stories in these three chapters may have given you more of an understanding about your own relationship to change. Want to improve it? In the next chapter we'll begin looking at specific tools to master change in your life.

Truth is so simple. So why doesn't everybody know it? Because it's too simple. Because we have our preconceived notions about what truth is or what it should be.

—Harold Klemp

Ask Yourself: How Would You Like to Move Forward in Your Life?

Write answers to the following questions. They may help you understand how to become more creative with change.

1. Is there anything you'd like to try but are afraid to? Define your specific fears with the new situation.

2. Have you considered a worst-case scenario as a way to give yourself confidence to make this change?

3. If you could come back to this life and be anybody (besides yourself) who would you be?

4. What kind of relationship to change does this imaginary person have?

5. Do you rely on hunches or "gut feelings" to help you make a change? What is your gut feeling telling you about this change? What would you need in order to trust it?

4

Change Your Relationship with Change

Adding to the Toolbox

*Our creative dreams and
yearnings come from a divine source.
As we move toward our dreams, we
move toward our divinity.*

—Julia Cameron

4. CHANGE YOUR RELATIONSHIP WITH CHANGE

*M*asters of any trade have tools. A master carpenter's toolbox is an array of precision tools for every possible situation that could come up in working with wood. A master painter has fine sable brushes, linseed oil, palette knife, and paints. A skilled computer programmer has code, files, and computer languages to build new programs. Each master in every area of life depends on certain tools to do his or her job.

I've often wondered, *Are there tools for handling change? What if someone were to hand me a toolbox that had everything in it I needed to handle change in my life?*

In looking at successful changes in my own life and others' lives, I've seen there are indeed such tools. People who ride easily through their turning points reach into a toolbox they have built over the years and use certain inner and outer tools. These are not hammers or sable brushes or programming code; they are often more spiritual tools. Like dream study, inner guidance, and a daily spiritual practice, such as prayer, contemplation, or meditation, that gives them strength, purpose, and direction. Change that would stymie another person might only confuse these people for a day—a week at the most—then they would almost visibly shake themselves and dig into their toolbox for something to help them get on with life.

In the next three chapters of this book, we'll learn about these tools and how to use them to work with change. By the end of this section, you may have accumulated new tools or reawakened your understanding of how to use those you've had all along.

While the body sleeps, we leave it for the inner worlds. The time spent there is called a dream.

—Harold Klemp

First Tool: The Power of Dreams

We all dream. And today more people are talking about dreams. In September 1995, *Life* magazine's cover story focused on "What Dreams Can Do for You." Listed as benefits of dreaming were (1) being able to detect illnesses before doctors can, (2) overcoming trauma and depression, and (3) unlocking the brain's mysteries. For me, dreams do all that and more. Dreams help me unravel the mysteries in my own life.

Because I have written my dreams down almost every day since 1974, I have found that I naturally look to my dreams for answers during tough times. And the answers are usually there. For example, during a difficult situation with a close friend I was able to see the future of our friendship through a dream.

This friend was going through a lot of major changes in her life, and so was I. Both of us were in our thirties, living in a new city, far from friends and family. We had met through work and grown closer through long talks and regular lunch dates. When tough times hit in our personal lives, it seemed natural that we would be drawn toward each other. I was grieving over the breakup of a three-year relationship, and she had just moved out from living with her boyfriend. Smarting from these sudden and painful changes, we decided to spend more time together to sort out the big question of life: Is love possible?

We combed antique shops, visited a health spa for her birthday, and spent many evenings talking, having tea, and exchanging stories. I was enthused about this new friendship blossoming just when I needed emotional support in my life.

About two months into our friendship, my friend hit a personal crisis at work. When it happened, I thought she would turn to me.

But she didn't. She crawled into a cave like a wounded animal. She wouldn't even tell me what had happened. No amount of talking could reach her. I was hurt and confused. Why had she excluded me?

I stewed about this situation for five days.

Whenever work slowed and I had a moment of peace, I'd close my eyes to relax a little, but all I could see was my friend's face. I felt such sorrow and lack of understanding about what was happening. I also recognized that I was caught in a morass of emotions about the situation.

I would have to free myself of the morass. But how would I do that?

By the end of the week, sick of the anger and pain I felt, I tried the Fear Room exercise in chapter 3 before bed. I wanted an answer to come in my dream, but I knew that the intense emotion I was feeling would make the dream unclear.

I saw my inner room filled with fog, but there was

Vision is the art of seeing things invisible.

—Jonathan Swift

also a coating of sticky black molasses all over the floor and walls. It was gooey and thick. I realized it represented the pain I felt.

So in the exercise I first imagined vacuuming out the fog of fear, then sending in a team of cleaning people to hose down the walls and floor. A river of thick molasses ran out into the street. It took quite a bit of time before I felt the room was clean of all the traces of this strong emotion.

By the time I fell asleep, most of the heavy emotion was gone. I felt much lighter. I asked inwardly for any further insight that would help me understand my friend's situation and the future of our friendship, then I drifted off to sleep.

A lovely dream came.

I do not know how to distinguish between our waking life and a dream. Are we not always living the life that we imagine we are?

—Henry David Thoreau

In the dream I was visiting my friend's house. She had two vacuum cleaners going, and she was racing around the house trying to clean huge piles of dirt. She hugged me but said she didn't have time to visit. Would I please come back later when she had finished cleaning the house? She thought it would take her about a week, no longer. When I awoke I knew the dream had given me both reassurance and an important message: My friend was cleaning out something in her life and couldn't be there for me right now. I relaxed, finally able to see the situation from a more compassionate viewpoint.

Then the most incredible thing happened. My dream proved to be prophetic.

Just as the dream had shown, within a week my friend called me. She was back—and thanking me for giving her space during that difficult time. As she told me what had happened, I realized her method of handling a problem was to retreat and take stock of her life. My style was completely different—I usually liked to talk it out. But now that she had explained things, I felt happy and close again.

Despite that brief week of trouble, our friendship had grown and strengthened. I was very grateful that my dream had encouraged me to be patient, to allow my friend the space and time she needed to clean out her life.

MAPPING YOUR DREAMS

Each morning as I wake up, my dreams flit across my consciousness. Sometimes they are vivid, earthshaking dreams like the one in the story above. Other times they are nonsense dreams—or so they appear at the time. Without fail, I write them all down. This is the key to remembering dreams.

A guest on call-in radio shows across the U.S. and Canada, I have fielded many questions about dreams from listeners. The main question people have is, "How do I remember my dreams?"

I tell them what I've learned, how it is essential to record your dreams regularly in some way: either by writing them, tape-recording them, or even drawing them. As you begin to record your dreams regularly, you will also begin to remember more details of your dreams. This is a proven truth in my life. When I neglect to write down my dreams each morning, I begin to remember fewer and fewer dreams. It's as if the inner memory gets rusty from disuse. Polishing my dream recall is the daily discipline of dream recording.

But dreams fly from the mind so quickly! So when I wake in the morning, I choose one key word or phrase

With every challenge you face, you grow.

—Susan
   Pilgrim,
   Ph.D.

from my dream to jog my memory when I sit down to write. If I had just had a dream about my grandmother's apartment, the key word might be *grandmother*. As a shortcut on a very sleepy morning, I simply give the dream an alphabet letter (*G* for grandmother) which will trigger memory of the phrase, then the dream, when I start writing. This is especially helpful if I have more than one dream to remember in the morning.

The other rule I follow is to write down all the dreams I have, even the silly ones.

Silly dreams can prove extremely useful when they are reviewed. They can yield important information. They can prepare us for events. One spring I was invited to New York City to give a talk at a conference. I had lived in New York when I was younger. Remembering only the high crime rate and other bad memories, I had strong fears about going back to the city. I knew I needed to get over these fears before my trip in the spring. Around February of that year, I began having regular dreams about Manhattan. I would be in a lovely restaurant, having dinner with friends, enjoying myself. Or I'd be in a crowd of friends, walking down one of Manhattan's busier streets. Each time I woke from such a dream, I wrote down the details.

As the trip got closer, I noticed that, strangely enough, my fear of New York had dissipated. I was actually looking forward to the trip! A group of ten friends had booked a table for dinner at a famous French-Asian restaurant for the Saturday evening of the conference, which also happened to be my birthday. And a trip to the New York Botanical Garden was planned. The whole weekend looked like such fun.

On my visit, I fell in love with the city that had so

Your everyday life holds much more that's worth your attention than you may have thought.

—David K. Reynolds, Ph.D.

frightened me for years.

When I returned home, I was very curious about what had happened. The outer experience had been transformed because—somehow—the inner fear had gone. But how?

Looking for clues, I reread my dream journal for the past two months, highlighting key phrases or interesting scenes with a yellow highlighting pen, as I usually do. I counted six separate dreams about New York City in the weeks leading up to my trip. Each dream was about having a great—and safe—time there. I realized that the dream experiences had slowly lessened the fear I had, allowing me to enjoy New York to the fullest. If I hadn't recorded those dreams, I might never have seen the role they played in my safe and enjoyable journey.

SPIRITUAL CONFIRMATION IN DREAMS

Dreams also help us make tough decisions or give confirmation at a crossroads.

Sarah told me about a dramatic dream that helped her make a life-changing decision. She had been married for years but was starting to feel crushed on all sides by the limitations of that marriage. For quite a while she had been wondering whether to get a divorce.

One night Sarah had a dream that helped her decide.

In her dream, Sarah was driving a car up a very steep mountain. The road twisted and turned, and as she came to each curve, Sarah knew she had to say her last name. This was the rule of the dream that she just knew instinctively. The right name would get her safely around the sharp curve. Each time Sarah said her married name, she didn't make it around the curve. The name was too long. When she said her maiden

As Soul, you are like a balloon that rises above the ground. The higher you go, the farther you can see. And the farther you can see, the better you can plan your life.

—Harold Klemp

name, which was shorter, the car took the curves beautifully. Sarah tried this over and over in the dream, and it kept working.

It took her a while to trust the dream's message and understand what this dream was all about, even after she had written it down.

The dream was telling Sarah that she wasn't looking at what was completely obvious in her life. The mountain represented her life, and she wanted to go up the mountain. But if she held on to her marriage she wouldn't make the turns of her life very well—if at all. Her marriage was holding her back, keeping her from the life she wanted to live. The dream confirmed her feelings that it was time to leave.

If we believe that we are loving, caring individuals who belong in this world, our reaction to the vicissitudes of life might be quite different than if we feel we are unloved and isolated.

—Rick Fields

As she thought about this vivid dream, Sarah says more was revealed to her. "It showed me that the dreams of my heart, conscious and unconscious, are reflected clearly in my night dreams," she says. "There's a strong connection between my daily life and my dreams; there's synchronicity. I felt a golden thread of love, looking out for my best interests, running through the dreams of my heart and the dreams of my nights. I got a lot of things from this dream—it wasn't just about the divorce."

Sarah is awed by the practical nature of life and how it is teaching her. "On one level there is the practical side, which helps me take a step in my life," she says. "On the other is the mystical side that teaches me about my relationship with God."

How to Decode Your Dreams

Dreams often work in symbols. What's the reason for this? Our mind, our internal censor, automatically blocks the real meaning of our dreams. Its purpose is to protect us from whatever images or experiences might upset us. As we begin to work with our dreams, we learn to decipher the symbols. We learn our own dream language.

As a result, our dreams become less jumbled, our learning more direct.

Although modern dream books often have lists that tell you what each dream symbol means, it is highly unlikely that a symbol would have the same meaning for everyone. To Sarah the mountain meant her life, but to another person it might symbolize a job, a steep learning curve, a rocky relationship, or an insurmountable obstacle. The best way to work with dream symbols is to create your own dream dictionary. I do this when I review my dream journal every month. I highlight the symbols and list them in the back of my journal by month.

Over time, the dream symbols that repeat are easily recognizable. They become important to me.

A recurring dream symbol I have had for years is my grandmother's empty apartment. She died many years ago, but I still see her empty apartment in my dreams. I wander around, looking into each room. There is a dead, stale feeling about the place, as if it has been vacant for years.

I wrote down these dreams, noting this recurring symbol in all its variations, for months. It wasn't until I looked back at my journal that I noticed a definite pattern: Each time I dreamed about my grandmother's apartment, something would change in my life within the next few days or weeks. One time, I got a new job. Another time, a new friendship came into my life. Or

To be receptive to a new way of seeing, we have to not only relax but also open ourselves and make room for the new.

—Susan
  Sarback

I'd go on a trip.

For my dream dictionary, my grandmother's empty apartment came to mean "a change is coming."

In my workshops, I often teach how to keep a spiritual journal, and a six-part dream-decoding exercise (see below). It has been very helpful to many people, especially to unravel the meaning of a complex dream.

Exercise:
Decoding Your Dream

1. Write down your dream in as much detail as possible. It's helpful not to censor yourself and to write as quickly as is comfortable.

2. List your feelings about the dream. You may have woken up feeling angry, peaceful, excited, optimistic. What strong emotion did the dream provoke in you?

Our dreams can be a source of genius for us.

—Bryan W. Mattimore

3. List the names of anyone who appeared in the dream, such as your friend John, your uncle, an old man in a white robe, your neighbor's dog, your fifth-grade teacher.

4. Give your dream a title, as if it were a story. Sarah's dream might have a title like "Up the Mountain of My Life."

5. Go back to the written dream from step 1, and underline any key symbols that pop out at you.

6. Formulate one question you'd like answered about the dream. Write down this question in your journal.

Here's an example of how these six steps can trigger understanding—through helping you get an overview of a dream.

Not long after I got my first puppy, I had a horrible dream where he was playing in a driveway and a car slowly started backing down the drive toward him. I tried to run to him but my legs were too slow, as if I was running through thick sand. I woke up, heart pounding, scared to death. The dream repeated several nights later. My puppy was fine, of course, but I wondered why I had had this recurring nightmare.

When I did the six steps, I uncovered some very basic fears about losing control in my life. Getting the puppy had been a tough decision. I've been a cat person all my life. Cats are very independent. Dogs demand an entirely different kind of care, and the added responsibility was scaring me to death—hence, the nightmare. Doing the exercise relieved my concern that the puppy would actually die, and showed me how it was symbolizing *my* life instead. It focused me on some work I needed to do: facing my own fears and attitudes about giving up control over small details and trusting life more. When I finally took care of this, I stopped having the scary dream.

If we regard all life as a dream, where outer experiences arrive in symbols and are teaching us too, the exercise works there as well. A Turning Points workshop participant told me about how it helped her understand three separate, and confusing, outer experiences she'd had recently and what they were telling her about her relationship with her children.

Lynn had three very odd experiences. The first

It is in acceptance that the mind and heart become free. For just as autumn yields to the coming of winter, so does winter receive the awakening of spring.

—John Robbins
and Ann
Mortifee

involved a robin pecking frantically on a window out-side a greenhouse at a friend's home. The robin was trying to get inside.

The second involved a squirrel who attempted to chew its way into the attic of Lynn's house.

The third was a spider determined to make his home on newly constructed walls, which Lynn was in the process of sanding.

Go to your bosom; / Knock there, and ask your heart what it doth know.

—William Shakespeare

Lynn felt these three incidents were connected. As she worked through the six-step exercise, she looked at the three characters in this story and realized they were all trying to get "home." But none of the creatures was doing it in a natural way; instead they were forcing entrance or building homes where it was impractical. Lynn looked at this as a symbol of something in her life and wondered, *Am I also trying to force something?*

Lately she had been having a difficult time with her three children, trying to force them to do things. She real-ized the three characters in her "waking dream" repre-sented her three children. From the exercise, she began to understand that she didn't have to force anything.

Why do we have such dreams and waking dreams? Dreams that are prophetic, dreams that help us unravel our lives?

In the waking life, there's often too much mental resistance to God's inner messages. As our lives speed up, we may listen less in our waking lives, so the only place these messages can come through is in our dreams.

Dreams are very practical. In my dreams, I'll get information about what to eat, where to go, who to be with. One winter, I was feeling lethargic, as if I had exhausted all my energy reserves. I had a nagging feel-ing I needed to change my diet; I felt there was some food I needed to eat to help me regain my energy. But I had no clue what it was. Then I had the idea to review my dream journal from this time last year. I read entries in November of the year before and saw the same symptoms. What had I done? A dream had come of standing in a field of greens—mostly kale. So I had begun eating steamed kale every night with dinner. And my energy had come back.

When I reread this entry, I was excited. Here was the practical information I needed. So I went to the store and bought kale. It worked! My energy level returned to normal.

An important thing to note: It's not just recording dreams, but it's also reviewing dreams that leads us to see our own unique patterns. As we review dreams, we see how the same patterns show up in our waking life. To save time, I chart both, as in the exercise below.

Dreams are important in terms of how they assist you creatively.

—Maurice Sendak

Exercise:
Charting Your Dream Patterns

1. For each month, make two columns: *Waking* and *Dreaming*.

2. Go through your journal entries for the month and circle or highlight any experiences, symbols, or phrases that stand out, whether from a dream or an everyday experience.

3. Write these phrases in the appropriate column for that month.

4. Highlight repeating patterns in your dream and waking life. What do they tell you about changes you need to make?

Second Tool: Daily Spiritual Exercises

I found a secret that has helped me with mastering change. It's the second tool in my spiritual toolbox: a daily spiritual exercise. This is a form of nondirected prayer where you listen to the guidance God is giving. Daily spiritual exercise helps me maintain a broader focus and perspective. And because of this, I can pay attention to my own turning points a lot better.

We work our physical muscles to get flexibility and strength; it makes sense that our inner muscles also need a regular workout. The people I know who handle change well often have a daily spiritual exercise they use to get clarity and peace inside. As we tone our inner muscles through the daily practice of spiritual exercises, they get stronger, able to lift more and propel us more quickly into the higher viewpoint of Soul.

What is a spiritual exercise?

It's simply a way to practice letting God work through us in every detail of our lives. During a spiritual exercise, we let go of our worries and the everyday world, and listen to life, or God. From the outside a spiritual exercise may look a lot like just sitting still, but inside it is much more active.

Anyone Can Do a Spiritual Exercise

Doing a spiritual exercise is easy. I make up my own as needed or choose one from Harold Klemp's *The Spiritual Exercises of ECK,* a book that contains 131 different exercises for most any type of situation. I know that, as Soul, I am creative. Each of us is. And each Soul approaches God in a different way. In their spiritual practice, some people like to use visualiza-

Quiet is not necessarily an absence of action, but an absence of negative thoughts running wild in a thought system that takes them seriously.

—Jane Nelsen, Ed.D.

tion, others work with sound, others experience a feeling of upliftment.

There are two basic guidelines that I have found to be crucial. The first is to do your spiritual exercise each and every day. The second is to set a length of time to do it, say twenty minutes, and stick to your schedule.

Why do your spiritual exercise every day?

If you stop your spiritual exercises, you may not notice a difference at first. Things will go pretty much as usual, but then you may start finding that life is slightly more difficult to deal with. While you were doing your exercises, you were tapping into a strong source of higher awareness. When you stop the regular spiritual exercises, you pull the plug and slowly lose this source of nourishment.

Most spiritual teachers recommend staying with a spiritual exercise for a period of time. Earlier in my life as I explored different spiritual paths, I tried out their practices and religiously followed them without variation.

If the practice worked—if it made me feel stronger inside and more able to cope with my life—I stuck with it. If not, I didn't. But I usually like to test things—even when they are working well. I'm not a devoted rule follower, unless I see the reason behind the rule. And even when I find a practice that works for me, I like to test it occasionally just to be sure.

I had used spiritual exercises daily for ten years, then one day I decided to stop and see what happened.

It was natural to stop doing my exercises that summer; I had just moved, and there was so much to do. The first few days I hardly noticed when I didn't set aside twenty minutes each morning; I just woke up and

If your belief in something is strong enough, if it's really right for you, or you feel you were meant to do it, then you will find the inner resources to make it happen.

—Paul D. Tieger
  and Barbara
  Barron-Tieger

began unpacking boxes. After a week of not doing the exercises, things started to become more difficult for me.

I was short-tempered with others, less forgiving of myself. It was hard for me to be detached from my stronger emotions. I put the blame on everyone else but myself.

Have you ever noticed how life can use its creatures to help us? Especially pets. My two cats were the ones who got me back on track. They loved doing the exercises each morning; they'd often curl up on my lap as I sat there. While the living room was in boxes, our favorite chair was not available, but still they sat hopefully next to it each morning at the right time.

On the sixth day the contemplation chair was finally unearthed, and my cats happily curled up at the appropriate time. Then they just stayed there.

I was still unpacking, but in a distracted and inefficient way, feeling worse about my life, my new home, everything. Walking through the living room, I finally noticed the cats. Everything hit at once.

It took me a few days to begin enjoying the exercises again. At first I was restless, not really sure why I was doing them, but the cats were solid weights on my lap so I stayed. Slowly the rhythm came back.

I began to experience the inner peace I had enjoyed before. I was convinced again.

This time, thanks to my brief lesson about the importance of doing the spiritual exercises on a regular schedule, I began doing them out of love rather than duty. I wanted the state of consciousness that came with them. So I did them every day. It was that simple.

I have also experimented with how long to do my daily exercise. I found that ten or fifteen minutes only

We all have beliefs and values that can enlighten us and provide strength during moments of confusion and despair.

—David D. Burns, M.D.

got me to the point where I was relaxed and ready to receive, like tuning in a radio. Thirty minutes left me groggy. Twenty was just enough. Now I set a kitchen timer to ring at twenty minutes, so I don't have to think about the time.

IMMEDIATE BENEFITS

Remember the exercise in chapter 2 about the overcoats surrounding Soul? The qualities of Soul shine through all these heavy overcoats, and they shine into our physical life as we practice these spiritual exercises. Most of the time I find flexibility, love, spontaneity, and generosity are part of my life—naturally.

Who wouldn't give twenty minutes a day for these kinds of benefits?

I really appreciate it when I am able to maintain a broader focus and perspective. I can see my own turning points coming before life has to shout to catch my attention. These are tangible rewards. But it's easy to talk yourself out of the time you need to put in to get these benefits.

The desire to practice spiritual exercises regularly is not something that can be imposed on us by another person; the love for doing them has to come from within. In my life I used to follow the routines of my spiritual practice or church out of duty rather than love; when I did this, I secretly resented it. I was more mean-spirited and had great difficulty handling change. But I had to learn this for myself. I had to try the exercises to see how much happier I could be when the desire to do them regularly came from my heart.

Spiritual growth must come from within us, rather than be imposed on us by other people or events.

Types of Spiritual Exercises

The three types of spiritual exercises I use most often are contemplation techniques, visualization techniques, and imaginative techniques. Sample exercises are scattered throughout this book and listed in the table of contents, or see page 353 for an entire listing.

1. Contemplation Techniques

Contemplation techniques are mostly listening exercises. I chant or sing a sacred word, quiet myself, give over my problem, then sit and listen. An example is below.

Exercise:
Hearing God Call Your Name

One day I was unhappy because of a series of setbacks in my life. As I sat in my living-room chair doing my daily spiritual exercise, I asked God, "How can I get back to love? I feel so far from it today."

Softly, gently, I began hearing my name: "Mary, Mary." It was so faint at first, I thought I had imagined it.

Then I heard it again. It came in waves to my inner hearing, like faraway wind chimes being brushed by a breeze.

Over and over I heard my name being called. With such deep love. I realized how much the Divine loves each one of us as spiritual beings, as Soul.

Try this as a spiritual exercise. Sit very quietly, and imagine God is calling your name.

2. Visualization Techniques

Visualization techniques work on the principle that we, as Soul, move where we focus our attention. I often visualize the Light and Sound of God (two ways God communicates with all life). I'd visualize it streaming in, healing and uplifting me. Below is an example.

Exercise:
To Regain Your Balance

When I was feeling very sad one day, I designed this exercise to regain inner balance.

1. Visualize being on board a sleek ship. The captain takes you to the control room, and you both stand before a large dial.

2. Ask the captain to show you how to adjust the dial to regain your balance. The needle on the dial might be all the way to the right or left, when it needs to be in the center. Adjust the dial.

3. Thank the captain, and open your eyes. Write down how you feel now, compared to how you felt earlier.

Be gentle with yourself. Treat yourself at least as well as you'd treat the family dog.

—Marshall J. Cook

Some people in my workshops have told me they have trouble with visualization techniques. They don't see anything. If you cannot easily visualize, try one of the writing techniques that are scattered throughout this book. Or adapt a visualization technique to use different senses, such as hearing. Each technique brings the same result—an increased amount of love.

3. Imaginative Techniques

Imaginative techniques use different senses—not just seeing but also smell, sound, touch, and taste. I might imagine myself sitting in a beautiful place, surrounded by the sound of tolling bells or wind chimes. I could imagine myself in a sailboat; I feel the boat rocking, and I smell the wind.

One purpose of a spiritual exercise is to create a receptive place for Soul to operate freely. Whichever type of spiritual exercise gives you a feeling of peace and an open heart is the right one for you. I tuck such places into my memory—a creek I sat by as a child, a room full of plants at the Minnesota Landscape Arboretum, a waterfall in Hawaii—and use them in imaginative techniques to bring the sense of peace I need for my heart to open.

The daily exercise of twenty or thirty minutes gives a better focus and a deeper strength to your life. It is what lets you be a living spiritual exercise the whole day long.

—Harold Klemp

What Can You Expect from a Spiritual Exercise?

When I first began doing daily spiritual exercises in 1975, I was just putting in time. I sat each morning, eyes closed and breath even. Not much happened that I was aware of. Sometimes a short flash of color would appear before my eyes. Sometimes I would fall asleep briefly and wake up marvelously refreshed.

But never did I have the incredible experiences others raved about—like being outside of my body, floating on the ceiling, or consciously visiting other worlds or levels of heaven.

Two years went by, and one afternoon I was talking to a friend who had practiced her daily spiritual exercises much longer than I had.

I hesitantly asked her what hers were like. Did she

have the extraordinary experiences I had read about?
She said no, she didn't.

I asked her why she had continued to do them if
nothing had happened.

She simply explained that the reasons for doing
regular spiritual exercises were more subtle for her.
Many wonderful changes had come about in her life,
and she saw this growth as the main benefit of her
practice. Who cared about floating on the ceiling when
one could have inner peace or an ability to deal with
conflict better?

*Faith is the subtle
chain which binds
us to the infinite.*

—Elizabeth
Oakes Smith

"Look at how you've changed," she added, turning
to me. She had known me at the beginning. To her, I
was now a different person.

Why have I kept doing them? Because now even I
see changes in myself.

DAILY PROBLEM SOLVER

Why start a spiritual exercise routine? Here's one
reason: it can be a daily problem solver. If you go into
a spiritual exercise with a question, it will often be
answered.

Training yourself to hear the answer takes time—
and discipline. Your outer ears are not easily tuned to
the whisperings of God. But day after day of practicing
the spiritual exercises will tune your inner hearing.

By the way, I recommend testing the information
and ideas you get in your spiritual exercises before
acting on them. Until you develop a sure link with God's
Voice, Divine Spirit, you must be certain where your
answers are coming from. I found that in the beginning
I would sometimes misinterpret what I heard, and the
results would come out skewed.

Start small in testing the answers you get. Maybe you'd ask what to have for breakfast to be your best that day. If an image comes, try it for a day and see if it helps.

Start with small questions then work up to bigger ones. See chapter 5 for more information on how to listen to the inner guidance.

Both big and little questions can be tackled in the exercise below. Unexpected results may come your way.

So absolutely good is truth, truth never hurts / The teller.

—Robert Browning

Exercise:
Asking God a Question

1. Close your eyes, and take several deep breaths to relax your body.

2. To relax your mind, visualize a very peaceful setting. I often imagine I am standing on the porch of the boathouse at my grandmother's summer camp in the mountains. I am watching rain on the lake, but under the porch roof it is dry and comfortable. The rain makes hissing noises as it hits the surface of the water. Use your own setting. In a relaxed way, get into a scene that will make you loosen your mental grip. This will allow images from a higher level to come through.

3. Now lightly place your attention on your question. Don't force your thoughts to go in any one direction, just let them ramble. Some unexpected image, feeling, or insight may pop into your consciousness. Is this your answer?

At first, you may have a tendency to disregard what you receive, or you may say to yourself, "How strange!" Practice a gentle acceptance of these fleeting messages. Don't judge them at this point.

When you come out of contemplation, take a minute to write down what you saw, heard, or felt—no matter how unusual it seems. If you'd like, pay attention to whether an image repeats during the day.

Often when trying this exercise, I get wonderful and unexpected answers to my questions.

CLEARING OUT LIMITATIONS

Two main limitations to benefiting from the spiritual exercises are inside us: our emotions and mind. If I sit down with strong feelings or mental worries, I cannot achieve an open heart. I end up feeling like a hamster racing in a spinning wheel.

But how do we clear out these inner limitations?

One morning not long ago I was feeling very sensitive to the emotional currents around me. My husband was a bit under the weather and had been very quiet all week. If I'm in a stable, balanced place this doesn't shake me, but this time it was awful. When I sat down to do my spiritual exercise, I knew the extreme sensitivity of my emotions would be disruptive.

So I decided my first task was to remove the obstacles standing between me and hearing the clear Voice of God.

First I used the exercise in chapter 3, the Fear Room exercise. I knew that behind my extreme sensitivity lay a certain amount of fear that other people's states could and would upset my own balance. Then I relaxed and inwardly asked, "What next?" The answer that came was surprising: "Reduce the amount of electrical current."

Immediately in my inner vision I saw a room surrounded by arcing blue electricity. It was arcing out of control. Out of range of the arcs, on the wall, was a dimmer switch, similar to those used for ordinary lighting. I got a second nudge: "Turn down the dimmer switch."

As I did this, the arcs of blue subsided.

The palpable tension that had been in the air was gone. I came out of my spiritual exercise feeling optimistic that the sensitivity would be calmed as well.

And it was. That day was the best I had had in a week.

Singing a Sacred Word

In many spiritual practices, students are encouraged to sing or chant a sacred word. It can be the name of a saint, God, or even *Amen*. A favorite of mine is the word *HU* (pronounced like the word *hue*), a sacred name of God taught in Eckankar. The idea is that the word becomes a focus for the attention, something higher than oneself.

It helps spiritualize the consciousness.

Beverly told me how HU helped her when her mother died. Her mother had been a very strong woman who controlled the household, and Beverly had often rebelled against this control. When her mother died, the emotional control was suddenly gone, and in the resulting emptiness, Beverly felt very depressed. She was working at home, but barely able to get dressed. Her husband's face would fall when he came home at the end of the day and found her still in her pajamas.

Beverly finally realized it was time to get her life back together, but how did she start?

All she knew was that singing the word *HU* had helped her before. So she set aside time each day to sing it to herself, quietly and gently, whenever she felt sad about her mother's death.

"Shortly after that," Beverly said, "a glimmer of light came in. And it built and built and built every day. And it built my life back up again."

In my spiritual exercises, I often ask for a sacred word to sing for strength or peace. This could be an ordinary word like *calm, peace, love,* or a combination of sounds that make me feel serene or uplifted. Once when I was feeling particularly stuck, I received a five-syllable word with the warning, "This word brings change!" Every time I sang it in the morning, some great change would happen in my life that day. Such a word is an empty vessel when first used. It doesn't mean much in itself. But as I begin to use it in my spiritual exercises, the word takes on power and life, like a battery being charged.

I swear to you there are divine things more beautiful than words can tell.

—Walt Whitman

Every now and then, I find a word's power has diminished. It's a sign that I have changed and I'm ready to move on. At first I just notice I don't get the usual lift of heart when I sing it. There isn't much there. At these times, I use a universal word, such as *God,* or *HU.* And I wait until another word comes.

And it always does, often as a sound or image during my spiritual exercise. Once it was the name of a popular brand of cat food! I can never predict what the word will be, but when I begin testing the new word, it almost always makes me feel uplifted, good, and balanced. It might fit me for a day, a week, a month, or several years. Then when I feel it has lost its charge, I ask for and get a new one.

Using a sacred word is a fine way to heighten the inner awareness, something that is very necessary when working with turning points. It becomes a vital tool in your spiritual toolbox and a great aid with the spiritual exercises.

THIRD TOOL: SPIRITUAL JOURNAL

Journal writing is a road to self-discovery. For many years I have taught workshops that include spiritual journal-writing techniques. Each time I am awed by the power of writing down thoughts, feelings, and dreams — and how these writings can be touchstones for mastering change.

Each morning I spend ten to fifteen minutes writing in my journal, anywhere from two to three pages of unconnected thoughts, dream recording, and ideas that have come to me in the past twenty-four hours.

Friends ask me, "How do you fit it in?" The extra activity fills my morning a bit, but it's a choice I made many years ago when I began to see how much happier and smoother my life goes when I devote time to journal writing.

I see so many benefits in journal writing as a daily activity that I wouldn't trade it for anything — extra sleep or more time before the makeup mirror or the chance to read the morning paper. And if I need confirmation, I just read my own journal to see what I have discovered about myself.

Many self-help and inspirational books and articles

propose daily journal writing as a great problem solver. Writer Joan Didion says in her essay "On Keeping a Notebook" that writing in a journal is a way she can "remember what it was to be me." An article in the January 1996 *Ladies' Home Journal* confirmed that women who wrote down their thoughts could be healthier than "those who sit and stew." Research showed that they're sick less and have fewer doctor's visits.

Journal writing is an essential tool for mastering change. The changes that we need to make are signaled in our daily journal ramblings long before any other outer signs are visible.

Journaling from the place of inner knowing takes you beneath surface concerns to the very heart of the matter.

—Joyce Chapman, M.A.

One winter I was feeling very cornered in my life by a lack of time alone. I have a wonderful marriage; my husband and I work together. We have smoothed out many of the traditional obstacles to this kind of arrangement, and both of us enjoy the companionship and our close-knit lives. But in my journal that winter I began writing more and more often about "the need for an hour alone." It surfaced again and again until I began to wonder what to do about it. Not long after, as I was setting some creative goals, I realized that I was eager to start another book project and craved the creative solitude I usually needed to mull over ideas for it. I worked out an arrangement to go to a nearby library or bookstore and write for an hour every now and then, and the urgency for time alone slowly passed. I was grateful that this sign appeared in my journal before the unmet need provoked real unhappiness.

I use the following three-part journal writing exercise to get this "story behind the story" when I am confused about some aspect of my life.

Exercise:
To Get to the Story behind the Story

1. Write for ten minutes in your journal. Time yourself with a kitchen timer. Write about an incident that provoked a strong reaction in you, something from the far or recent past. Don't edit or censor your writing, and if you get stumped and the writing stops, write the words "I don't know what to write about this. I don't know what to write about this" until the writing flows again.

2. When the timer rings, turn to a new page in your journal. Choose one person or place from the writing you just did. Put that name in the center of your page, and do the Turning Points exercise from page 55 with that name as the seed.

3. Turn to another page in your journal, and write for ten minutes again on the topic *Why I am grateful to this person or place.*

I taught this exercise recently in a spiritual writing workshop. The group of twenty-five was very positive afterward. One woman got a whole new perspective on a relationship. Another saw clues as to why closure was so hard for her. It's a powerful exercise.

If you're just starting journal writing as a spiritual tool for mastering change, start slow and easy. For beginners, five to ten minutes is plenty of writing time for one sitting. You may want to draw or doodle in your journal, make lists of things you really love or want to do sometime, or write notes about your creative projects.

Remember to review your journal. I do this on the same day of every month. It takes me about an hour in the evening once a month. I use a yellow highlighting pen to highlight anything unusual that has occurred. Another color highlighting pen can be used for things I want to do, which can get transferred to a to-do list later.

Journal writing teaches me perspective. Good happens. Even when my life is at a low ebb, reading my journal reminds me that everything changes—anger, loneliness, hurt, sadness, and pain pass eventually. And they pass much more quickly when I can write about them—"get the garbage out" as one of my writing students said. Writing down your thoughts and feelings can unravel the fear behind anger or loneliness. So you can deal with it. And move on.

The next tool to develop is inner listening. We'll cover this in the next chapter.

Ask Yourself:
What's in My Toolbox?

Answer the following questions to identify a few spiritual tools.

1. Does anyone you know rely on hunches or nudges to make decisions? Do you? What do you think about this?

2. What were some of the best changes in your life? How did you handle them? Was there any connection between the importance of the change and the level of fear you experienced?

3. What is one talent you have that other people admire? Is there some way to use this special talent for yourself to help you make a change?

5

$\mathscr{A}$wakening the Listening Heart

Mastering Change in Your Life

*Nearest to all things is that
power which fashions their being.*

—Henry David Thoreau

5. Awakening the Listening Heart

When I was four years old, I spent most of my weekday mornings at my grandmother's. I loved visiting my grandmother. She baked me cookies and brownies, took me for walks down by a stream behind her apartment building, and let me play her piano.

Her name was Helen Hartz, and everyone called her Hartzie, even her four grandchildren. She was in her sixties then, a very robust white-haired woman, with years of experience organizing people and planning projects. Each day she would sit for about forty minutes in silence, often with her eyes closed, sometimes jotting notes in a small black binder she kept close by.

My mother explained this was how Hartzie got her spiritual guidance. This was her quiet time, when she listened to God's instructions for her that day.

When pressed once, she explained the process to me in words a small child could understand: She'd simply think about a topic or a problem, letting it loosely roll around in her mind, and suddenly "guidance" would come. It was often no more than a subtle feeling to do

Guidance to the broader, deeper, richer view of life is available to all who ask — and who are willing to let go and hear.

—Mary Pat Fisher

this or that: often an idea that she had not even considered would float into her mind. She believed sincerely that the guidance was celestial. Unlike most of us, she had no doubt in herself as being worthy of this kind of special attention from the Divine. Hartzie taught me that we are all special to God.

Because of her daily spiritual guidance, Hartzie had always been very good at change. She would often recognize turning points before they arrived.

She'd get hunches or feelings about some event or decision. She'd wait until the time felt right to act or speak. She'd ask for counsel but always make the final decision after a brief moment of silence or a night's sleep.

I realize now how much early tutoring I had in recognizing the inner guidance all around me—Hartzie lived and breathed according to this guidance.

The movement of life has its rest in its own music.

—Rabindranath Tagore

Why Listen?

Developing a sense of inner guidance is probably the most important tool you can add to your toolbox on handling change. It's a graduation to a new level of awareness of personal turning points. And you get better at listening by practicing the spiritual exercises every day.

But exactly how does inner direction come to a person? What are the ways you can develop more of this inner sensitivity?

First, inner guidance is not the same for everybody. Some get nudges; others get images, a sound, or a subtle feeling. Each of us has the ability to listen and receive our own individual guidance. The trick is being able to tune in and stay tuned. That takes practice and trust.

In my family, probably because of my grandmother's influence, inner guidance was a practical and common spiritual tool. My mother would get nudges to call me long-distance, often when I was down in spirits. We used to joke about her "inner link" with family members.

As I learned to develop my skill with this inner tool, I noticed that sometimes the inner guidance came very strongly, other times more subtly. I began to see that certain practices helped my tuning in and others hindered it.

Inner guidance comes without warning, so there's little way to predict when it will come—just ways to stay receptive. I practice listening during my daily spiritual exercises, which are often similar to my grandmother's quiet time. I keep a notebook handy to jot down any ideas that float through as I sing HU or another sacred word. Sometimes the ideas are unexpected answers to problems I've been stewing over. Sometimes they are as simple as a friend's name—and when I'd follow this nudge and call the friend, she would tell me how much she needed to talk just then.

I never had the experience of looking for God. It was the other way round.

—C. S. Lewis

Decision Making

My friend Sondra had been working on her house for what seemed like years; the remodeling-project-without-end had taken over her days. The place was a disaster: walls torn out, carpet a mess from ceiling repair, contractors not fulfilling their commitments, no running water. She was in despair and often wondered if she should abandon the project and try to sell the house—just to stop remodeling and have some peace again!

"A friend from Europe told me about an exercise she does when things get confusing and she has a decision to make," Sondra said. "When she goes to sleep at night, she fills her heart with love and sincerely asks God for guidance on the problem. She knows that when she gets up in the morning, the answer will be there.

"So before sleep one night, I filled my heart with sincere love, and I asked God, 'Should I sell my house?' So many decisions, so much inconvenience, so much money has gone into it, and it will be months and months before it's all done."

That night Sondra had a dream where someone came up to her and asked, "Are you selling your house?"

Love comes when we have developed our capacity to feel love within.

—Ruth Ross, Ph.D.

"Don't ask me yet," Sondra told the person in the dream, "I haven't woken up yet."

The dream seemed funny to her until she fully opened her eyes the next morning and saw the mess again. It hadn't gone away overnight. And there still was no clear guidance in her heart about selling. So she got up, showered, and dressed. As she was putting her handbag over her shoulder to walk out the door, she turned and looked at the remodeling mess once again. And suddenly she knew.

"I'm keeping the house," she said out loud. It was a very strong feeling.

"Yes, and all the problems that go with it," an inner voice chuckled softly. She smiled.

Things didn't get easier in the way you would normally think. There was still a lot of work. But when Sondra stopped debating about selling the house, she realized how much energy she had been wasting on worry and complaining. This energy, when redirected to finishing the projects before her, suddenly gave her much needed strength and courage to complete the task.

When we last spoke, she said the remodeling was almost finished. She's delighted she listened to her inner voice and kept the house.

If you'd like to try the exercise Sondra used to get her answer, here it is.

Exercise:
To Get Answers While You Sleep

Before you go to sleep, gently ask for an answer to a question. Try to frame the question simply, like Sondra did in the story above. Then give the problem over to God, and go to sleep.

The next morning, does any solution or decision come to you? Write it down.

TESTING YOUR INNER GUIDANCE

As I mentioned in chapter 4, it's always good to test the guidance you receive. Small instances, like choosing one of two equally good routes to drive to work, can become the testing ground. I ask inwardly, "Which way today?" then take the road that comes to mind. Often I can find no difference between the routes, but sometimes I avoid accidents or construction delays that might have made me late.

The guidance comes more and more frequently as I listen more carefully and use what I receive. When I ignore this guidance out of tiredness, stress, anger, or fear, I regret my decision often enough to return to listening.

I find that guidance comes through most steadily and clearly when I am in a relaxed state and neutral in my attitude.

To maintain this as much as possible, I practice my

We are not accustomed to thinking that God's will for us and our own inner dreams can coincide.

—Julia
  Cameron

spiritual exercises for twenty minutes every day. I also record my dreams and any experiences that seem significant, since they often hold clues to guidance. As I mentioned before, I now trust the process enough to scribble down meaningless dreams in the middle of the night when they wake me. Even in the morning light these experiences may not make much sense, but I often find their meaning at a later date. I discover that it was a spiritually significant dream.

I also pay close attention to any event or conversation that causes a strong reaction, either unexplained repugnance or attraction. If I can, I write this down. It might be alerting me to a future turning point.

To believe with certainty we must begin with doubting.

—Stanislaus I of Poland

If you'd like to start working with inner guidance, try the exercise below. It can help enhance your natural ability to hear inner direction from life.

Exercise:
To Strengthen Your Guidance

For a day imagine that each decision—as small as what to eat for lunch or what clothes to wear—is really important to your life's plan. Spend a second asking inwardly which breakfast food to eat, which pair of shoes to wear, which route to work to take, which chair to sit in at a meeting—and take note of the subtle images or feelings that come to you.

If nothing comes at first, be patient and practice the exercise another day. Write down whatever results you have. Did you receive any inner guidance? Did you follow it? What happened when you did or didn't? By keeping a log of your progress, you may realize that you have been working with inner guidance all along.

The stories that follow give examples of how guidance is always present during times of change.

TO LET GO OF THE PAST

Diane is a talented musician who sings part-time and works in a publicist's office. After many years of marriage she recently got divorced, moved out of the house she and her husband owned, and found an apartment.

She debated about how to handle the divorce, how to get what she felt was her share of the marriage assets. Her friends and a lawyer urged her to go for more, that she had a good case. But her ex-husband was putting up a lot of resistance to each change.

She decided to ask only for the bare minimum in order to settle easily and smoothly. But Diane often debated this in her head: Was she not being assertive enough?

As she drove home one afternoon, thinking about all of this, she kept taking the wrong freeway exit. She'd turn the car around, get back on the freeway going the other direction, and try again. But it happened over and over.

After the fourth time, Diane was exasperated. What was happening here?

She pulled over to take stock of the situation.

What had she been thinking about when she kept making the wrong turn? Her divorce. Trying to get more money. Where had the turn been taking her?

Even the most mundane activity . . . contains spiritual principles. How did you handle it? What did you learn?

—Harold Klemp

Toward her old neighborhood. Diane laughed at this. The message was pretty obvious.

What was this experience trying to tell her?

Diane realized that if she concentrated on getting all the money she felt she deserved, it would just embroil her in her past. She'd never be able to make the right turn. She could spend all her energy in the past, or she could use it to move forward into her new life.

So she stopped debating with herself and settled the divorce.

Later she realized how smart that decision had been. She felt free to move on very quickly and focus on her new life.

How to Begin Listening

The best way to begin to develop your awareness of inner guidance is to realize you already have it. Just assume that, as a spiritual being, as Soul, you are connected to the source of all creation which is guiding you through your turning points. This doesn't mean walking around hearing voices all the time. To me, inner guidance doesn't come as a clear voice. It's more often a subtle nudge or a passing idea.

Lee is a chiropractic physician who uses inner guidance in her practice and daily life. She shared some examples.

"A lady came in to my clinic with a work injury. She had worked in a dental office. While moving a large X-ray machine she had hurt her back. It hurt terribly. She had gone to a doctor who told her it would heal and gave her a muscle relaxant, but the pills didn't work. The pain kept getting worse. A month later, she went to a different doctor who told her she had a

We are dancers joining the dance of our life as it is going on, and continuing it toward its fulfillment.

—Ira Progoff

ruptured disc. She got very mad at the first doctor who had told her she was OK.

"The pain was so bad, the woman was off work for three years. When she came to my clinic and spoke about the first doctor, her face got very stiff. She looked about as mad as a person could get. I got an inner nudge just then to say to her, 'You need to find a way to forgive that doctor before I treat you.'

"She came back the next day. She told me she had forgiven the doctor, and I began treating her. Within three months the miracle happened. She was pain free and back at work."

Lee also told me about a man who had come in to the clinic after he hurt his back when he was bending to tie his shoelaces. He couldn't even move. Someone got him into a car and brought him in. His pain was terrible.

Lee again had a strong inner nudge. "What's going on in your life?" she asked the patient.

The day he hurt his back, the man told her, he had just received a bill for $65,000. He was so afraid he might not be able to pay the bill. He was a building contractor and many people owed him money, but he was reluctant to call and collect because he was equally afraid of losing business. This put him in a dilemma.

After talking with Lee, the man came up with a way to ask his friends to pay their debts.

Lee saw the man several times after that, and he seemed to be changing rapidly inside. The back pain went away completely the day he wrote the check for $65,000.

Lee marveled at how inner guidance helped her ask just the right questions. In both cases, the patients were able to take care of unfinished business in their lives and heal themselves.

It is the heart always that sees, before the head can see.

—Thomas Carlyle

SELF-DEFEATING BEHAVIORS

If I don't pay attention to inner guidance, I can get very comfortable in a familiar job or situation and not notice that my inner life has gotten stale. When I finally listen—and change something—everything is fresh and new again. But usually the change is not easy.

If I listen carefully each day and take action when I get the inner nudge to do so, the change is much smoother. I can prevent the time lag and a host of other problems.

For Henry, a talented musician, inner listening taught a great lesson about how true this guidance can be. And he almost didn't hear it until it was too late.

Henry had just changed careers, studied computer programming in school, and upon graduating had been hired by the same school to automate some of their departments.

He'd worked at the school for about a year when he began to hear that little voice whispering, "It's time to move on to another challenge." *No,* he thought, *not just yet.* He was comfortable there, the job was secure, and he was reluctant to change anything so settled. *I'm in the middle of a project,* he told himself, *so I'll just wait.* The nudge persisted, and Henry continued to ignore it.

It wasn't long after that he unknowingly became involved in a power play at work and ended up in the school director's office. The director asked for Henry's resignation.

"Go clear out your office," the director told him, "then come back here to return your keys."

Henry was stunned and shocked. How had this all happened? One day he had a fine job, the next day he was fired. It felt as if someone had pulled the rug out from under him. *What will I do about my financial responsibilities? What will I tell my family?* he worried.

"We talk about having faith and confidence in the justice of God," Henry said later, "and now was my opportunity to walk the walk instead of just talk it. So I put my attention back on God's guidance as I walked back to my office and started putting my things in a box."

Before he went back to the director's office, he asked God, "OK, what's the next step?" He was ready to listen now.

When Henry returned to hand in his keys, the director surprised him again. "This unpleasant situation doesn't reflect on you," the man said. "I was caught in the middle of something. And by the way, keep your keys. I want to hire you as a consultant to complete the project you're working on." And the director named a significantly higher consultant's fee.

Henry was also teaching a night class at the school, and during class that week he got another call to come to the director's office.

"While you were working here as an employee, I couldn't have given you this job referral," the director told Henry. "But here is a great creative opportunity." It was a job designing a course to teach hearing-impaired adults computer programming.

Henry went for an interview, determined this time to listen better "to the whisper of God."

When he got there, he realized this was not just a job opportunity; it was a huge step for him on many levels, a spiritual opportunity beyond his wildest dreams. His heart filled with so much love he could

We become just by performing just actions, temperate by performing temperate actions, brave by performing brave actions.

—Aristotle

hardly speak during the first interview. When the school called him back for a second interview, they told Henry they had already picked their final candidate, but they wanted to put Henry and the other candidate on a panel and let the students interview them.

Henry didn't know sign language or very much about hearing-impaired students, so he just decided to talk to them as spiritual beings, Soul to Soul, with great respect and love.

"My mind and emotions got the best of me after the interview," he said, "and I was full of doubt. But I knew I had followed my inner direction and did my best to work from a loving heart."

The school called him the next day.

The students had chosen Henry over the other candidate because of the respectful and loving way he had treated them during the panel interview. Henry loved his new job. It was better than he ever imagined.

Knowledge comes, but wisdom lingers.

—Alfred, Lord Tennyson

CLEARING THE CHATTER

Sometimes we are talking to ourselves so loud and fast that it's hard to hear the inner whisper of God.

A friend bought a fixer-upper home and decided to do the remodeling herself. It was a huge job. She learned about putting in electrical outlets, new windows, and kitchen cabinets. She was often up until 1:00 or 2:00 in the morning after a full day of work, fixing one more thing.

One night, she was trying to connect a copper pipe under the dishwasher, moving the wrench in a very tight space. The pipe started leaking, then came a flood of water. It was very late, and she was very tired. She turned off the water and just lay on the floor, totally discouraged.

She asked God, "What am I doing here? What do I need to do now?"

"Go quiet," said the still small voice inside.

But after so many hours of work, she couldn't do it. "Bring your scattered energy into the center," continued the voice. Finally she was able to do this, but it felt like she had to use all her energy. *This is much harder than connecting the pipe,* she thought.

But as soon as she followed the inner direction, my friend saw an inner picture of the pipe and how she could connect it. It was as clear as day. She rolled on her side, put the wrench into the space exactly the way she had seen it in her inner vision, and the pipe tightened perfectly.

"Once I was able to focus my energy," she said, "I was able to get the guidance. But first I had to clear the chatter inside."

The small voice can be very quiet. It is almost like tuning a radio to a faraway station. If we can become still inside, we hear better.

Each time I practice my daily spiritual exercise, I develop more of an ability to hear this still small voice. But sometimes life is so busy that the outer noise is louder than the inner voice. At those times, I use a special spiritual exercise to help clear my mind and emotions of busyness and noise. I've adapted it over the years, and it's a very effective calming and quieting practice for me—especially after a very hectic day. It's almost like taking a minivacation. When I finish I am completely refreshed and revitalized, both physically and spiritually. And with a clearer heart I can hear

Elected Silence,
sing to me.

—Gerard Manley
  Hopkins

the small voice inside.

To prepare for the exercise, find a quiet place to sit or lie down for twenty minutes. Imagine relaxing your body; if it helps you can tense the muscles in each part of your body for a few seconds, then release them with a big sigh. Imagine all the tension leaving you.

Exercise:
To Quiet the Heart

Visualize your mind as a big movie screen. You're watching a movie on the screen, the characters rushing around and chattering. Slowly the last scene of the movie ends, and the credits come up. Then the screen goes blank.

There's nothing but silence.

Feel the silence deepen inside you and all around you. You may be aware of a slight humming in your head, like the sound high-tension wires can make. Or the faint sound of music.

Rest in this stillness for as long as you like.

When you are ready, open your eyes.

Don't abandon the vital, vivid present for the vague vapors of the future.

—Marshall J. Cook

HOW GUIDANCE HEALS US

This all-powerful guidance is in our lives at every moment. It gently directs us toward whatever we need, directs our attention to whatever weakness we must look at and strengthen within ourselves. And each situation God sets up for us is custom-tailored to show us what we need to do next.

Linda, an award-winning playwright, told me this story about the healing of a lifetime of deep anger and pain. The surprising gift came while she was holed up in a mountain retreat finishing a play.

Linda had carried a truckload of anger toward her parents because of pain she'd been through while growing up. As an adult, Linda was drawn to the theater and playwriting. Soon after starting a career as a dramatist, she won a grant to write and have a reading of a play about her childhood.

"A few weeks before the play was due," she told me, "I decided to go to a mountain cabin to finish it. The writing required me to relive my youth, scene by scene, but the process also allowed me to rise above the pain, even finding humor in tragic situations.

"One night after working on the play, I dreamed that my mother confronted me, very upset that I was airing family secrets. I woke from the dream very troubled. But each time I asked for inner guidance, the reassurance came to keep writing."

Linda decided to contemplate on the disturbing dream. When she finished her spiritual exercise, there were no new insights.

But when she opened her eyes, she saw a three-foot-wide ribbon of termites streaming from the interior wall of the cabin!

Quickly she called the maintenance person. When he arrived, he explained that since it was spring the termites were moving outdoors. It was a springtime ritual in these mountains, he assured her. She had never seen anything like it.

Linda moved to another cabin, determined to finish her play. As she stopped for the day and took a long walk

Love is unto itself a higher law.

—Boethius

to stretch tired muscles, she thought about her play and all the grievances that had been eating away inside her for all those years. She began to cry as she realized that through the play, God was slowly guiding her to untie the knots of anger that she had held inside her for so long. And she began to feel the faint stirrings of love toward her parents, for the first time in many years.

The next morning, as Linda prepared to write the final scene of her play, she was in for another surprise.

When she turned on her computer, all the files were gone! Quickly she inserted the backup diskette, but it too was completely blank.

"It felt as if the room were reeling," Linda said. "I left the desk and fell on the bed. All that work—a year's worth. And I'd have to give back the grant money. I cried out to God, 'Why did you tell me to keep going on this project?'

"And a soft voice answered, 'Now you can write the play.' "

Linda remembered the thousands of termites marching out and realized that the anger, pain, and blame that had eaten away at her were gone too. The writing project and trip to the mountains had changed her life. *If I have to return the money, it will be a small price to pay for this gift,* she thought. But the grant people told her she didn't have to repay a penny. The money was to help promising artists become better at their work—and this experience, they told her, certainly had.

Nothing gives rest but the sincere search for truth.

—Pascal

Exercise:
Going to a Spiritual Spa

Before you fall asleep, ask to be taken in your dreams to a healing place in one of God's heavens.

Imagine you are arriving at a beautiful Grecian temple, bathed in soft colors by the evening sun. You are escorted into the temple, and you lie down on a low bed in a room with tall windows. Let the golden light of the setting sun flowing through the windows bathe your body. Imagine a special color of light focusing on your heart, to promote peace and well-being.

When you finally fall asleep, keep this image of the healing temple.

After trying this exercise, be sure to write your dreams down when you wake.

HELP WHEN WE NEED IT MOST

Sometimes we may not know what we need, but God does. All we have to do is ask for help. Then listen.

Dick is a documentary filmmaker. A number of years ago he found himself in a bind. Although he had a desire to be very connected with other people, he found himself feeling increasingly isolated. He felt he simply wasn't communicating well with others.

Dick didn't know what to do. A senior editor for a national computer magazine, he had been trained to figure out everything intellectually. But he couldn't solve this problem with his mind.

Dick tried the exercise in chapter 4, "Asking God a Question." In contemplation he asked, "What should

I do about this?"

The exercise and question Dick asked set in motion a number of events.

"I met a fellow on a business trip who said he was an adult child of an alcoholic," Dick says. "I hadn't known what this was, but it's a person who had a parent who was an alcoholic, as I had. A short time later someone gave me a book about adult children of alcoholics. Soon after that I picked up a brochure about personal-growth classes. When I got home and read the brochure, I learned there would be a seminar for adult children of alcoholics, and the description of the topics they were going to cover were all the things I was feeling at the time.

"It was almost as if someone was knocking on my door three times, saying, 'Pay attention.' "

This became a major turning point in Dick's life.

We should not let our fears hold us back from pursuing our hopes.

—John F. Kennedy

Your Special Relationship

Many people have had a special relationship with God when they were growing up. This connection may have been encouraged and fostered by church, a parent, or a grandparent. Or it might have been discouraged and became a refuge from loneliness or pain.

My friend Becky, a musician and artist from New England, was a very sensitive young girl in a family of five children with not enough love to go around. She often felt alone and afraid, but every night before going to sleep, she made a connection with a very loving presence she thought was God. They would "talk," and she would feel God's love and reassurance around her like a warm blanket.

I use Becky's image as an exercise. When I'm feeling

lonely or troubled or apart from God, I imagine God's love reaching down from heaven like a huge blanket settling on my shoulders, keeping me warm. I feel enormous arms wrapping me in the folds of the blanket. I rest there, like a child being rocked to sleep. It's an intensely comforting feeling.

Whatever brings you closer to God will also help you develop your ability to listen to God's Voice.

GUIDANCE THROUGH SYMBOLS

Some people enjoy working with symbols to help them develop the skill of listening to life. One friend chose the symbol of a blue feather to remind herself of inner guidance.

She wanted to make a big change and start a new creative project but wasn't sure if she had the stamina or if it was the best direction for her at the time. So she made a pact with God. If she was supposed to start the project, God would send her a sign.

It is the heart which experiences God, and not the reason.

—Pascal

She chose the blue feather. It was an unusual symbol, and she felt that if a blue feather came to her attention, it would be more than simple coincidence. That week, blue feathers began popping up everywhere. Standing in line in the supermarket, she noticed that the woman in front of her had blue feathers printed on her dress. A friend sent her a letter and a gray-blue gull's feather. Walking on the beach, she found another blue feather. The collection was growing. Within a week she started her creative project.

Another friend, Alison, told me about her search for an apartment that was close to where she worked. It fulfilled a goal she'd set twenty years before, and the search was confirmed by symbols of a blue heart and a blue star.

Traveling to and from work on the freeway each morning was the worst part of Alison's job. It was a forty-five-minute commute with stop-and-go traffic both ways.

One day she thought, *I really want a nicer place to live. And I want to be closer to work.*

She had just pulled up to a stop sign. The car in front of her had a blue star and a blue heart hanging from its rearview mirror. These were important symbols for Alison; for her they symbolized her inner spiritual guide. She took this as confirmation that she was on the right track. She immediately began looking for a new place to live.

At first she thought she would try to find a house to buy. She looked at a lot of places, but none were right for her. While she was looking at homes near her office, she'd often driven by a lovely apartment complex. Several times she'd called to see if they had vacant apartments, but the landlord either didn't return her calls or the building was full.

One lunch break, while daydreaming about her move, Alison got an inner nudge: Call the manager of this apartment building again.

This time, to her surprise, the woman was in. Yes, she said, they did have a vacant apartment! It had been rented but the agreement had fallen through at the last minute. Alison could come look at it right away. She did and loved it.

After she had settled in her new home, Alison realized that twenty years ago she had written a wish list. One of her goals had been to work in a job she loved and live nearby. The two had never come together until now.

The symbols of a blue heart and a blue star had given her the encouragement to take this important step.

Ideas are born, they struggle, triumph, change, and they are transformed.

—Eugenio María de Hostos

Creating a personal symbol can help you learn to recognize and work with turning points—and remind you of life's constant guidance.

Exercise:
Choose a Symbol of Your Turning Point

1. If you are unsure about a change or turning point that you see coming, choose something as a symbol that will remind you of your turning point.
2. Record in your dream journal the symbol and the turning point the significant change in your life—that it symbolizes.
3. Commit yourself to taking careful notes each time you see or hear your chosen symbol.
4. After a period of time (one month, two months, six months) review your journal notes. How often does your symbol appear? Did it lead to a turning point?

The secret of success is constancy to purpose.

—Benjamin Disraeli

This exercise puts you on the alert. It allows God to begin working with you to further develop your awareness of how to master the changes in your life.

SPIRITUAL SETUPS

My husband coined the phrase "spiritual setup." To us it means that God has set up a lesson for us to learn. All the players and props are arranged perfectly. We enter the scene, and the learning begins.

Often, spiritual setups are only humorous when they're over and you look back to see what you learned. But if you retain your sense of humor, there's usually a great gift in the end.

One hot August evening, a group of girlfriends and I set out across town for a concert at the Minnesota State Fair. We were going to sit in the bleachers, eat corn dogs, get rowdy listening to Mary Chapin Carpenter and Suzy Bogguss, and totally relax from work. Another group of coworkers would drive separately and meet us by the ticket booth an hour before the concert so we could get good seats.

Unfortunately, I'd neglected to remember rush-hour traffic and the hassle of finding a parking place close to the fair entrance.

We left late and became even later as the traffic moved at a crawl through Minneapolis and into St. Paul. My Honda's air conditioning roared, barely keeping us cool. My friends chatted about the concert, and I kept the car moving ahead, listening mostly to their chat and not really paying attention to the dashboard gauges.

By the time we reached the fairgrounds we were very late. And there was nowhere to park.

"Dear God," I said under my breath, "isn't there someplace to put our car?"

In about the same degree as you are helpful, you will be happy.

—Karl Reiland

As I rounded yet another corner in the residential area near the entrance gate, huge clouds of steam began pouring from under the hood. The car's temperature gauge had sailed over into the red, and I hadn't even noticed.

I turned the engine off, jumped out of the car, and watched in dismay as the radiator boiled over and dumped its water onto the ground. Now our evening was really in tatters. No way to move the car until it cooled off, no place to park it, the concert starting in fifteen minutes, and our friends waiting.

Just then a friendly looking fellow in a truck drove

up with his young daughter in the seat beside him.

"Need help, ladies?" he asked. This was Minnesota, and most people are extremely friendly.

We walked over and explained what had happened, that we were late for our concert.

I don't remember the man's name, but he was truly a knight in shining armor for us that evening. He and his family lived around the corner. He helped us move the car to his driveway, let us park it there for the concert, and promised he'd refill our radiator with water as soon as it cooled down.

We couldn't believe this kind of good luck.

All through the concert we joked about friendly Minnesota rescuers and marveled at the timing of this wonderful man's arrival. The radiator was full and the car was ready to drive when we returned from the concert at midnight.

I worried that some damage had been done to the engine. Would I have to repair anything, replace a leaky hose? But nothing was wrong on the ride home or the next day.

That's when I knew it was a spiritual setup. I had asked God for a parking place, and God had provided one in a very unusual way. The car was fine, as if the incident had never happened.

What did I learn? One, to pay better attention to the time and the road. Two, that people are really good-hearted, more often than not—an idea I needed to be reminded of. Three, that if I ask, there's usually a solution to most any problem.

Spiritual setups are a kind of tongue-in-cheek learning experience. They usually are too perfect to be co-incidences.

There is in the worst of fortune the best of chances for a happy change.

— Euripides

Exact Timing of God's Plan

Sometimes we are clueless about the timing of our next step. All we can do is follow the inner nudge we are given, take one step forward, then see where the next nudge takes us. This was beautifully illustrated by my friends Sue and John.

When we do the best that we can, we never know what miracle is wrought in our life, or in the life of another.

—Helen Keller

Sue had doubts when she received the inner nudge that her husband John and she might enjoy moving from Minnesota to Virginia a few years ago. In her spiritual exercise one morning, Sue had stepped through a golden door and gotten a new sacred word to sing. Then the nudges started coming: Move to Virginia.

Although John was agreeable, he did have a good job and they both had wonderful friends they would miss. *Why in heaven's name Virginia?* Sue wondered. Here's how God answered her concern and set up the lesson that followed.

Even though it seemed foolish, there was no way she could ignore the pull of her heart toward this new place and the people there. A visit with friends in Virginia that month cemented the decision. When Sue came home, she set about the business of moving. And when they made the decision to go, it seemed God began providing everything: a new job for Sue, a place to live. The feeling of closeness to God intensified.

But Sue still had plenty of doubts; she especially wondered if this was the right move for John.

The move itself went smoothly—except for a strange occurrence the day they left, which brought its own confirmation. They packed the twelve-foot cargo van one hot and humid morning, the first day of a mid-July heat wave. Sue remembered a special prayer she'd heard recently: "Bless this day and those I serve." It seemed like a good declaration to God that she was still listening, so she went about the heavy work singing this under her breath.

John took the first turn driving the van. Sue drove their station wagon, and they communicated by CB radio. Less than two miles from the house, Sue heard the CB crackle.

"I think something's wrong with the van, like a loose belt," John said. "It's making a loud high-pitched noise, like a lot of crickets."

Sue groaned. What a way to begin a trip! They pulled over. Sue listened carefully to the van's motor but couldn't hear anything unusual. "Everything sounds OK to me." John backed away, and stood there, chuckling. He could still hear the crickets. "It's not the van," he said. "It's the Voice of God I'm hearing." They felt that such inner sounds were important symbols that they were on the right track. *Bless this day,* Sue thought. Another confirmation that God was with them.

Two months after they arrived in Virginia, Sue started to see that her new job was temporary, but she was gaining a tremendous amount of confidence and strength from it and being in a corporate environment. Then there started to be a sense of things not working anymore, doors closing unexpectedly. Sue and John teased each other: "We could always move back to Minnesota." Then more seriously, "What if we did? Our old friends would laugh, and our new ones would be sorry to see us go. But things here are changing. What if God's telling us something—again?"

Unexpectedly Sue's job ended.

She had a dream that night. She was with John and her spiritual guide. They were discussing their future.

As a man thinketh so is he, and as a man chooseth so is he.

—Ralph Waldo Emerson

When Sue woke up, although she didn't remember details of the dream, she realized it was time to choose again, to set a goal. The answer came: "Move back to Minnesota."

Where the heart lies, let the brain lie also.

—Robert Browning

John readily agreed. They moved back within a week. Shortly after, Sue found a job, and John got his old job back.

"I must always follow my heart," Sue told me, "no matter where it leads. I've learned that as long as I'm acting responsibly it doesn't matter what anyone else thinks. The move to Virginia prepared me in many ways for my current job—I needed exposure to corporate America—as well as giving me many other needed experiences."

This was a true spiritual adventure, born of listening to inner guidance. Not all of us would want this kind of adventure, but Sue says, "Each time, following the guidance was like coming out of a long, intense struggle. I knew I would never for one second doubt or question our decision.

Change is not made without inconvenience, even from worse to better.

—Samuel Johnson

"Life is to be lived without fear. If you make a decision based on love, it cannot be wrong, it can't be a mistake."

When All Else Fails, Listen

At a time in our lives when we could ill afford it, my computer started to break down. I have a notebook computer, not a new model but one that has helped me write almost one thousand newspaper columns, four books, and half of a fifth.

My husband, Tony, is a clever handyman and can usually fix most things that break down in our home, but the computer's erratic behavior had him baffled. He spent a lot of time running one diagnostic program after another, attempting to decipher the problem.

When we finally found a local company that serviced this type of machine, they told us it was definitely the extended memory board. They said it couldn't be repaired, but they could order a new one. But there was no guarantee that it would fix everything. The new memory board was expensive, more than the notebook was worth.

I carefully figured out how to use our old 8088 laptop computer. But the repair shop kept my notebook computer for one week, then two, then three. I managed to make each writing deadline, but a new project was coming up soon. The old laptop wouldn't be enough to handle it. Should we just get a new computer?

On each new notebook we looked at, the keys on the keyboard were positioned differently. On our current machine, the keyboard setup was ideal and familiar. So buying another computer was not the solution I wanted, even though ours looked destined for another month in the repair shop.

Inwardly, when I asked for guidance on what to do, I kept getting, "The computer is not broken. It will be fine." Was it possible?

Tony researched some more and found a company in California that might be able to help. We reclaimed our computer from the repair shop and sent the memory board out via overnight shipping the next day. Not long after, we got a call from California. "The memory board is fine," the woman told us. "We resoldered a loose connection, and we're returning the memory board to you at no charge." Free service and shipping from a company we'd never dealt with before?

The computer was repaired and back on my desk

He that will not sail till all dangers are over must never put to sea.

—Thomas
   Fuller, M.D.

a day before I needed it to start my new project. I was grateful for the reassurance I had gotten. *If inner guidance can work with computers, it can work with anything,* I thought.

Listening to God is a lifelong adventure, and it will take you places you never dreamed of. As you practice inner listening, you may notice more changes in your life, but you'll also notice that your path through each change is smoother.

But don't expect success overnight. It often takes a lot of practice to become confident that God is indeed taking the time to talk to you, that you are worthy of this kind of attention.

In chapter 6, we'll explore the next tool for your spiritual toolbox: goal setting from a higher viewpoint.

As you come to see more of the spiritual horizon of your own life, you find you have a greater capacity to plan and live a happier life.

—Harold Klemp

Ask Yourself:
How Does Life Speak to You?

1. Are you a good listener? If so, how did you become one? If not, how do you suppose you'd improve this skill?

2. Do you work with gut feelings, nudges, or hunches when you have to make a decision at your job or at home?

3. Has a change ever been fun for you? Did you work with hunches or inner guidance at all during this change?

4. How do these hunches come to you? Has the way life communicates to you changed over the past few years?

6

How Life Works with You If You Work with It

Goal Setting for Successful Change

*Fear is a condenser; love, an expander.
This means that fear can create a world
as small as a thimble, while love is
able to open us to the fullness of living.*

—Harold Klemp

6. How Life Works with You If You Work with It

*G*oals are part of life. And setting goals helps us handle change successfully.

Consciously or unconsciously, we set goals every day. We figure out the best way to drive to work during rush-hour traffic, to close a deal at the office, to negotiate child care with our spouse or partner, to get dinner made before the guests arrive. Just the act of dreaming about and focusing on what we want—the essence of goal setting—starts a chain of events in motion that brings us closer to that result.

If we don't dream, reach for the dream, and grow, we become stagnant and dead inside. I've met people who have set goals, failed to reach them, and never attempted such dreaming again. This lack of dreaming and reaching for goals brings boredom with life—and ourselves.

A great example showed up on an episode of the TV show *Star Trek: Voyager*. The Q continuum, a group of beings that have routinely annoyed the *Star Trek* crew with their great powers and immoral antics, are amused by humans because they struggle with growth. The Q cannot die; they've lived for billions of years and have run out of things to do. One member of the Q continuum took the Voyager crew to a gas station in the middle of a desert to show them the downside of living forever. A road stretched east and west; as far as the eye could see there was nothing but empty desert. One man played a pinball machine, another sat in a rocking chair. The continuum took turns being the person who played pinball or the person in the chair, the dog, or the scarecrow; after a few billion years, even the idea of annoying humans had charm.

Seeing this show reminded me that it's essential to the well-being of each Soul to continually grow and change. And one way we do this is through setting goals.

It is neither wealth nor splendor, but tranquility and occupation, which give happiness.

—Thomas Jefferson

To those who have failed with goals and never want to try them again, I'd say: Goal setting is a process. Like any process, it has a learning curve. It demands adjusting and readjusting as we figure out (1) what we really want, and (2) the best way to get it. Those people who seem to magically achieve their dreams, over and over, usually view goals as a process and make these adjustments. They set smaller goals within the larger goals. When a smaller goal isn't effective, they adjust their dream.

The best goals are goals that satisfy a basic need. What does this mean? A goal that satisfies brings you the qualities of life that allow you to blossom, like a garden flower.

Nick told me about a job he dreamed of, worked hard to get, and finally was hired for. But when he got the job, after all those months of work, he realized he didn't want it. He had grown during the process, and what he wanted from his work had changed. The job now seemed like a straitjacket rather than an opportunity.

How do you set successful goals that will grow as you grow? There are three essential elements: (1) an awareness that life, God, the higher power, helps you reach your goals; (2) an understanding that the goals that really satisfy are those that fulfill your purpose in life; and (3) the constant inner listening that allows you to adjust your goal to match your growth.

Many people don't understand that apparent failure is part of the process, a necessary part. They set a goal—to get a new job, a new home, a new relationship—but something changes in the process of getting there, and when they don't reach the goal they see this as a flaw in themselves or believe that goal setting doesn't work. But failure doesn't mean that either you or the goal is flawed. Failure might just mean you need to change direction, make an adjustment. Actress Emma Thompson, interviewed in the February 1996 *Vanity Fair,* said, "I've discussed the value of failure in creative work. Failure is terribly important. . . . The notion that failure is a negative thing is wrong." Bernie Siegel, founder of Exceptional Cancer Patients, writes that "failure [is] a redirection that leads to good things." If we don't reach a goal, we may need to ask ourselves some questions: Was the goal inner-directed (something we wanted) or was it other-directed (something someone else wanted)? Were the benefits worth the effort? Did the goal limit our or others' freedom? Were the obstacles manageable? Did we set an unreasonable goal?

Goal setting is a process, and it can be easier if you

Excellence does not remain alone; it is sure to attract neighbors.

— Confucius

examine these questions before you begin. Start by looking at how you've handled past changes; and with the following exercise, take inventory of the change skills you currently use.

Exercise:
Your Change Skills Inventory

1. Think of five changes you've been through in your life.

2. Describe them on paper by writing a paragraph about each one.

3. Then list the change skills you used to get through the change. You may remember using skills like: patience, compassion, listening to others, listening to God, writing your thoughts and feelings, working to remove inner emotional blocks, or others.

4. Congratulate yourself for each change you made it through. Acknowledge your current skills.

Often, we don't realize our limiting assumptions until we begin to try to see without them.

—Susan Sarback

TURNING GOALS INTO GOLD

Penny and Mark, good friends who've experienced a lot of adventures in their lives, shared a great story about their goal-setting process. The three most important principles they learned during a recent move from Connecticut to Colorado were (1) to keep adjusting and reviewing their dream, (2) to stay open to all the unlimited possibilities life gave them to manifest their dream— as well as unexpected resources—and (3) to continually ask themselves if this is what they really wanted—a process of adjusting their goals to their growth.

Although it had been their home for many years, Connecticut was a tough place for Penny because of the wet climate and her allergies. And lately Mark had been experiencing winter blahs. Slowly the feeling grew that they should move to a drier, summier climate. Like they usually do in their goal-setting, Penny and Mark followed this inner nudge with a spiritual exercise. They wrote a wish list of all the aspects and qualities they'd like in their new life: where they wanted to live, what their new home would be like. They followed up with journal-writing exercises where they picked an item from the list, contemplated it in silence, then wrote about it afterward. As they went through this goal-setting process, they kept checking: was the nudge to move still there? Each time they looked inwardly, the move was a go.

Penny's career as a classroom teacher was blossoming in Connecticut. She had been a sought-after teacher and now was beginning to move into administration. She even took part in a national training film for teachers. With both Mark and Penny prospering professionally, friends and family wondered why they would want to move.

But the inner nudge persisted.

So they took the first step: selling their home. Though interest rates were high and housing prices soft, their house sold within two months at a price where they neither lost nor made money. In the interim, they rented a small apartment and looked for jobs farther west.

It took two years, but in 1993 Mark was offered a transfer within his company to Boulder, Colorado. Mark and Penny were ecstatic at first. But Penny began to get cold feet. Now that the move was a reality, Penny debated, "Why should I give up my career for my husband's? Am I really willing to start all over again?"

Mark understood. He said, "We can give up the idea of moving. It'll be your decision."

Penny did another spiritual exercise to review the goal again and get more guidance. She remembered her constant allergy headaches, the initial reason to move. They were still a big problem. And the nudge to leave Connecticut was still strong. So Mark accepted the job transfer and not long after, they found an apartment in Boulder.

Each weekend, they explored the area to fulfill their wish-list dream of buying a new home. One day they found a new housing development with a spectacular view of the Rocky Mountains, prairies, and farmland. Nearby was a quarter horse ranch and new public golf course. Penny and Mark loved horseback riding and golf. They decided they wanted to buy a lot in the new development. It seemed their dream was coming true.

But things began to slide around that time. Penny found out Colorado would not honor her teaching certificate from Connecticut. It would take a year to get certified. Meanwhile Mark's company fell into financial trouble and issued across-the-board pay cuts. Buying a new home was now out of the question. As Penny said, "It was as if a big hand were crossing items off our wish list." First her career and Mark's previously larger paycheck, then their dream home.

They began to wonder, *Did we make a huge mistake? Perhaps we misunderstood the guidance we were getting.*

But instead of looking at these setbacks as failure, they took stock of where they were and realized they had achieved their primary goal: living in a drier,

Your eyes need to remain fresh and alert to the dynamic dance around you. . . . No one solution lasts forever.

—Terah Kathryn Collins

sunnier climate. Penny's allergy distress had been greatly reduced and Mark's winter depression had disappeared with all the Colorado sunshine.

Turning back was not an option at this point, so they decided to make some adjustments in their plans and be patient.

For a while things just kept getting worse, though. Mark saw his company's fortunes fall dramatically that summer and finally decided to contact another company in Boulder that had offered him a position in the past. It so happened that they needed a director of engineering. He was offered the job along with a handsome salary increase. Things were looking up again.

They decided to move from their apartment and look for a home to rent, but rents were outrageous. Just by chance Mark and Penny drove by the home sites they had seen a year before. The same smiling sales agent greeted them.

He was nearing the end of his sales cycle, and negotiations over the remaining four home sites had left him frustrated. Since he liked working with Mark and Penny, he said, "I'll let you have the lot of your choice." They were prime lots, much nicer than the one they had selected before. They decided to buy, and they moved into their beautiful open-plan home in 1994.

Good fortune comes in multiples, and not long after that Penny happened to be talking to someone in the education system who told her, "You can get an emergency teaching certificate using your Connecticut license." No one had even hinted before that this was possible. Penny eventually got her permanent certification, and in the summer of 1995, she was offered a job teaching fourth grade.

Life is a very real dream world. Everywhere we go is a spiritual occasion.

—Harold Klemp

Both Penny and Mark gained plenty of experience with goal setting and the process of achieving a dream. As Penny assured me, "The road was difficult all along." They learned that letting God arrange their lives in God's own time is not an easy process but it brought them many more blessings than they had anticipated.

Goals Set for the Greater Good

Goals that fulfill our heart's desire, that satisfy who we are as spiritual beings, are the most important goals. If we set those goals first, they can become the foundation of our other goals. They bring more satisfying, more lasting results. Penny and Mark did this by constantly checking their goals through spiritual exercises. And remember Jack's job-change proposal in chapter 2? In creating his new job, the changes were of long-term benefit to Jack—giving him more confidence that carried over into other areas of his life.

Setting goals and directing your life through inner planning and spiritual exercise allows you more mastery of change. And when we direct our lives from this higher level, we can work for the greater good rather than selfish desires.

You may scoff at this: Is it practical to work for goodness in the real world? Does it pay to have a spiritual goal in everyday living? Does this kind of inner-directed vision work in corporate business, for example?

You bet.

Just read one of the many articles appearing lately about how corporate spirituality is enlightening the bottom line. The June 5, 1995, *Business Week* discusses new approaches to management at major companies like Boeing, AT&T, Lotus Development, and Med-

There are people who convince themselves that they can't do anything with their lives because of what's happened to them—and they're right. They can't. But the reason is that they've told themselves they can't.

—Wally Amos

tronic. CEOs are answering their top managers' question: Why do I feel so unfulfilled in my job now that I've made it to the top rungs of the corporate ladder?

Perhaps a spiritual principle will shine through: The realization that if I set a goal to climb to the top of the corporate ladder but I do it by stepping on others, the fat bank account and power I gain will bring me little happiness. A goal that is purely self-serving, that takes away other people's freedom, also limits my own in the end.

This leads us into a new area: how to set a goal based on an inner direction and higher values, yet stay open and flexible to the changes life might bring. And not become tied up in the inflexible desire to have things just one way—our way.

DESIRES VERSUS PREFERENCES

It is said that desire is the root of all pain. I believe this is referring to anything that has such a gripping hold on the heart that it won't let go until it's satisfied.

When my goal is to work in harmony with life and the good of the whole—God's plan—strong desires can act as distractions and keep me from the inner listening that lets me adjust and redirect my goals. Desires can keep us from hearing God's more subtle directions. Desires can be very inflexible. Once a desire is set, my mind locks it in, and it seems impossible for me to be neutral or detached. It feels impossible to place an outcome in the hands of God, no matter how many spiritual exercises I do or how much I talk about detachment.

I've learned the hard way to try to have preferences rather than desires. Preferences are gentle requests of life, without the inflexibility of a desire.

I may prefer that something happen, but I have learned that God has a much broader vision than I do. I can imagine an outcome and state my preference for it—"I'd like this job"—but I do not fuss and whine if it doesn't take place.

Who knows? I might get an even better one.

Goal setting with this point of view can be more challenging. The process is not easy, because you have to work very intentionally with preferences rather than desires. And you have to be willing to let go of the outcome if necessary.

Once, I had to let go of a nice-sounding freelance job that unexpectedly fell through. Yet it allowed me to take two jobs at twice the money several weeks later. I had really wanted that first job. But after a bit of internal struggle I was able to let go of it because from past experience I knew that if this deal fell through, a better one would be around the corner. I'm not always able to hold this attitude, but when I use it to work with goals I am much more flexible.

As is our confidence, so is our capacity.

—William Hazlitt

The funny thing is—when I am truly flexible and trusting of life, my dreams almost always come true.

YOUR CURRENT SKILLS

People in my Turning Points workshops often ask me, "How do I start getting some of these goal-setting skills—the inner flexibility, the higher viewpoint on my life? I could sure use them with the changes I'm going through right now."

I tell them, "You probably already have these skills to some extent."

As a test, ask yourself, *How did I get to where I am today?* Most of us have handled a lot of big and little changes in our lives. People in this fast-paced era experience much more change—marriage, divorce, moving, buying homes, having children, job changes—than earlier generations did. You handled these changes in some way. You got to the other side. How did you do it?

Did you use dreams? Journal writing? The inner skill of listening to your gut, to your intuition, to God?

Take nothing for granted.

—Rick Bass

You can always learn something new based on your current level of understanding. To get better at anything, you begin with the skills you currently possess. And the resources you have around you.

Whenever I am going through a change, I lean heavily on my resources. I interview friends who have gone through something similar. I reduce the learning curve of a new skill by reading books, taking classes, listening to audiocassettes. I brainstorm in my journal about who could offer guidance. I've found that there may be many people in my life who can help me with each major or minor change—I just need to ask.

You have these resources too. What resources from the list below might have helped you with a past change? Which could you call upon to help you now?

1. Family
2. Friends
3. Priest, minister, spiritual teacher
4. Inspirational books and scriptures
5. Workshops and classes
6. Mentors in your field
7. Libraries and bookstores
8. Businesspeople in your community
9. Your writing journal
10. Dreams
11. Inner guidance
12. Spiritual exercises or other spiritual practice(s)

To further explore resources available during change, a friend taught me the following exercise. It's very subtle but causes a powerful shift in my attitude whenever I use it.

Exercise:
What Can You Control?

Turn to a clean page in your journal. Draw a vertical line down the center to make two columns.

Write at the top of one column: *Can Control.*

Write at the top of the other column: *Can't Control.*

Now explore a change you're currently going through. Assess what you can control about the situation. Jot these things in the first column. Look at what you cannot control about the change, and write them in the second column. Review what you've written in each column about the change — and how much you feel victimized by it.

Finally, list your past patterns in handling change. Imagine times when change came — a job change, for example, or a relationship break-up. What did you do? How can you do something different this time around?

When old words die out on the tongue, new melodies break forth from the heart; and where the old tracks are lost, new country is revealed with its wonders.

—Rabindranath Tagore

WHAT DO YOU REALLY WANT?

There are goals that truly satisfy. Goals that serve the whole person, including the spiritual being. These goals usually have to do with improving a quality of life. You can discover more about them through an exercise a friend shared with me, a kind of inner searching he called *envisioning.*

Envisioning means becoming open to receiving what God wants for you, the gifts God brings you in whatever form, not just in the limited form you can see at the time. What area of your life could use a little upgrading? A little less fear? Is there an area of your life that could be more creative and free?

Exercise:
To Envision the Qualities of Life You Want

1. Turn to a fresh page in your journal. You'll be evaluating an area of your life that you'd like to infuse with this high level of love and well-being. It can be physical health, finances, a relationship, a friendship, family, emotions, mental learning, spiritual advancement, or whatever you have a nudge to improve.

2. Write a short paragraph or a few sentences answering this question: How do I see this area of my life now?

3. Start a new paragraph, and answer this question: How would this area of my life look if it was filled with well-being and love?

4. Write the answer to this question: What actions can I take to bring this about? List one or several things that come to you, even if they seem silly or irrelevant. Have any signs appeared lately that might give you clues as to what actions to take? These can be subtle indications of a turning point.

5. Look at what you must surrender to bring this about. What old beliefs or attitudes about yourself or your life could be tossed out now? What must be changed to fit your new vision?

In order to create there must be a dynamic force, and what force is more potent than love?

—Igor
  Stravinsky

When I tried the envisioning exercise to set a goal for my career as a writer, I found myself quite surprised by the "goals" I wrote in each category.

First I did a spiritual exercise to attain the highest point of view I could. From this high viewpoint I envisioned a quality, a state of being, such as serenity, peace, fulfillment, courage, love. These were my goals, the inner states I was trying to achieve. Then I visualized the outer situations that would naturally reflect those inner states. For example, when I set a goal for balance and satisfaction in my career and home life, I envisioned a work situation that would allow me to leave my job at the office at the end of the day and have plenty of time to relax with my family. A job that kept me running with no rest did not reflect an inner state of satisfaction, serenity, and fulfilled purpose that I desired. See how it works? You have to really home in on what you want.

To list outer situations that would be reflections of these inner states, I used one page in my journal for physical, another for emotional, a third for mental, and a fourth for spiritual goals. Each is important.

As I did this exercise, I suddenly realized that making a lot of money has never been an end in itself for me. It's important to be comfortable, but just having money is not my purpose in life. I certainly don't want money at the expense of more intangible goals, such as a fulfilling marriage or satisfying, purposeful work. This was a truth I had overlooked.

As I applied this exercise to my freelance writing career, it totally changed what I was willing to do to achieve the next outer goal I had—to get published in higher-paying magazines.

Creating a successful life might be as simple as determining which moments are the most valuable, and seeing how many of those I can string together in a line.

—Pam Houston

I realized what I really wanted in terms of my work life was not more money or my name in *People* magazine, although that could happen. I actually desired to learn more courage and honesty in my writing and in my life. I wanted to overcome the barriers of fear that stood in my way.

I saw how less fear and more courage was a lot more important than getting my byline on some glossy pages. If fame and fortune came as a result of overcoming fears, so be it. But those were no longer the primary motives. I breathed a huge sigh of relief when I finally figured this out.

A strong feeling of freedom flowed through me. I relaxed inside. It was wonderful. I totally trusted life to bring me whatever was needed to achieve my inner vision of myself as a courageous, honest writer.

And life brought it in a very unexpected way.

The Gift of Receiving

About three months later, when I had totally forgotten the exercise I had done, I got a call from Laurence, a friend from England. He was visiting the United States for the summer and was taking a writing course from a university in the area.

Laurence was very excited. Could we get together so he could tell me about the writing course?

Laurence's story was to be a mirror of my own. He had asked a friend to sign him up for a creative-writing class. He hoped to learn how to incorporate spiritual principles into fiction stories. But instead she had registered him in a course that taught how to sell nonfiction articles to magazines. The first evening, he was surprised and slightly disappointed that the content was to be so different from what he had anticipated. But something inside urged him to stay.

The writing teacher proved to be one of the best he had ever met. She had published hundreds of magazine articles on a multitude of topics. She had also authored at least one book and was writing a magazine column.

As she put the students through their paces, those who stayed learned the fine art of querying magazine editors and composing copy that really touched the reader.

As a result of that class, Laurence sold his first article to a large U.S. magazine. He was able to research a spiritual subject—dreams—and include interviews with experts in the field. He was also able to include his own spiritual experiences with dreams, including several exercises he loved.

I was impressed with what Laurence had accomplished and decided to try the course myself.

I wondered what I would get out of the class, but it seemed to fit my new goal of learning courage and honesty in my writing. After the first meeting, I realized why. This class would be tough. But it would also be the vehicle to teach me what I needed to learn about courage *and* allow me to break into the higher-paying magazine markets.

Within six months I had sold twelve articles, most to magazines I had been afraid to contact before the class. The instructor and I became friends, and at her urging I joined a national organization for magazine writers, which brought me two more writing assignments. A year later, when I looked back at the goals and dreams I had written down, I had to laugh.

I had achieved exactly the goals I had set in the envisioning exercise.

I was feeling more creative freedom as a writer. I felt less fear. I could feel my inner wings unfolding. It was a huge relief to stop operating from the tight, cramped place I had been in before.

This really works! I thought. Setting my goal in this new way, I had reached the inner dream of more courage and honesty in my writing. I had also gotten the outer results. I was getting pieces in bigger magazines—and book contracts.

I use the envisioning exercise on an ongoing basis to set new goals for myself and review past ones. It's also a simple way of ridding myself, layer by layer, of old useless beliefs. Practicing this exercise helps me realize how I can set spiritually successful goals in my life—if I take the initiative. Some tips to succeed with this exercise:

1. Find a quiet place to be alone for twenty or thirty minutes. Take your journal with you.

2. To prepare for the exercise, close your eyes and relax as thoroughly as you can. Set aside all your worries, concerns, and problems for this period of time—you can come back to them in half an hour.

3. To achieve the higher viewpoint you need to do this exercise, it helps to open the heart. To do this, imagine a person, animal, place, or object that you love more than you have ever loved any other person or thing. Focus on that feeling of intense love—it can be in your past or present. Feel the love roll through you in great waves.

Nothing strengthens the judgment and quickens the conscience like individual responsibility.

—Elizabeth Cady Stanton

Now take the object of your love out of your vision. Just feel the love itself. This love is very pure. It has no object, no desire to change anything. It just loves. There is a great feeling of peace that comes with it because no action decision, or movement is necessary. You feel safety and great well-being, as if all is right with your world.

When you feel this love and you feel refreshed by it, open your eyes and continue with the exercise.

Most of the limitations we have are self-imposed.

—Les Brown

Whenever I work through this envisioning exercise, I put the notes away then look at them six months later. Just as my desire to become a better writer brought me the special writing class, life inevitably brings me a way to break through the limits that are holding back the well-being I want in any area of my life.

You can do this exercise each day for a different area in your life, making even finer distinctions within categories.

I have found that consciously deciding to set goals for the greater good makes my turning points into slight shifts on the road rather than bumpy potholes and sharp curves.

What Is an Action Plan?

Through envisioning, you've set a goal of the qualities you want in your life. Now you have to take that goal and break it into workable segments. This is sometimes called an action plan.

Action plans are a great way to speed your goals along the road to becoming reality. They can be as detailed as you wish. Some people, like my friend Dave, make them into an art. Others prefer a looser, more open-ended approach. Let's look at both.

Dave believes his very detailed action plans are the key to successfully achieving goals. Here's his approach in a nutshell:

1. Developing an action plan is simply setting a specific goal then breaking it into workable sections to accomplish.

2. To be sure he maintains balance as he works toward the goal, Dave considers how the plan affects all the different areas of his life — physical, social, mental, financial, spiritual, family.

3. Dave likes to use a notebook or create a filing system to keep his goals and action plans in one place, where he can review them often.

Dave has had such success with this process that he even sets goals as to how often he works on each action plan, so he knows he's on track with what he wants to do. He personalizes his plans: "I sat down one day and wrote out what I'd like my plan of action to look like. I make the process really enjoyable, really me," he said. "I like variety, so I try to make each goal look a little different visually. I know numbers and charts motivate me; if I can chart something, if I can see how close I am to the top, I know I'll stretch to meet that goal. When I noticed how eager I was to get home and put each day's number on the chart, I realized this was a good motivator. I knew money motivated me, so I taped a $20 bill to the cover of one plan of action.

"When I get bored with the plan as it is, I shift it around. I try and shake things up. I draw pictures. I decorate it to give it a little flair."

I never lose an opportunity of urging a practical beginning, however small, for it is wonderful how often the mustard-seed germinates and roots itself.

—Florence
Nightingale

Dave also said that a key to success is building flexibility into the plan. "One time I felt an area of my life was out of balance: I was watching too much TV instead of starting some other projects. The things I really wanted to do just weren't getting done," he told me. "So I set a goal to watch less TV. My action plan was to limit myself to less than twenty-five hours of TV a month. But I knew that if the plan was too rigid, I'd rebel. So I added flexibility: two days a month when I could watch as much TV as I wanted. The real objective here, the real goal, was that I wanted to spend more time on things other than TV. And I accomplished that.

"It's like having a business plan for your life," Dave said.

Not everyone I know likes the detail of working with this approach, and I tell people in my Turning Points workshops that it's just one kind of road map to get you to your goal. Another is making what I call a "qualities collage" (the next exercise).

The collage exercise is a great follow-up to envisioning. It's the hands-down favorite exercise from my Turning Points workshops—a fun way to creatively remind yourself how to continue to focus on the higher good in your life. Participants have told me, "Doing this collage made my goals less serious and heavy; it allowed me to play, and yet I was able to see many aspects of myself and my life."

To use your collage as an action plan, post it somewhere visible and regularly study it. Ask yourself, How can I bring more of these qualities into my life today?

Exercise:
Making a Qualities Collage

1. Collect five magazines or colorful catalogs and spend a half hour cutting out images and words that attract you, ones that relate to the qualities you described in the exercise above.

2. Then take a large sheet of paper and create your own collage by pasting or taping the pictures in any arrangement that pleases you.

Nothing is so much to be feared as fear.

—Henry David Thoreau

WORK BACKWARD FROM THE FUTURE

A third way to develop steps, or actions, toward what you want to bring into your life is to work backward from the future. It's my most successful method of dispelling the natural fear connected with bringing a dream into reality. People in my Turning Points workshops tell me this technique works miracles for them.

I imagine a goal has already been achieved in the future, then I work backward from that point.

One workshop participant tried this technique and was jubilant about its success in his life. Months later he told me, "It's now essential in my goal setting to see what I want as already complete. Looking from this completed state to the present takes some of the pressure off."

When the pressure to achieve your goal goes away, so does any fear. Since fear blocks our inner listening, it keeps us from what we really want. When the fear is gone, we hear God better. Here's an example:

Several years ago I had become restless in my job,

wanting to begin another project but not sure what direction to go in. I started the envisioning exercise. I decided that I wanted my new project to serve more people, reach a wider audience. I also saw how I wanted to be respected and recognized in my work, more than I was at that time. So I began with that future and worked backward, imagining what would have to happen to me, both personally and professionally, in order for me to feel completely satisfied with my progress. I looked three years into the future and wrote out a page-long description of myself in relation to my goal. It was as if I were seeing my project completed and those qualities actually in my life.

Exercise:
Working Backward from the Future

1. Imagine yourself in the future: five years, three years.
2. What would have to have happened personally and professionally in order for you to feel satisfied with your progress? Write a one-page description of your life as it would be with the qualities you set in your envisioning exercise. Be as specific as you can—include details.
3. Do the same for one year, one month, one week, and one day from now.
4. Now pick one action you can take by each of these dates that would help bring the qualities into your life.

Doing the above exercise was amazingly easy. I could even think of specifics—what kind of project I'd like to have completed, what response it would get, how it would enhance my career and reputation.

Then I moved the goal forward to one year. I again imagined the qualities, how far along I'd be at that point. I wrote a short description of my life one year from now. I repeated the exercise for one month, one week, and one day from now.

After I had finished envisioning these future dates and their qualities, I asked myself, What is one step I can take to achieve each of the qualities for each date?

Immediately answers came. The next day's action would be to lead a meeting I had scheduled and to do it well; in the meeting I would practice and refine an exercise I wanted to use in my project. For the next week, my action was to write a timeline for the project. Next month, I wanted to begin researching the project and set up file folders for each segment of the project to gather and sort my notes. By the end of the year, I wanted to have tested the idea in the work environment. In three years, I wanted to have the project finished.

Once I had set this action plan, I wrote the steps in my calendar where I could remember and review them, and check to see what I'd accomplished as the dates arrived.

If you do the work of envisioning what you want—even if you don't know how it will come—and you begin to take action, life will take care of the results. This principle worked for me in a way that was almost miraculous.

As soon as I had set my goals and action plan from the future—as if the goals were already achieved—the pressure I was feeling dropped. And things began to happen. Within a week I got three phone calls from

Growth is demanding and may seem dangerous, for there is loss as well as gain in growth. But why go on living if one has ceased to grow?

—May Sarton

Seattle, San Francisco, and Toronto, all from groups wanting me to talk at conferences or meetings. This was an amazing first result—in such a short time. Within a month, a manuscript based on the project was written and reviewed. And within a year it was published. All my goals were reached within two years!

What Do You Really Want?

A woman in one Turning Points workshop told me, "This kind of goal setting was very new for me. It taught me first to think of a goal more as a quality, to realize what I really wanted." She saw how many of her past goals had been based on other people's dreams, not her own.

The challenge in successful goal setting is to explore your own dreams, then set goals based on what you really want in your life. Asking what I really want helps me whenever I'm not sure what goal to set, if too many crowd my mind, or if I need to sift out other people's influences. It gets me motivated whenever I feel frozen by indecision.

The last time I asked myself, What do I really want? it brought to light two long-lost loves in my life: music and art. I had done a lot of drawing and painting in college, and I had loved being in choirs or singing with friends. But I had forgotten these loves. The exercise inspired me to join a local choir and take life-drawing classes. It felt wonderful to bring these hobbies back into my life, to expand into new areas. I realized the urge to learn and grow in other ways than through my work had been missing for about two years—so no wonder I was feeling a little stagnant. Just by asking the question I also discovered how much I wanted to teach again, and within two days I got a call from a local bookstore asking me to lead a writing workshop for them.

This kind of inner research may sound very simple, but it works. So I created the following exercise.

Exercise:
What Do You Really Want?

1. In your journal, list five goals—things you'd love to have if you were not limited in any way.

2. Next to each goal, write the quality of life it holds for you. For example *a great job* might have the quality of "fulfilling your purpose" in life or "helping you be more creative." *Travel more* might have the spiritual quality of "freedom," "new ideas for your work," or "a chance to visit family."

3. Do this exercise once a week for a month. If any goal repeats itself, circle it.

4. At the end of the month, choose the goal that appeared the most often in your exercise.

5. Write this goal in the center of a piece of paper. Follow the instructions for the Turning Points exercise on page 56 and write any ideas that come of a step you can take toward your dream.

CRISIS AND OPPORTUNITY

The stories in this chapter illustrate how goal setting is a process that often includes challenges and the need for adjustment. The challenges can make us stronger if we look deeply into ourselves—and see our true dreams and goals.

In the January 1996 issue of *Natural Health* magazine, Nathaniel Mead writes, "Personal growth can arise from what is otherwise a negative experience. Sometimes life brings difficulties that are the starting points for a new and better phase in one's life."

Marjorie Kelly of *Business Ethics* adds, "It's at the time of falling apart that we make the choices that build our future. We create the future as we go. . . . Our deeper self comes awake—bringing us flashes of insight, powerful dreams, or deep intuitions."

When my husband and I sold our house, the same house I mentioned in chapter 3, it was one such challenge—a traumatic experience because I had to let go of something I had dreamed of and developed for four years. But as Mead said in the quote above, as the old dream crumbled, a new one—a better one—took its place. The story shows how life really does look out for our highest good—if we follow our dreams.

When you get into a tight place and it seems you can't go on, hold on, for that's just the place and the time that the tide will turn.

—Harriet Beecher Stowe

MY DREAM HOME

That home had been my first solo purchase, one that I had made before our marriage. I had poured so much love, time, and money into it, trying to create a beautiful refuge from the world through interior decoration and exterior gardens. I imagined growing old there.

My pride and joy was my flower garden which stretched the length of our driveway and along the street. Enlarging it a little each year, I had carefully chosen perennials that flowered in contrasting colors to create a beautiful array from June to September. It was a bright spot in the neighborhood, one that made passersby stop and comment. In the fall of our fourth year in the house I planted two hundred spring-flowering bulbs in patches around the house. It would be beautiful in May, I imagined, loving my home and garden even more.

In January my husband suggested we think more seriously about moving. We both commuted about forty minutes each way to our jobs, and in winter the roads could be hazardous. In my mind's eye I saw the two hundred blooming daffodils and tulips waving in the May breeze.

The idea of moving—of leaving all that I'd created—was too much. I burst into tears.

It was a stormy weekend. At night, I tossed and turned, grieving over each flower, mentally walking through my gardens. By Sunday night, just to get some sleep, I did a special spiritual exercise.

I asked for help to say good-bye to the house. I imagined walking through my gardens in full summer. I said good-bye to each lily and spring bulb.

The next morning, I felt more positive. Following a nudge, I began the envisioning exercise, then wrote a wish list of all the things I could possibly want in a new home. I wanted space, coziness, plenty of light, privacy, something close to work, a lovely garden, woods. I let my imagination run wild as I described a terraced garden, with plants cascading down to an enclosed lawn or patio, like a Mediterranean villa. I also wrote that I'd like to see my present garden in bloom one last summer or take part of it with me to the new house.

My husband called a real estate agent. The agent

Every thing teaches transition, transference, metamorphosis: therein is human power. We dive & reappear in new places.

—Ralph Waldo Emerson

reasoned that the house could take as much as three or four months to sell. No need to look for a new house until we had a firm offer.

Four days later our plans changed.

The agent called, surprised. "There are possibly two offers on your house," he said. Our For Sale sign wasn't even up. "One couple is very serious," he said. "Your pictures sold them." On an impulse, I had left an album of summer garden photographs on the kitchen table.

Our house sold the next day. We were grateful, but the gratitude was tinged with panic. What if we couldn't find a new place we liked? My husband reassured me: "Look how fast our house sold! That was a miracle. The perfect house is just waiting for us."

We arranged to go house-hunting the next morning, but the agent had only two homes to show us. A drop in interest rates had made more houses available in our price range, but the neighborhood near work was still very expensive. I came back to the office depressed; neither home we had seen was half as nice as what we were leaving.

That afternoon I talked about our problem with a coworker.

"Oh, I just saw a lovely house that's going up for sale," she said. She described the size and price of the home, the large two-car garage, the backyard. "It was under snow, so I couldn't see what they had done out back, but it's lovely inside," she added.

I felt a tingle of excitement. "Where is it?"

"About a mile from here." She gave me sketchy directions.

I called our agent first thing the next morning.

"There's a house down the road that sounds good; it's in our price range," I said. "I don't know the street number. Can you look it up in your computer and arrange for us to see it?"

"Nothing's listed in the area," he said after a moment. "If it's really for sale, it'll show up soon. I'll call you."

I tried not to get my hopes up. God would take care of it. We felt tremendous pressure to find a place fast, but I reminded myself that achieving goals is a process and God had guided us this far.

That same day I went to lunch with a girlfriend. As we drove through a residential area on the way to a restaurant, we passed an attractive house that had often caught my eye. A car from a local real estate company was in the driveway. A woman I took to be a real estate agent was putting a lockbox for a key on the house.

This must be the home for sale! I could hardly believe it. My friend pulled the car over.

Running up to the woman, I asked, "Is this house for sale?"

"Yes," she said. "It's just going on the market this week. The family was unexpectedly transferred back east, and they have to sell in a hurry." I arranged to see it the next morning.

MY DREAM COMES TRUE

That night I had a dream of a turning point to future happiness. It helped confirm for me that my goal was the right one. In the dream I was walking through a beautifully remodeled home that was full of light. The living room was trimmed in teal blue, the floors were gleaming hardwood. Best of all was the summer garden

When one door of happiness closes, another opens; but often we look so long at the closed door that we do not see the one which has been opened for us.

—Helen Keller

out back. Could this be our house? I scribbled down the dream on awakening.

When we walked into the house the next morning, I couldn't believe my eyes.

Teal blue trim edged the living room, and there were the gleaming hardwood floors. It was my dream house. Although the backyard was covered in snow-drifts, on the kitchen counter were six snapshots showing a terraced garden waiting to be planted. My wish-list garden come to life!

I made one of the fastest decisions of my life. Moving into the living room where my husband and our agent sat talking, I said, "This house is going to go fast. We need to put an offer on it today, now." They looked at me in surprise.

"This is my dream house," I explained, telling them about my dream.

Our agent had never heard of someone buying a home based on a dream. My husband, however, knew me well enough to agree to the idea. We signed papers and a check.

Sensing that there would be competition for the house, I suggested offering more than the asking price. The agent called us later that evening to say that there was one other very interested couple, and the sellers would make a decision the next day.

That night I had trouble getting to sleep. "It's the perfect house, your dream house. It would be so terrible if the sellers didn't choose you," my mind worried. "It's in your price range. And think of that garden."

But I knew I had followed my spiritual guidance each step of the way, down to offering more than the asking price. It was now out of our hands.

We do not succeed in changing things according to our desire, but gradually our desire changes.

—Marcel Proust

The agent called us off and on all the next morning as the owners met with their agent and tried to decide who to sell to. "It looks good," he'd say, "your income is more stable." "Not so good," he'd call back the next hour, "you have another house being sold. They're worried that deal might fall through."

By noon, we were nervous wrecks. I made lunch and sat at the kitchen table across from my husband, pretending to read a magazine. The phone rang; we both jumped. It was our agent again.

"You better sit down!" he said. "You got the house!"

We moved into our new house the week before my birthday. *It is quite a birthday gift,* I thought, as I watched the snow melt and found a few plants coming up in the flower beds. Best of all, as part of our selling agreement, the buyers of our old home let me come back one day in May and dig up a carload of perennials for my new garden.

When I look back on all the things that could've gone wrong in the sale and move, I shudder. Sure, there were unexpected problems that came to light after we moved in—an ancient hot water heater that needed replacing, for instance—but that's part of buying an older home. The unexpected benefits were much more numerous: the very private backyard, the feeling of country living near a big city, the practically sound-proof family room (perfect for evenings when my husband wants to watch TV and I want to read upstairs). The entire experience was an exercise for me in setting a goal from the highest point of view, adjusting as the goal manifested, and listening to God's direction despite my doubts.

Live all you can; it's a mistake not to.

—Henry James

When We Move from Panic to Power

When we take these steps toward mastery and begin directing our lives and setting our goals from the inside instead of the outside, we move from a position of panic and "Life doesn't make sense!" to one of resting in God's arms.

This is an important survival tool. If you master it, you can move through all kinds of tough situations with more serenity—even when life throws you a curve ball.

The best way to successful change is to look into your heart, face your change, and set goals for your life from the highest viewpoint you can.

As we've learned in this chapter, the most successful goals are based on qualities—whatever would make you more of who you truly are. They allow you—and encourage you—to take responsibility for where you've come from and where you want to go. And when you take that first step toward this kind of freedom, life responds.

Life also brings you an amazing number of resources to help you with this kind of goal. In chapter 7 we'll look at the really big challenges that come into our lives to help us master change—how difficult turning points become blessings.

Ask Yourself:
How Do You Set Goals?

1. How have you set goals in the past? What were the results?

2. Would you change how you approached setting goals based on those results?

3. Have you ever achieved a goal you felt was particularly successful, in that it enhanced many areas of your life and made you a better person?

4. How did you achieve this goal?

5. Can you apply the same steps to a change you're currently facing?

7

$\mathscr{L}$ife's Greatest Challenges

Learning via
Difficult Turning Points

*If we want to live fully, beyond the life we
have today, we must take risks, stretch
ourselves, move past what we are now.*

—Marsha Sinetar

7. LIFE'S GREATEST CHALLENGES

———— 🖋 ————

*S*oul, the real you, always has an answer. The mind and emotions are sometimes so loud, Soul cannot express this answer in a way that it can be acted upon. It can be especially hard when changes force us to face a part of ourselves. The story below is a personal example.

When I first wrote about this turning point, which involved the dramatic failure of a business I had begun, I became very ill. I had not talked about the experience for almost five years, except with my husband and two close friends. I had even avoided thinking about it.

Why? It was just too painful. The whole situation was like a wound, painful to touch.

Life was asking me to face something in my past, a very unhappy time, but a time of great growth. It was a time when I believed I had failed miserably at a valued dream and hurt many other people in the process. So looking at it was something I had avoided for five long years.

When I finally faced this situation and the memories, I began the process of healing. It was an amazing experience.

Not long after I wrote about it, I was asked to tell my story at a spiritual conference of three thousand people. Backstage, waiting to go on, I was trembling and more scared than I had been in many years. Onstage, I told the story in the simplest words I could. But the emotions I felt from the audience made it hard to keep from crying. Afterward, as I walked out of the auditorium, many people came up to me to thank me for sharing what was "their" story too.

I'll never forget one young man who simply stood in front of me for a long moment, then gave me a hug. Tears were in his eyes as he whispered, "Thank you," then quickly walked away.

Speaking and writing about a painful turning point, exploring the lessons it had brought me, began the healing for me—and for these others too.

Writer Gabriele Rico's book *Pain and Possibility: Writing Your Way through Personal Crisis* talks about this: "Paradoxically, by letting go, by externalizing feelings in words, we gain a greater ability to take charge of our own lives, and begin to see the patterns within the seeming chaos." This is what happened to me.

The Courage to Live Your Life

In 1980 I met a man who worked as a chef in the restaurant where I waitressed. As passionate about food and cooking as I was, Eric wooed me on one of our early dates with an elaborately garnished home-cooked meal. We were soon married and living in Portland. We both got jobs in a booming natural foods store; I as an instructor for cooking classes, and Eric in the company's public relations department.

I designed the curriculum, taught, and hired other

To know the universe itself as a road, as many roads, / as roads for traveling Souls.

—Walt Whitman

teachers, and organized the classroom kitchens. Backed by plenty of company money, my classes were well advertised and quite successful.

Proud of our success, Eric and I thought having our own school would be fun, possibly our gateway to fame and fortune. So we packed our bags and moved south to the San Francisco area to try our luck.

Both Eric and I believed strongly in inner guidance, and in this venture the instructions were coming fast. Both of us got daily nudges, ideas, and obvious hints to talk to certain people, investigate certain locations, check certain sources of financing. We saw a path in front of us, and we followed it. It was a very exciting time.

A dream was coming true.

To live is so startling it leaves little time for anything else.

—Emily
Dickinson

Exercise:
Finding Your Dream

1. List ten things that bring you joy.
2. List ten things that you do well and give you satisfaction in your life.
3. List five things others tell you you're good at.
4. List ten creative things you'd like to do with your life if you had no limitations of time or money.

FINDING YOUR OWN PATH

The path appeared paved with gold—from conception to manifestation. A 1200-square-foot storefront housing the cooking school and cookware store took just under six months to open.

We poured all our time and resources into the school. Other than three years I had had in vitamin sales, neither Eric nor I knew much of anything about business, but we believed in our idea, and we found backers who believed in us.

On opening day, the store was flooded with people who had seen our ads and my hand-lettered flyers. We served fresh cookies and cider, gave sushi-making demonstrations in the school kitchen, held a raffle for gourmet cookware, and took in sales beyond our wildest dreams.

All the month's cooking classes filled in a week.

Innocent of the changing times, neither of us could predict the recession of the early 1980s that would begin just a year later.

Foolish people imagine that what they imagine is somewhere else. That stuff is not made in any factory but their own.

—Henry David Thoreau

At opening, the school was an instant success. California is always looking for novelty, and we were in the spotlight for that time. A major U.S. newspaper ran an interview, I was featured in a syndicated food column in forty-six newspapers, people flew in from as far as Switzerland to take our two-week intensive course on natural foods gourmet cooking.

The classes kept filling. Eric and I worked very long hours and began to pay back our investors. Success lasted through the end of that year; and when the year turned, it brought personal turning points.

I was beginning to discover that I still loved teaching and was passionate about food, but I hated running a full-time business. We had three employees but no bookkeeper. Neither Eric nor I had had much experience with managing cash flow or other business necessities. We knew enough to draw the first round of customers, but not enough to sustain them on the long haul.

By the beginning of the fourth year, both our marriage and the business had fallen apart.

The school was bringing in enough money to cover the monthly overhead of rent, supplies, and our small staff, plus meet our payments to investors. But salaries for Eric and I were almost nonexistent. A bicycle racer, Eric finally decided to get a full-time job at a bicycle store nearby, and I began to run the school alone. That meant eighteen-hour days, six or seven days a week. When we had a party to cater, I was often working until 1:00 a.m.

I was young and energetic, but the heavy workload began to take its toll. Eric had recently become interested in setting up his own graphics business, and our lives grew more and more separate. Most days we barely saw each other from morning till evening.

Stress ate away at any foundation of our relationship. We argued more than laughed as the weeks went by. With no time or understanding of how to shore up our shaky marriage, we decided to go our separate ways in the spring of the cooking school's fourth year.

That summer, my life started to close in around me. Eric had found a new relationship, and his graphics business was growing beautifully, while I felt more and more trapped, looking to a future with no hope. Each day became a struggle. Meeting our investors' payments and salaries was about all I could manage each week. Indebted to many suppliers with no way to pay, I kept hoping for a solution—a new investor? A sudden flood of business?

Over and over I asked myself, *Why didn't it work?*

Both Eric and I had listened to our spiritual guidance, had done everything we could each step of the way, and had had the best of intentions. Yet, due in part to economic times, failure was imminent and seemed beyond our control.

I spent long sleepless nights.

I had reached a small crisis in faith. All my life I had believed that if I followed God's Voice, I would be guided to do the right thing. But now I was in a mess. I railed inwardly at my ex-husband, myself, and God, feeling victimized by a business I now dreaded facing each morning. And all these people who depended on me, who had backed our idea! What about their hopes and dreams for the school?

There seemed to be no solution in sight.

No man can produce great things who is not thoroughly sincere in dealing with himself.

—James Russell Lowell

Exercise:
Dialogue with a Dream

Imagine a conversation with a significant project or endeavor that failed and caused you disappointment or pain. Ask the experience, What did you teach me about myself? Write this question in your journal.

Now imagine the experience answering you. Write anything it tells you.

Next ask, How did you strengthen me?

Write down the answer.

From this exercise, review the experience again and see it from a different perspective. What did you learn?

Difficult Crossroads

One August evening I went over the figures again. Each month the school had fallen further and further into debt. There really didn't seem to be any way out of the mess. I had tried every possible trick to boost sales and class attendance, offering discounts and bring-a-friend programs. It seemed as if everything was against the success of the business.

But I wanted to keep trying, not give up yet. *There must be an honorable way out of this,* I thought. *God will show me the way to solve this.* And again and again I said to God, "Thy will be done."

By then I had hired an accountant. He called unexpectedly that evening to discuss the books. Overwhelmed by the dead-end situation I faced, I asked him if there was anything we hadn't tried. Were there any ideas he could think of to get the business back on its feet?

"Is that what you really want?" he asked.

"No," I answered slowly, realization dawning. "I've had enough."

"Then there's always bankruptcy," he said.

When he said the word, I felt the world stand still. If I had known what I know now about turning points, I would have recognized one — a big one, a life-altering one — facing me at that moment.

Everything in my being shouted no at the thought of bankruptcy. I was sure this wasn't the way God would've selected. My spiritual understanding at that time said it was wrong, a terrible choice, creating worse karma, or spiritual debt, than I could ever repay. I believed that bankruptcy did not exist in the spiritual worlds.

I also remembered my growing up years, the principles that had been drilled into me by my grandmother about carrying through. Bankruptcy was certainly not carrying through! It was leaving the toys out in the rain, not cleaning up the kitchen, and worse. I could feel Hartzie looking down on me at that moment, shaking her finger.

Then I realized the worst part: Bankruptcy would be giving up my dream. It would be telling the world I had failed.

My accountant waited through my long silence, while these thoughts churned in my head. Quietly he reminded me that this was a business decision. Emotions must be put aside. He knew a little about my spiritual beliefs and my strong sense of right and wrong, payment of debts being one of the strongest.

"These are not decisions to be made lightly," he said, "but if there is no other recourse, the physical world has provided this as a way to start fresh. Part of business is the risk of failure. You knew that starting out, didn't you?"

I hadn't. I realized I had gone into this business with just my enthusiasm, a few skills, and little detachment.

This was a real shakeup in my attitude toward my goal. I needed to look at some of my beliefs about failure and consider the consequences of such a step. So I told him I would think about it.

I sat down that night and did the Turning Points exercise from chapter 3. I closed my eyes and focused on God for a moment, to help me get to the highest state possible, above all the turmoil of my emotions and doubts. Since it was so much on my mind, in the center of my page I wrote the word *failure*. I saw that my understanding of failure was the key concern here, central to my fears, the heart of my turning point.

Lightly, I put my attention on this word. Images started flooding my mind: my grandmother shaking her finger at the five-year-old who hadn't put her toys

The saddest day hath gleams of light, / The darkest wave hath bright foam beneath it.

—Sarah Winnemucca

away, my parents' disappointment, embarrassing questions from friends. I wrote anything that came into my mind about the word *failure*—thoughts, feelings, a person's name, places in my life, special objects, even colors, smells, and remembered words people had said to me—drawing lines to connect these new items with the center. I was careful not to censor myself. I knew that unexpected concepts or images may be coming from a higher place than the mind's censor, and as Soul, I had access to that higher place.

Exercise:
Exploring a Difficult Turning Point

In the middle of a clean page, write the word *failure* or whatever word best describes the problem you face. Now write any thoughts or ideas or situations that come to mind when you think of that word.

Explore one of the ideas by writing about it for ten minutes. Time yourself with a kitchen timer, and keep writing until the timer rings.

Throughout history the human mind and the human spirit have overcome and endured problems and situations that seemed insurmountable.

—Les Brown

As I was doing my Turning Points exercise, I unearthed some very deep feelings about the decision I was about to make.

Part of me believed that Eric and I had made a mess and would need to be punished for it, to lie in the mess for a while, to suffer. Another part of me questioned this idea: "Was it all my doing? Hadn't I really done the best I knew how each step of the way?"

I also looked at why I had started the business in the first place and found I hadn't had many goals of my own—I was following Eric's lead. I wanted to share what I loved with others; I really wasn't after fame, fortune, or huge success. I just wanted to make a living doing something I enjoyed.

The exercise allowed me to look at what I had learned so far. Now I needed a solution. I could see no way out that wouldn't hurt someone. What would cause the least amount of damage?

It is as if one has a storage room where you have informa- tion that you can't reach when you're awake. . . . Then, in that dreamy state, somehow you can reach in the darkness and find some- thing like a treasure that is hidden in this storage room.

—Isabel Allende

Doing an exercise where a turning point and its lessons are explored can be a key aspect in recognizing the purpose of more dramatic turning points. On the surface these may look like disasters. Often the out- come is out of your hands. Your only job is to do the best you can at that particular moment, then watch as life shifts the pieces on the chessboard in front of you and opens up new options.

As I did the exercise, a truth emerged from the turmoil of my shame and negative feelings about bank- ruptcy: "If I learn something important here then per- haps it is the best choice."

The years of suffering with a failing business had taught me so much about money management. Was that really the lesson here? Could I take this new understanding of finances and live my life differently, start afresh? I was still very unsure of what the karmic payback of this action would be.

The answer came unexpectedly that night in a dream.

DREAM ANSWER

In the dream I was standing in line at a super- market checkout. Harold Klemp, my spiritual teacher and the leader of Eckankar, was standing next to me. The cashier had just totaled my purchases. "That comes to $400," she said. This was much more expensive than I had expected, and I knew my bank account would be severely depleted. But even in the dream I was willing to pay whatever I owed and began writing out the check.

"Wait a minute," Harold said. "I think we've been overcharged."

He pointed to an advertising coupon. "This coupon entitles us to a reduced price at this time. And someone else must have added these extra items to the order; we really don't want them. Shall we return them?" he asked me.

"Sure," I said.

After the cashier had corrected the bill, the total was much less. Harold and I walked out of the store with very little to carry. I felt light and free, as if a heavy burden had been lifted.

When I woke I knew immediately that the dream was significant.

At the time, the number four signified something important for me: In my study of Eckankar, I had graduated through four levels of spiritual initiation, or growth. I was now at what was called the Fourth Circle. *Four* also reflected the four years I had been in business. I felt the cashier was symbolic too. She was like an impartial judge in a courtroom, only this was a higher court which assessed karma, or spiritual debt. She was ringing up the total I owed karmically from my four years of experience with the school.

At first the total was very high, an amount that would almost deplete my karmic account (my checkbook). But rather than just accept this at face value, my spiritual guide pointed out some errors in calculation.

Do you believe you deserve to have what you desire? If you don't, you won't allow yourself to have it.

—Louise L. Hay

And the amount I actually paid was far less, something I could afford spiritually. The consequences of the bankruptcy would be something I could handle.

The dream stayed with me for hours that next morning, and the more I thought about it, the more I saw it as a good sign. I felt sure God was telling me to go ahead with the bankruptcy and trust that it was the best option.

I slept one more night on the decision, and in the morning I knew it was the only path I had the strength to take now.

I filed for bankruptcy in late summer.

PAYING BACK THE DEBT OF FAILURE

Despite the dream, I still believed I had violated some spiritual code. Inwardly I waited for a heavy load of karma to fall on top of me and crush me. And many things appeared in my path that were obviously paying back the bankruptcy.

They didn't always appear in the arena of money, however. Sometimes it was illness. Or a gift of aid to a friend.

Once the school closed, I had no income. My first challenge was finding a job. But before I could even finish writing my résumé, I got a phone call from a respected doctor in San Francisco.

He had read a review of my low-fat cooking classes. He was working with a university hospital studying heart disease, and he needed someone to run the food program. Would I be interested?

The next door that opened for me was an almost more astounding gift.

I had always wanted to write a cookbook but hadn't found either the time or the skills to put one together. I couldn't imagine how to go about contacting a publisher or writing a proposal. But during the next month, totally out of the blue, a large West Coast publisher called me.

They had also heard of the school and wondered if I would like to put together one of their cookbooks. The writer they had hired had changed her mind, and they were desperate for someone to take over the work.

SEEING A BIGGER PICTURE

By telling this story, I don't want to imply that the ends justify the means.

For me, bankruptcy was a very serious step. It cannot be taken lightly. In most cases, quite a few people are hurt or at least inconvenienced. In this way, it is not a positive option for most of us.

But in the larger picture, I made a decision that was the best possible option for me at the time.

One reason was this: Interwoven in my experience were old attitudes about success and failure that I needed to rid myself of. As I did the Turning Points exercise, and in the ten years that followed the bankruptcy as I slowly rebuilt my credit history and my understanding of business, I saw what a lopsided view of failure I had held—all or nothing. Black or white, no gray area for the natural learning curve.

It took me a while to forgive myself and my ex-husband for the failure of our business. I eventually saw how young and enthusiastic, but naive, we were. I saw the mistakes we had made in the first successful years and how they led to the eventual depletion of our resources. I spoke with some of my creditors from those days and got a new viewpoint on the rise and fall of small businesses. The exercise below helped me enormously during this time.

Exercise:
On Forgiving Yourself

Imagine you are just beginning this life. Write a letter to God with a wish list of qualities you'd like to have learned by the time you are ready to leave this life.

Which qualities from your wish list has a most recent problem given you?

Since it was part of your original plan with God, forgive yourself for any "mistakes" regarding this problem that you might still feel ashamed of. Do this in writing or some other creative, playful way.

Men are like trees: each one must put forth the leaf that is created in him.

—Henry Ward Beecher

Another important lesson emerged from this experience, a lesson about money. How to use it wisely and how to budget, how much I can really afford to risk on a business venture, how to keep a good financial foundation as I try new things in my life.

As I gained this overview, I forgave myself for disappointing and hurting the other people involved in the school. The emotional sting of letting friends and coworkers down stayed with me for many years, and forgiving myself was one of the hardest parts of resolving this turning point, something that came much later than my growing understanding about financial balance.

All of this happened over ten years ago. It was a major turning point in my life. Life had taught me a severe lesson with the business I built and lost so quickly. And I don't know if I could've learned in another, less painful way.

The severity of such an experience often depends on one thing: How fast can we recognize the experience as one of positive growth and change? And how fast can we see the lesson behind it?

A speaker I once heard gave a good analogy of the growth that can come from crisis, like grief over a loved one's death or the failure of a dream. Life continually hands us the bricks and mortar of experience, he said. If they are left lying around and not used, they will harden into obstacles. And whether we build a wall or a walkway with the raw material is entirely up to us.

In other words, our approach determines our experience.

I believe God is very committed to each of us and our spiritual development. Hard lessons and difficult turning points can bring us the strength we will need later. In my story, a painful experience — losing a lot of money — gave me a more conservative streak and a new attitude about saving. A very difficult path can prepare you for survival. But how do you take the leap in understanding and learn to see something beneficial in what appears to be a negative experience?

You have to give up your old ideas. You have to embrace new ones.

And this can be the hardest part of all.

That voice which speaks in your conscience and in some of your intensest joys . . . is in fact the closest contact you have with the mystery.

—C. S. Lewis

Embracing New Ways

As John Welwood, Ph.D., says in *Journey of the Heart*: "This kind of growth is challenging because it often costs us what we hold most dear: namely, our old ways. . . . Yet the promise in such a situation is equally powerful: If we open up in the ways it requires . . . we will broaden out as human beings, becoming more flexible, loving, and responsive to life as a whole."

The Sunday, September 26, 1993, edition of the Minneapolis *Star Tribune* ran an article by a travel photographer who had been on assignment in Borneo when she faced a situation as transforming for her as mine had been for me.

On their way to the Djakarta airport for a flight to a jungle camp in Borneo, she was helping companions load baggage into taxis when she realized she didn't have her camera bag with all her film. She got to the airport in time to see her camera bag, piled with the rest of the group's luggage, go through the security X-ray machine.

X-ray machines in Western countries are film-safe for speeds up to 1000; her film was 1600, and this was a developing country. Sick, she turned from the group to contemplate her loss. Now she had no film for the story she was supposed to shoot in Borneo. Deep in the jungle there were not likely to be camera shops.

After being flown halfway across the world, how would she complete her assignment?

Friends tried to comfort her, but during the plane ride to a small village, she fell deeper and deeper into her greatest fear as a professional photographer: coming home with nothing.

To calm herself she turned to a book of meditations

If you want something from life, first of all you have to earn it. But you also have to be open to the gifts life is willing to give you, and that means you have to ask for them.

—Harold Klemp

a friend had given her before she left. One sentence jumped out at her: *You can choose how to feel.* She had never believed that. But now she tried. Repeating phrases from the book over and over to herself, she tried to flood out the worry with uplifting words.

And to her surprise, it began to work.

"Without the usual self-torture," she wrote, "I had room for other thoughts—not how awful the past event was, but what to do next."

A friend leading the trip counseled her to not give up. "Why don't you shoot some of the film and get it developed—find out if it really is wrecked?" she suggested.

Surprisingly, even though they were now in the deep jungle, there was a photo lab in a village downstream.

The woman quickly shot a few rolls of the film, handed the boatman the equivalent of twenty dollars, and watched him slip down the river. She crossed her fingers and kept practicing her new vision: You can choose how to feel.

It took two days for the boatman to return, but when he did he was carrying a package of prints. The film had come through unscathed.

To the travel photographer, it was nothing short of miraculous. Which was the greater surprise, she wondered later, finding out that there was a working Fuji photo lab in the jungles of Borneo or learning that she could choose how to feel—a miraculous turning point in itself?

Such experiences as my bankruptcy and the grief it brought, even the photographer's near disaster, are ways God touches us. Life, through pain and heartache, through giving up a long-held belief or dream that we really want to keep, teaches us how to be greater vehicles for love.

In the next chapter we'll talk about the major spiritual leaps such crises create for us.

Ask Yourself:
What Do You Learn from Tough Changes?

1. What is the worst-case scenario in a current change you're facing? Do you have the strength to see it through if it came about?

2. What is the best-case scenario?

3. What keeps you from accepting life's challenges with love and grace?

4. Does your history tend to repeat itself?

5. What effect will the choices you made this week have on your life next week? Next year?

8

When Big Changes Bring Big Gains

Facing the Fear of Death

*That which has hitherto been
most feared . . . may be thereby
transformed into spiritual strength.*

—John Layard

8. WHEN BIG CHANGES BRING BIG GAINS

*E*very day people face the possibility of death through disease, war, accident, or other disaster. Many crumble. Yet many come through the experience with renewed strength—and faith that a divine hand was guiding them even in the darkest moments. What quality of character makes the difference here? An attitude of seeing the blessings within each experience life offers.

Ann's car accident turned her life upside down. But for some reason the morning of the accident she had woken with a sense of joy, as if great blessings were about to enter her life.

That evening, she put her two-year-old daughter into the front seat of their car, snug amongst a huge bag of laundry, then drove off for home.

On the way, they were hit head-on by a truck.

Miraculously, Ann's daughter Sarah remained unhurt, protected by the laundry bag. Ann, however, had not gotten off easily. She was rushed to the hospital where doctors gingerly extracted slivers of glass from her tongue and stitched the cuts on her head. Focusing on God and singing HU quietly to herself, she was able

As you chant the name of God, with love . . . the bindings and bands that constrain Soul will begin to unwind.

—Harold Klemp

to calm herself as the doctors did their work. She made it through the emergency, and in time was on her way to full recovery.

When she got home from the hospital, she saw the letter she had written the morning of the accident, thanking her spiritual guide for the blessings about to come into her life.

How was a near-fatal car accident a blessing? she wondered. The answer came in the next few months. Recovery gave Ann plenty of mental and emotional rest and Sarah special time with her father. The situation was indeed a blessing.

It only took a different viewpoint for Ann to see past the trauma of the accident to the gift, a gift she might not have been able to receive another way.

First Comes Crisis, Then Comes Opportunity

In a workshop, students were asked to graph the highs and lows of turning points in their lives, including supposedly disastrous ones such as accidents, divorces, marriages, job shifts.

Their graphs showed an interesting pattern.

Participants usually marked their crises as low spots on the graphs. The teacher noticed that the lower the dip to the crisis, the higher the upswing that followed. Each major upheaval in the form of disaster, disease, or disability was followed by turned fortunes and new understandings.

In my life, crisis appears to be particularly useful in two situations: (1) when I need a good shaking up, a spiritual wake-up call, when old patterns that no longer serve me have gotten too deeply rooted and need to be weeded out. Or (2) when a large amount of karma, or spiritual debt, presents itself to be worked off, as in the following story.

When I Learned I Had Cancer

It all began with a routine blood test. I had been feeling tired, and at my checkup the doctor ran a thyroid panel. The numbers showed possible malfunction of the thyroid. On the advice of the doctor, I made an appointment with an endocrinologist.

The specialist dismissed the blood-test numbers but was immediately curious about my thyroid, which protruded slightly on the right side of my neck.

"What's this lump on your neck?" he asked.

"Oh, it's been there for years. Probably a result of a car accident; the muscle's strained."

"Not a muscle strain," he said. "I'll be right back."

He stepped out of the room and returned with a lab technician. "This might be a tumor," he said. "We can perform a biopsy right now and see what the tissue looks like."

Later that week, I called the clinic for the results. "The tissue shows abnormal patterns. It could be cancer," my doctor said. "We'd like to do a radioactive scan on the tumor. Can you come in next week?"

My mind was awhirl. I was seeing my life change before my eyes: disease, death—my worst fears were being realized. *Cancer,* I thought. *Oh, my God.*

No passion so effectually robs the mind of all its powers of acting and reasoning as fear.

—Edmund Burke

Death and Rebirth

I closed my eyes and desperately asked for help and guidance through this ordeal.

The reassurance came from my inner guide, "I'll be there. Go ahead with it." I asked the doctor for some time to think this over. His parting admonition was not to take too much time. The scan later that week showed a good possibility of a malignancy, and an operation was advised.

Life was beginning to stir something in myself that I had been afraid to examine: fear. I didn't know what exactly was happening inside me, but the fear was monumental. With one part of myself, I observed dispassionately that feelings were going to be examined, old behavior patterns would surface and burn off, and those fires would change me deeply. But most of my being was just very afraid. The fear kept returning, as one dire possibility after another surfaced.

Who wouldn't be shaken by such a diagnosis? In our modern era, cancer is a death sentence for many people. My secure marriage, lovely home, safe family, and great job shrank in importance as I imagined what life would be like as I dealt with this disease. Would I have surgery, chemotherapy, radiation treatments? Should I try the route of natural healing without surgery or drugs?

There were so many decisions, and I really didn't think I had the strength to make any one of them by myself.

I began to work each morning with the Fear Room exercise from page 76, trying to lighten the inner atmosphere so that I could choose a clear course of action. I wrote at length about the cancer in my journal, trying to see the lesson behind it. But most of all, I kept asking, silently and otherwise, for help.

As decisions were made I marveled at how the event was bringing members of my family closer. Despite our occasional differences, we really pull together in a crisis, I realized. My mother and I consulted each other

Mastery and surrender are the same process, seen from two different perspectives.

—John Robbins and Ann Mortifee

over each aspect of the surgery and treatment. She suggested flying to Baltimore, Maryland; the family knew doctors at Johns Hopkins Hospital. We would find the best surgeon, the best oncologist. The telephone wires hummed between Baltimore and Minneapolis almost every night, as my family rallied to my support.

Although I had for years been a fierce proponent of natural healing, I felt a strong urge to go the allopathic route, see a regular oncologist, and then decide on treatment. This was a surprise. I often wondered if I had chosen the right route. Then I had to laugh: My primary doctor turned out to be named Dr. Allo, a bit of confirmation that I was taking the right course. It brightened my darker moments.

The day of the surgery I was in a daze. Feeling my inner guide quite close, but palms sweaty with fear and an even bigger lump in my throat, I was wheeled into the operating room.

That was the last thing I remembered.

Immediately I was out of my body, enmeshed in an experience like a dream—but infinitely more real.

I found myself in a beautiful city in another world. All my dreams had come true. I had somehow escaped all fear, pain, and death. A young Adonis romanced me. He said he loved me and wanted me to stay forever in the lovely place he had created. In return he promised to take away all the fears that had clouded my life on earth. The inner world was huge, light, and happy; people lived by creating music and art instead of working. It seemed as though I had everything, but a thought kept intruding: *Where was my inner guide?*

The young man showed me the place where I would

live. I was entranced by the spaciousness, the lovely feeling. At one point I put my hand in my pocket and was surprised to find a folded slip of paper with two words on it: *Tony* and *Mahanta*. They were two things I loved very much in my life on earth. Tony was my new husband, and *Mahanta* is the title of my spiritual guide in Eckankar.

It was tempting to stay in this place of beauty and light, where I knew no fear, but I had to return to earth to continue my learning with these two people. I knew I had far to go in my understanding of love, so I chose to complete the work I had begun. Reluctantly I told the young man I had to go back.

He protested and tried to keep me; I realized later this was my struggle to reenter the physical body.

Healing through Emptiness

Although only hours had passed, it seemed like days. I was floating above my body as it lay in the recovery room. I knew I had to go back, although it took all the effort I could muster to move my hand and slowly come back to physical consciousness.

Later my mother told me it had taken hours to revive me in the recovery room. I had been so pale and appeared deathlike. She never knew how close to the truth that was. All that night I struggled with the choice I had made, the choice to live. The beautiful inner world where my fears had miraculously dissolved seemed even more appealing now. Dying seemed a positive choice when my body was so full of pain. Everything hurt, and I was nauseous from the anesthesia. My throat felt empty, as if more than a cancerous tumor had been removed.

Whoever loves true life, will love true love.

— Elizabeth Barrett Browning

The loneliness of returning to this gray world was overwhelming. That first night, as I came back to my body and began to realize where I was, remains one of the bleakest in my memory.

I still only understood a part of what had happened; more of the spiritual reasons behind the disease would reveal themselves over the next few months as I endured the radiation treatments and healed from the operation.

The gift of the experience would slowly emerge as I wrote about it.

As I remembered and wrote down the strange out-of-body experience I had had while on the operating table, I saw one of the gifts right away. God, protecting me, had been there all along—not visible, but in those two written words. I later came to understand that the place I had visited while my body lay unconscious was one of the lower heavens; the young man had tried to trick me into settling for less than my destiny. My sense of obligation to return, to work out my fears, had saved me from a beautiful trap. Although living was the more difficult road, I knew that in my earthly life I was experiencing great tempering as Soul.

ILLNESS AS A TEACHER

It was not until months later that I began to piece together the puzzle of this important turning point. It felt like a weight had been removed from me and also that I had passed a test of courage: I gained a chance to reach a much higher heaven than the one the beautiful young man had offered me.

Part of my decision not to die was a feeling of responsibility to pay back debts I'd incurred and to finish learning the lessons that accompanied them.

Most people have to delve into the dark areas and go through them before they reach a state of freedom, light, and serenity.

—Christina Grof and Stanislav Grof, M.D.

During the months following my operation and treatment, I was able to let go of very deep-seated fears about myself, as well as reunite with my family.

One of the major fears was tied up in many other spiritual lessons I've encountered: learning how to express myself as Soul. I had always been very outspoken, sometimes to my own and others' harm. It had taken years to learn how to temper my sometimes severe way of expressing myself into something equally direct but more respectful of other people's feelings and space. It seemed appropriate to me that the cancer would lodge in my throat, the seat of vocal expression.

I also had a vague feeling that I had somehow paid back some debt I had incurred during the years I had the cooking school. God chose this very efficient way to handle both in one short life-and-death experience.

Another gift that came in the months following the operation and treatment was a growing compassion for others who were healing in some way. I remember sitting in the airport, resting between flights on my way from Baltimore to my home in Minneapolis. Behind me were seated two elderly women, each complaining about some ache or pain or illness that plagued them. Months earlier, I would've been less than sympathetic with their health problems and pain, but now I sincerely felt for them.

The insights and healings that followed my summer of cancer were indeed highs on my graph for that year. I watched myself changing, becoming softer.

In an article in the November 1995 *New Woman* magazine, Judith Levine wrote about her dad who has Alzheimer's disease. She told of how her once demand-

Not until we are lost . . . do we begin to find ourselves.

—Henry David Thoreau

ing father had become "more 'here' than ever before. Not bulldozing forward or expanding to take up all the space, this manageable-size Dad leaves room to approach him. And then, to move closer."

So my cancer was a gift for me. I have watched life move closer, and I've welcomed it with open arms.

LEARNING TO TRUST

When I was young, my mother would drive us kids each July from Baltimore to upstate New York where we attended my grandmother's summer camp. On one part of the New York State Thruway, we had to drive through a long tunnel. Mom hated tunnels. So she sang her way through them.

One must learn to be a more active giver of love.

—Gina
   Cerminara

Perhaps she was afraid of getting stuck in the darkness and never being able to find her way out. Through my cancer experience, I understood that feeling.

Sometimes it was as if I were singing in the darkness, trying to get through the tunnel of the experience. But since I was given the blessing of my experience with cancer and made a conscious decision to stay and finish my work, I no longer view life as a tunnel to be sung through. Instead, my life has become one of steps from one experience to the next.

This understanding wasn't instantaneous or neatly packaged. It came to me very slowly, through months of recording my dreams and daily experiences. It came because I wanted to know. And because I trusted life to tell me.

DEATH OF A LOVED ONE

A dear friend had to face death at an important crossroads in her life—the death of her beloved husband of many years. Normally this would be devastating, and this is not to say that it was easy for her. But because she was paying attention, life prepared her in an unexpected way for this major turning point.

One Saturday morning, my friend was on her way to the post office when she took a wrong turn. Instead of turning left, she turned right and had to double back through a series of unfamiliar roads.

As soon as she turned down the unfamiliar route, she felt a holy silence everywhere. She rounded a curve and saw a man lying in the middle of the road. Her first thought was, *He's a runner who's had a heart attack.* She parked her car at the side of the road and got out to see if she could help.

When she stepped out of the car, she saw his terrible wounds and knew he'd been hit by a car and there wasn't much time.

She looked at him. "I'll be right back," she said. "May the blessings be." This is an ancient blessing in Eckankar. The equivalent of "Thy will be done," it helps release the outcome of the event, however traumatic, into the hands of God.

She ran to the nearest house, yelling, "Call 911! Call for help!" They did. Then she ran back to the man and knelt beside him, singing HU.

The first few notes came out as sobs. My friend heard her inner guide chide her, "You have a task to do. Focus on it." So she centered herself, and the HU came out as clear as a bell.

The man's body suddenly stopped spasming. He turned and looked my friend in the eye. She knew Soul was recognizing the beauty of God in the HU she sang.

Suddenly my friend's inner hearing opened, and

she could hear the man speaking. His only concern was for his family. "My wife, my family," he said silently, "please let them know."

She said aloud to God, "How can I do this? This man doesn't have any identification on him."

The next minute, a man stopped his car and ran over. "Can I help?" he asked. Then, as he knelt down beside my friend, he gasped, "Oh, my God, it's Stan."

"Do you know this man?" she asked.

He nodded yes.

"Please, go get his family. He wants his family to know."

The man turned to obey, and the injured man relaxed as soon as he knew this was taken care of. His next concern was voiced to her silently: "I need the blessings of God." My friend felt strength surge into her heart. In a clear voice she said, "You have earned the right to walk in the presence of God. You have learned love and compassion, and giving of yourself in this lifetime. You will forever live in the worlds of God."

Soon the paramedics came and put the man in an ambulance. My friend continued to kneel on the side of the road, silently singing HU. A few minutes later, a branch fell from a tree and landed gently beside her.

She knew this Soul had translated from this world in the process we call death.

My friend's life was changed by witnessing the passing of another person in such a dramatic way. A few short weeks later, her own husband died. His death was not unexpected since he had been in and out of hospitals for kidney failure for many years. But their love for each other was a strong bond, and his leaving shocked her to the core.

Should the ECK, or Holy Spirit, ever touch your heart, you realize there is never any turning back on the path to God. Ever.

—Harold Klemp

Comfort to the Heart

One day, not long after her husband's funeral, my friend received a letter from the wife of the man who had died on the side of the road.

In the letter, the wife explained she had read an announcement about my friend's husband in the paper. She wanted to express her sympathy and also tell my friend how much it had meant to her to have my friend's support when her own husband, Stan, had passed away.

The two women shared a common experience. For both, losing a beloved spouse was life-changing, shocking, and the last thing they had wished for.

But it was not life-destroying.

Because of the belief that their spouses had in some way chosen to make this step, each woman saw a spiritual side of the experience of death, believing that Soul continues to live on.

Death makes us feel very vulnerable. It reminds us that despite our best efforts at controlling life, there are certain things beyond our control. Yet both myself and the two women in the story above have learned that Soul, the essence of a person, does have a choice when death comes. Death is another turning point, a door to the next room. We can choose how we view the process of death.

Choosing Love over Fear

My friend Sondra is a competent physician, a very organized and efficient woman who has just remodeled her own home and built her chiropractic practice from the ground up. Looking at her you'd never imagine she had to face as dire a problem as my cancer—but she did. It came on the emotional and mental levels: fear.

She said it began one night when she was with

Working on self-knowledge is not easy. Often, the harder it is, the more important it is.

—Jennifer James, Ph.D.

friends. "I want to study fear," she proclaimed, "since fear is the only thing that can keep me from God." And so life obliged her with the following lesson.

In the middle of the night, Sondra got up to use the bathroom when she was confronted with a bizarre inner vision: It was a horrible battle scene. In the battle, she was being beaten. Blood flowed everywhere. The scene only lasted for a second, and then it was gone.

"What was that?" she cried out loud.

She put her attention back on the inner world, and there it was again. She checked a third time. *This is awful,* she thought. Sondra began to sing HU. Inwardly she heard, "Good!" And the battle scene faded. But she had a strong feeling the experience wasn't over yet.

The following night she was watching TV alone in her house when the fear came again, in a different guise.

Suddenly, Sondra felt like something evil was waiting outside the room and if she left that room, it would get her.

Sondra is not a paranoid person. As I said earlier, she is an efficient and responsible doctor. But this experience shook her to the core. She said she sat in that room for hours, thirsty, wanting to go get water, but afraid to move. Finally she got up the courage to go to bed then lay awake for hours, wondering what in the world was happening to her.

The next day, it happened again. Coming home from work, she puttered around her house for a few minutes, when all of a sudden she felt there was some-one outside, looking in the window and trying to open it. She looked. No one was there. But the feeling was very strong, and she couldn't shake it.

Each day the fear became more intense, and by the end of the week, it was like a thick blanket around her, everywhere. At work, she was fine. But the instant she got home, it was back. This unexplained fear was taking over her life.

She began trying different spiritual techniques. One would work for a while, giving temporary peace, then the fear would return.

When she went to bed at night, she'd lie straight, like a mummy, afraid to move, shivering with fear at the slightest sound, and finally falling asleep from sheer exhaustion a few hours before the alarm would wake her.

About a week into this terrible experience, she began repeating a sacred poem by a spiritual Master from ancient China, Lai Tsi. This helped her a bit. She sang her sacred word. But her mind and will were so weakened by the experience, nothing helped for very long.

Lai Tsi's Prayer

Show me Thy ways, O Sugmad*;

Teach me Thy path.

Lead me in Thy truth, and teach me;

On Thee do I wait all day.

Remember, O Beloved, Thy guiding light

And Thy loving care.

For it has been ever Thy will,

To lead the least of Thy servants to Thee!

---

* A name for God.

Finally two weeks into the experience, she asked God, "Why am I having so much fear?"

Suddenly, in her inner vision she saw a conduit, a long pipeline. Light was flowing through it in a brilliant, fast stream. She decided to jump in. Immediately she was flying down the conduit, faster than a jet, passing scenes that she instinctively knew were her own experiences of fear. Small and large fears, fear of losing her car keys, fear of getting sick, fear of losing a loved one. All these fears added up over many lifetimes.

How have I had so much fear in my life? Sondra asked.

And suddenly, she was sick of it. Sick of the fear. She wanted to be rid of it. Now.

"How do I get rid of this fear?" she asked.

The answer came: "Know you are worthy of God's love."

Sondra realized that she'd held herself back because of her fear; it made her feel inadequate, unworthy. And because she felt unworthy, she justified going off on her own spiritually, doing what she wanted, instead of listening to God's will.

She cried, "I *am* worthy! I *am* worthy of God's love. No matter what." This was the first turning point.

The next days were easier. Slowly courage returned. When the fear came, she fought it by saying, "That's an illusion." Sondra was starting to feel stronger, but her heart, closed by weeks of fear, was still feeling empty and hollow, with a cold wind blowing through. Living and working all these weeks with paralyzing fear had taken everything out of her.

In a final turning point one night, she faced the fear in its most potent form.

Asleep in her bed, Sondra had a lucid dream. She was awake within the dream, and everything was very clear. In the dream she saw a werewolf. It had sharp claws, and it was tearing her apart. The pain was unbelievable. It was so powerful and strong, she felt she couldn't do a thing to stop it.

She woke, drenched with sweat.

Although she was afraid to fall asleep again, Sondra knew she had to go back and face her demon, and as she drifted off once more, she tried to consciously fill herself with love. Fear cannot come where there is love, she knew. So she put everything she had, all her love for God, into one sound and sang it: "HU-U-U," asking for God's divine protection and guidance.

"There was an incredible transformation in me at that moment," Sondra remembers. "I was suddenly in a place of absolutely no fear, in the heart of God, totally protected.

"When I went back to the dream, the werewolf was still there, waiting for me. But a strong force surged through me. The force and I were one. And the werewolf couldn't touch me. I had no fear. When it couldn't get at me, it stopped attacking. And we began to talk.

"It told me I had created it from all my times of fear in the past. It was the sum total of all my fear. It said fear would always be my adversary, but I was strong enough to handle it now."

When Sondra woke the next morning, there was a feeling of strength and freedom inside her that she couldn't have imagined. Something heavy she had carried all her life was gone. She realized a healing had taken place. God's love was strong inside her. And it had replaced fear.

We live in two worlds, the waking world with its laws of science, logic and social behaviour, and the elusive world of dreaming.

—David Fontana

Exercise:
To Combat Fear with Love

1. Make a list of everything in your life you are grateful for.

2. Now list everything in your life you give love to. It can be as simple as a plant you water, your body when you feed it well, a friend or family member.

3. Ask, "How can these blessings in my life bring me out of the darkness of fear? What is one thing I can do today and each day this week to combat fear?"

4. Listen inside. Write down the answer. It may be simple. Do it.

A child who smiles in his sleep lulks with the angels.

—Irish folklore

ENDINGS AND BEGINNINGS

For many of us, losing someone we love is the most fearful experience of all. But the love we have for that Soul is also a key to transform the fear. That's what Linda found out in the following story.

"As I look back on it," Linda said, "I see now that our dog Prana came to us when the family was ready to go through a big change. Two years before we moved to Minnesota, we visited a breeder who had a litter of golden retriever pups. Every one of them was just as cute as could be. We wanted a puppy but had no idea which to choose."

So Linda said to the puppies, "One of you is going to have to choose us." And sure enough, one of the pups immediately came over to Linda's husband, Allen, and untied his shoestring. When Linda asked her if she was the one, the puppy wiggled and squirmed excitedly.

So they took her home.

"I asked her what she wanted us to call her," said Linda. "Immediately the name *Prana* came to mind. It's not a common name, not one I would have chosen. It means 'breath of life.' That's what she became for our family, my two children and Allen and I. She taught us how to love."

The family moved to Minnesota soon after.

Allen's job at the time included opening and closing a beautiful temple situated on rolling prairie. He took Prana to work with him each evening, and she loved the place. Off her leash, she would run like the wind through the tall grasses.

Animals are such agreeable friends— they ask no questions, they pass no criticisms.

—George Eliot

"One weekend, we started noticing she wasn't feeling very well," Linda said. "She was sleeping a lot, not having any energy. We took her to the vet, and when they X-rayed her, they found a big obstruction in her intestine which meant she would have to have an operation. Allen took her to the temple the last night before the operation, but by then she was so sick she couldn't run anymore. She just got out of the car and looked around quietly."

The vet called the next day. Prana had advanced cancer, so far gone it was probably best to put her to sleep.

"Everyone at the vet's had grown attached to her. She was such a special dog," Linda remembered. "The vet was crying when he called us. It was very hard on everybody. The vet said it was the most unusual thing: Prana had tried so hard to stay alive that her intestinal wall had started to grow around the tumor. But it just wouldn't work."

About a year before this, Linda and Allen had

gotten a new kitten, Feisty. "One thing Prana did before she left was raise this kitten as a dog," Linda said. "Prana let Feisty eat her food. Feisty learned Prana's generous ways. He would follow her to the door to greet us when we came home—which is a very uncatlike thing to do!"

It was a very sad time for the whole family when Prana left them. Even the kitten appeared to mourn.

Teach us Delight in simple things.

—Rudyard Kipling

About two years later, Linda had the nudge to get another puppy. Both Linda and Allen had had dreams with Prana, especially right after she died. They'd seen her at a temple in heaven, one of the temple guard dogs, loving what she was doing.

They decided they were going to get a yellow lab retriever. The night before they were going to pick out the dog, Allen had a dream.

In the dream, Prana went out into a huge ocean and when she came out of the ocean, she was carrying a puppy in her mouth. It was a little yellow lab. She gently placed the puppy at Allen's feet.

The next day when Linda and Allen went to the breeder, they again faced a litter of adorable pups, each as cute as could be. How could they choose the right puppy?

Suddenly one of the pups came over and untied Allen's shoelaces.

"This was Prana's signal to us," Linda said. "The pup looked just like the one in Allen's dream. And in the first two weeks she was with us, Taylor did the exact things Prana would do, as if Prana had coached her and showed her how to fit into our family."

Linda said she learned so much about love through the short life her beloved dog shared with them, and the dreams that showed her Soul never dies.

Here is an exercise you can practice to become aware of your existence as Soul and overcome the fear of death.

That in order to form a habit of conversing with God continually, and referring all we do to Him, we must at first apply to Him with some diligence; but that after a little care we should find His love inwardly excite us to it without any difficulty.

—Brother Lawrence

Exercise: To Overcome Fear of Death

Each night before sleep, ask a spiritual figure you trust, "Please take me on an inner journey to the heavens of God. Take me to that place which will benefit me spiritually."

When you wake, make careful notes of any and all dream experiences you remember.

This exercise will bring results, but they may be subtle, like incomprehensible pieces of a puzzle. You may not get any clue about the inner heavens until you have noted the images or feelings from several weeks or months of nighttime journeys.

There's an ancient Hindu proverb that says that if a fish swims up the mountain stream, it will be bruised against the rocks, exhaust itself, and dislike the journey. If the fish swims with the current, however, it easily avoids the rocks, travels swiftly, and enjoys the journey.

The stream doesn't care which way the fish swims.

Life is the stream that pulls us along on an inevitable course that leads to the death of the physical body. There are ways to delay death but no way to outsmart it. And why would we want to? What we have here is not anywhere near as wonderful as what we have in the higher worlds. The goal is not to avoid death but to make our swim in the stream of life easier, by going with the current.

One way to do this is to live life fully and prepare for the ultimate spiritual turning point that awaits us. This is not to condone a morbid fascination with death and dying. Life is for living fully; that's why we're here.

In the next chapter we'll learn about the teachers, mentors, and spiritual masters that work with us through change, to help us live life more fully.

Ask Yourself:
What Blessings Come from Great Changes?

Write your answers to these questions. They may help you understand the blessings you've received from life-and-death changes.

1. What do you imagine the transition of death will be like for the oldest person in your family? The youngest? Yourself?

2. What would keep you from accepting this transition with love?

3. What was the toughest life-and-death change you've faced in your life? What spiritual skills did you use to move through it? How could you have handled it better?

4. Can you think of three blessings that came from this change?

5. What do you imagine will be the next greatest change in your life? What blessing would you like to gain from it?

9

The Journey and the Teacher

Those Who Teach You about Change

*The true master is one who knows
how to steer others toward
their own experiences of truth.*

—Mary Pat Fisher

9. THE JOURNEY AND THE TEACHER

———— 🌀 ————

A friend told me an interesting anecdote about a famous statesman. It seems a young assistant to the statesman was asked to research a project and prepare a report. After several weeks of work the young man finally came to the statesman and placed a large folder on his desk. The statesman thanked him, and the young man went away. The next day, the statesman called the young man into his office.

"Is this the very best you can do?" he asked, pointing to the report.

"Well," said the young man, "maybe I could research it a little more."

"Please do that," said the statesman, handing back the folder.

Two weeks later the young man returned. Again the statesman kept the report overnight and in the morning called the young man into his office.

"Is this the very best you can do?" he asked again. The young man hemmed and hawed, then finally agreed to work on the report a bit more. The statesman again handed it to him, and the young man walked out.

Several days later the young man was back. The

Things do not change; we change.

—Henry David Thoreau

process was repeated, and again the statesman kept the report overnight and then asked, "Is this the very best you can do?"

"Yes, it is!" the young man exploded. "I have slaved over that report, researched everything I could think of, and rewritten it four times. It's the very best I can do."

"Very well," said the statesman, "I'll read it now."

How Life Brings Its Teachers

We all have people in our lives who teach us these kinds of pointed lessons, lessons which can be turning points in our lives. I've written several times about my grandmother who taught me so much when I was a child.

One of my grandmother's favorite slogans was "carry through." Her grandchildren were taught exactly what this meant. When you spilled something, you cleaned it up. When you finished playing, you put your toys away. When you said you were going to be someplace, you were there, and on time. My grandmother valued dependability above everything. And I was the grand-child who exemplified it for her. I grew up with these qualities she so loved engraved on my heart: account-ability, being on time, orderliness, and organization.

This was my foundation, until another teacher came along who showed me the missing piece needed to balance my grandmother's teachings.

In my late thirties I became friends with a woman I'll call Rebecca. We were drawn to each other, pulled almost across the room at a meeting. We both ended up working in the same office.

Our working relationship got stronger, and slowly our friendship did too. We discovered we had a lot in common.

But as the friendship grew, snags kept arising.

I would expect something from her, based on something she had said or a promise made, and she would not carry through. The biggest disappointment was when we agreed we would meet regularly to work on writing projects, but she fell in love about that time, and the meetings dwindled to nothing.

Anger at these disappointments grew slowly in me and became like a knot in my chest. I kept my contact with her to a minimum until eventually we were barely speaking, only making connections in our work.

Why had I trusted her when I knew she was so changeable? But I found I could not just let our relationship die, even if it was hurting me.

One evening after Rebecca failed to show up for yet another writing meeting with me, I began to write about the situation, how it angered and frustrated me, how I felt so cast aside and dishonored by her lack of carrying through. I wrote her name in the center of a piece of paper, then did the Turning Points exercise in chapter 3 with any words or phrases that came to mind.

Love is a great beautifier.

—Louisa May Alcott

BEEN THERE, DONE THAT

As I did the exercise, the intensity of my feelings surprised me.

I felt completely and utterly betrayed by something as small as a missed appointment. I knew that Rebecca was in my life to teach me something, however painful it might be. But for the life of me, I couldn't figure it out.

Sitting in the living room that night, I thought hard about this relationship. At first I was sure I knew what the problem was: Rebecca's behavior. If she would only do what she said she was going to do, our friendship would be all roses.

But then I wondered, *If I took to heart my premise that everyone in my life was here to teach me, what might I learn from Rebecca?*

Was there a more significant aspect to our relationship that I was overlooking?

I worked my way around the page, surprised to find images of my grandmother surfacing, along with notes of her disappointments in life. So many people had disappointed my grandmother—why was that? Were her goals of carrying through and accountability not worthy ones? There was a puzzle to solve here, a link between what I had learned from my grandmother and what I was learning from Rebecca.

Interested in solving the problem and understanding the turning point, I began listing the positive traits of our friendship, what I felt I gained from knowing this woman.

Flexibility was one. She found it easy to change, which was a virtue in most cases. In fact, the thing that had attracted me to Rebecca in the beginning was her fluidity, creativity, and easygoing nature. *She also found it easy to forgive,* I thought somewhat shamefaced, as I suddenly recalled all the times I had canceled dates with her.

It took time, but finally the real problem emerged. I realized that along with many virtues a pattern of rigidity had been passed down from my grandmother to me. Yes, the values my grandmother held dear were worthwhile ones, but along with them came a lack of flexibility. I remembered how hard it was for my grandmother to forgive someone who had wronged her, however slight the mistake.

In its deepest essence, the creative process is the same as the process of spiritual growth. Both involve struggle and have as their goals truth, beauty, simplicity, and . . . love.

—Bryan Mattimore

My attraction to this friendship with Rebecca made sense now. I was inwardly pulled toward those people who could balance out the potential for intolerance in my nature.

Exercise:
Have You Been Here Before?

Often we repeat our lessons again and again.
Ask yourself these questions:

1. Is there anything familiar in the qualities of this situation? Does it remind me of any other time in my life?
2. What did I do then?
3. What did I learn then?
4. What action can I take with the present situation that would bring a different result than in the past?

With understanding, you can actually influence whether or not a change will repeat in your life. Once you understand it, you may not have to experience it again.

Anything we're trying to change away from will keep coming back unless we replace it with something new.

—Allen Fahden

EVERYDAY SACREDNESS

Sometimes when I meet someone, I have a certain feeling about them: *This one will be an important teacher for me.*

The feeling is not always altogether pleasant, because there is also the foreknowledge of a turning point and possibly some hard lessons to come. The process of living grinds away our rough edges, and many of the people we meet act as sandpaper to further smooth those edges. Somehow this or that person would be the sandpaper to my rough edges.

One such trait of mine that took some sanding in my twenties and thirties was the need to rearrange my outer life when I became uncomfortable with a slow cycle. In the worst of times, when my job, marriage, or a friendship seemed to bog down, I might rearrange the furniture in the entire house before my roommate got home from work. I remember the face of one such partner, arriving home early one evening and doing a double take as he caught a glimpse of the totally different living room.

I even recall him checking the number outside to make sure he had the right apartment.

In those days, I moved around easily. I would quit a job, end a relationship, move out of an area whenever things got uncomfortable. This is the change for change's sake syndrome we talked about in chapter 1. I was a master at it. My slogan seemed to be, If change is coming, I'm going to beat it to the punch. And usually I beat it by many months.

In other words, I didn't work with the pace of life, I pushed the envelope. I rushed scenes, I pushed climaxes, and I often spoiled the final act of the play.

Some people have no trouble with this, but it was slowly making me very unhappy. I didn't realize that I was living on an edge of impatience, that I was changing for change's sake, moving furniture and partners to avoid working with the natural flow of life. It wasn't until my midthirties that I began to get an inkling of what truly happy people understand with their whole being: that life has a natural order and flow.

In can be no dishonor / to learn from others when they speak good sense.

—Sophocles

Change happens more easily when it is right in the larger sense.

It was not long after this concept found its way into my heart that I met my husband, Tony. The first time we dated was a paradox of uneasy and rapturous feelings. The uneasiness was born of a brief moment when I felt like I was drowning. I knew I was in over my head with him from the start; he would teach me plenty.

The first difference I found in my relationship with Tony was the way he seemed to get to know me in a much deeper way than I had experienced before. I thought myself to be a private person, unwilling to let someone else see my really low times. But with Tony, I felt like I could trust him to stick by me even when the going got rough. And it really did. I knew this person would be a great teacher for me, and something in me wanted to rush to start the lessons.

So, in a typically compulsive move, I quit my job, found another one in the city where he lived, and hired a moving van to pack with my furniture. Then I flew in, with my two cats, to arrive on Tony's doorstep.

I remember the day the van drove up a week later, the movers unloading box after box into the garage and roomfuls of furniture into his once-spacious, one-bedroom apartment. Immediately I set about arranging everything, like a demon whipping through the apartment as my future husband looked on. Finally he stopped me.

"Let's do this together, think a little about where things should go," he said. This was a new concept: planning from the inside out, not the way I had always done it. Our first lesson began.

Over and over in the first three years we were to-gether, he gently but firmly showed me how much easier life could be when one listened to and followed life's natural rhythm. Each time I wanted to rush my fences, he presented a different option—usually waiting.

Many times I have looked at my own relationships and the various partners my friends have chosen, wondering what in the world drew me or them to such a polar opposite. Why do we pick people who have such different approaches to life? Often, for me, it is the easiest and most efficient way to get a new viewpoint, to balance something in myself gone awry. And in the perfect plan of life, we end up being teachers too, so nothing is wasted.

By asking, you have reached out and taken the initiative— a first step that will lead you to the next answer.

—Harold Klemp

Exercise:
Who Have Your Teachers Been?

1. List ten people in your life, from early child-hood until now, who have been the best teach-ers for you. They may have been people you loved or didn't care for, but they taught you something important.

2. Next to each name, write what quality or les-son that person taught you.

3. Circle the qualities that have helped you handle change in your past. Why were these qualities important?

LEARNING FROM ALL LIFE

During the experience with my friend Rebecca, I was suffering from too little of a quality that is common to people who face turning points easily. This quality is spontaneity. Spontaneous people are often more alert to turning points, willing to let go of what they have to get something better.

To foster spontaneity, life brought me another teacher in the form of a small dog named BJ.

My husband first broached the idea of getting a miniature longhaired dachshund puppy. Being a cat person, I had never spent much time around dogs and was both excited and hesitant. Wouldn't a dog cover my clean white sofa with muddy paw prints, wake me up in the middle of the night to go out, and generally disturb my carefully wrought patterns of living?

BJ did all this and more. He turned my life upside down for the three months of his first winter with us. And despite my irritation and despair over the sofa and my lack of sleep, I knew this little dog was to be an important teacher for me. The main lesson he began teaching me every day was how to be full of joy and spontaneity.

BJ teaches by example. Whenever we meet, he greets me like a long-lost friend. No matter how my day has gone, he always expects the best from me—a pat on the head, a session of catch with one of his tennis balls, his dinner. There is no doubt in his mind that I love him and I will give him the best I have.

BJ's arrival changed other members of our household as well. Our two cats, Sasha and Sushi, had settled into a comfortable hierarchy, with Sushi definitely being top cat. When she first saw the tiny puppy, she knew her life had changed—and she decided it was for the worse. Irritated that we had brought this stranger to live with us, Sushi retired to the basement and

No man can reveal to you aught but that which already lies half asleep in the dawning of your knowledge.

—Kahlil Gibran

backyard for three months.

Sasha took a different tack. He became the kindly uncle to BJ.

It was amazing to watch the thin, eight-year-old cat escorting the young puppy around the house. Sasha even tolerated BJ's playful rolling and tumbling, tennis-ball-chasing, and mild biting. The cat made it his job to show BJ the spots for afternoon sunning, the windows with the best view of passersby, and the most comfortable cushion for morning naps.

My joy in learning is partly that it enables me to teach.

—Seneca

Before BJ, Sasha had been extremely fearful. He was always startled when someone came in the room; if I dropped a book on the floor, he would dash downstairs. The sound of the vacuum cleaner or other noises terrified him.

Maybe it was because Sasha felt responsible for BJ, but the puppy's noises never startled the cat. And this new bravery leaked over into the rest of Sasha's life.

Now he sits placidly when we vacuum, not even moving a whisker.

Sushi finally came out of the basement one weekend. She too had changed. Having ruled the roost for eight years, she had grown used to ignoring the people in her life except for basic needs, such as food and water. Now she was less sure of her position in the hierarchy. She realized she needed more than food and water: she needed love.

Moving quickly from haughty to ingratiating, she began spending mornings in the kitchen, waiting for us to wake up so she could tell us the happenings of the night in her loud Siamese voice. BJ had opened her eyes to what she could contribute to the family as well as receive.

Exercise:
Learning by Observation

1. For an hour or a day, watch a child and/or a pet. How do they go about their day? What spiritual qualities can they teach you about living life with more grace?

2. Write about the experience in your journal.

3. List ten qualities that you'd like to have from this experience.

RESOURCE FOR SELF-DISCOVERY

Lyndra told me a story about a lesson she learned from a great teacher in her life, her dog Jackson. Jackson is a golden colored beagle, and Lyndra has been his companion since he was two. They go everywhere together, and Lyndra loves Jackson like he were her child.

It was a warm October day in Vermont during a hike that Lyndra almost lost Jackson and learned a tremendous lesson about love.

Lyndra and her friend Sandy decided to take Jackson for a hike up nearby Mount Philo. There are signs on the trail saying No Pets but Lyndra knew the trails had officially closed Labor Day, so she didn't worry about Jackson being there. He loved to run but had no sense about cars and roads; since he was hit by a car four years ago and almost died, Lyndra has kept him on the leash on walks.

But as they started up the road, Jackson was so eager, pulling on his leash and choking himself, that Lyndra decided to let him run. He'd scamper up the road, always coming back when Lyndra called. He'd wait

*The dog
. . . is
the god of
frolic.*

—Henry Ward
　Beecher

ahead until the women were in sight, then run some more. Each time Lyndra would nervously look for him, but Jackson came faithfully each time he was called.

On the summit, they were surprised to be greeted by a park ranger.

Life only demands from you the strength you possess.

—Dag Hammarskjöld

"The mountain is open another week," he told them, "so you'll have to take your dog home immediately or I'll have to fine you." Without stopping to enjoy the view, Lyndra put Jackson on the leash, and the little group started down the mountain.

Jackson was again straining to get off the leash. Sandy suggested that it might be OK for the return leg, since the dog had had his fill of running on the way up the mountain and was probably tired. So again Lyndra let Jackson off the leash, with misgivings.

Immediately the beagle ran into the woods.

Within seconds, Jackson began frantically barking. Lyndra could hear him, but she couldn't see him. She was afraid he had gotten into a fight with a larger animal. She hurried down the trail and Sandy ran through the woods, both women calling to Jackson. They met at the road. Still no sign of the dog anywhere.

The women spent the next hour searching for him. They got the car and drove around the base of the mountain, asking at nearby homes if anyone had seen a golden colored beagle.

Lyndra's heart was breaking. This situation was all her fault. She should never have let Jackson come on the hike, never let him off the leash. What if he were injured, lying somewhere badly hurt? What if he were dead? Would they ever find him?

Lyndra decided she would hike back up the mountain to the last place they had seen Jackson in the woods. Sandy would keep driving Lyndra's little red car along the road and look for Jackson down there.

Lyndra's heart was pounding as she reached the section of woods where they'd last seen Jackson. She searched for Jackson's body, any sign of struggle, but she found nothing. Then she hiked back down to the road, calling his name and checking the woods on either side of the trail as she went. When she reached the road, there was no sign of Sandy either. What to do next? Feeling at a total loss, Lyndra sat down on the side of the road and waited.

A beautiful panorama of Vermont hills stretched out before her, but she felt miserable and alone. Next month she was planning to move across country after thirteen years in Vermont; her house was sold, her job ending.

But to leave without Jackson!

She had relied on him for so long to be her companion, and his company had made the idea of moving away from friends seem much easier. She couldn't imagine what her life would be like without his love. But she had done everything she could. Now it was in God's hands. To ease her heart, Lyndra began to sing HU, the sacred name for God she often sang as a prayer song. As she sang with all her heart, the sound emerging from the depths of her and flowing out into the surrounding mountains, she felt she was resting in the arms of God.

She imagined Jackson, wherever he was, in a protective circle of light and love. She spoke silently with him, telling him to stay away from cars and large hungry animals.

We look for good on earth and cannot recognize it / when met.

—Euripides

Then she sat silently. *What should I do?* she asked God again.

An answer came: *Stay calm, stay close. Don't give up yet.*

Moments later she saw a small red car coming around the bend; a woman was driving and there was a small golden dog in the front seat. Lyndra's heart jumped, but as the car approached she could see it wasn't Sandy and Jackson but another woman and dog.

Lyndra sat down and tried to regain that connection with God. She began to think about times in her past when such hard lessons had hit, how they had been good teachers for her, and how, despite the pain, things had always worked out. She realized that nothing had ever happened to her that wasn't good for her spiritually.

Maybe if she could figure out the lesson here, Jackson would come back. She closed her eyes and tried to relax.

As she sat there with her eyes closed, Lyndra suddenly realized that she had to let go of her need for the dog. If Jackson's time had come, she had to let him go. Deep in her heart, she knew he was Soul and would live on. She suddenly realized that she would be OK, that she could move across country by herself—without Jackson. A peaceful feeling came over her as this realization swept through. It was a sense of complete surrender to God's will.

In the silence after this thought, Lyndra suddenly heard the tinkle of a dog's collar.

Slowly she opened her eyes and stood up.

In the far distance, a small animal was walking toward her. Bedraggled and tired, but still alive, it was Jackson.

You may not be completely delighted by what you have created, but be assured, you have created it for one reason or another and that means you can also change it.

—Debbie Johnson

Lyndra began sobbing with relief and gratitude. Her friend was alive and had come back. She rushed toward him, and they rolled on the ground together, Jackson enthusiastically licking her as if to say, "I'm OK, Mom! I'm OK."

The experience on the mountain that day stayed with Lyndra for many months. She saw a wonderful lesson about the love God has for all creatures in Jackson's disappearance and her inner struggle to let go. She knew the love she had for Jackson had to be unconditional and that he would have his own experiences in life, both as her teacher and as her companion.

Bees sip honey from flowers and hum their thanks when they leave.

—Rabindranath Tagore

Exercise:
Writing a Thank-You Letter

Gratitude can turn misery, blame, and resentment into an openness toward whatever it is that a difficult situation is teaching you.

1. Choose a person, place, or time in your life that was very hard for you to deal with. It can be anything from childhood to the present.

2. In your journal write a thank-you letter. Thank this person, place, or time for what you learned, what you became. What strengths did this part of life give you that have been useful since then? How did you change as a person?

GIVING AND RECEIVING WISDOM

Often the best teachers in my life have been the hardest ones. This is also true for my friend Carol and the tough lessons she has gone through with her family.

Growing up, they were the first Asian family in that Chicago neighborhood. Carol's parents felt the family had to be an example. Carol was pushed to get the best grades, excel at everything she did. Her work was never good enough because her parents always felt it could be better. In addition, her parents had grown up during the Depression, and Carol's mom was very frugal, causing Carol a lot of anguish with stringent rules.

Twenty years later, the pain of her upbringing still hurt, and she harbored a lot of resentment toward her parents. In a church class one day, the teacher mentioned that we choose our teachers and our family is no exception. As Soul, as spiritual beings, we choose each situation we enter. We even choose what family to be born into.

This idea was radical to Carol. How could she blame them if she herself had chosen her parents?

All at once she saw how the hurt and resentment she had harbored against her parents was harming her, causing her heart to stay closed. So she did a spiritual exercise. She listed all the traits she had and traced them back to their origin. Who had given her these traits? Each one came from her parents. They had made her who she was.

For the next Christmas, Carol made an audiocassette recording of all the positive things her family had given her. Then she gave it to her mom and dad.

"It changed my dealings with them dramatically," Carol said, "but it still doesn't make it easy to go home. I still fall into a few childhood patterns. But I appreciate my parents and all they gave me growing up. Each lesson had a positive side: striving for excellence, frugality, humility, a softer heart. So I am, in the end, grateful to have chosen them."

Try Carol's exercise with a tough teacher in your life.

Exercise:
What Are Your Roots?

1. List your strongest personality traits.
2. Now write the biggest influence in your life for that trait.
3. Are the traits that make you who you are directly traceable to anyone in your childhood?
4. Write a thank-you letter to that person. You can mail it or keep it in your journal as a reminder.

One must take all one's life to learn how to live.

—Seneca

A NEW WAY OF LEARNING

Good teachers, like Carol's parents, give us strength and shore up our weak areas. Often we don't even know we have these weaknesses. We struggle through the lessons, resenting the teacher. Then one day we look back, as Carol did, and are very grateful.

When I was a high-school student I had a tough but kind teacher named Claire. Claire taught Russian and history in the small Quaker private school I attended in Baltimore. I was a pretty good student, above average, with a love for languages and art. I decided to focus on Russian in ninth grade and make a career out of it.

Russian is a terribly difficult language to learn—at least it was for me. I loved reading about Russian history, and I loved listening to the spoken language, but mastering the Cyrillic alphabet and learning the complicated verb forms was a headache. Luckily, I had Claire.

Unto whomsoever much is given, of him shall much be required.

—Luke 12:48

A brilliant but exacting teacher, she was my own personal cross to bear for four long years of Russian class three times a week. I had transferred from another school when my family moved from New York, and I wound up in Claire's homeroom, slowly realizing in those first weeks that I had missed a lot of the groundwork she had already given the rest of the class. Two counts were against me: Not only did I have trouble with the language to start with, I had to struggle to keep up with a class that had been with Claire since sixth grade.

All this combined to make Claire focus her attention on me—or at least I felt under the spotlight each time I made a mistake. My grade average plummeted as I struggled, and she spent extra time helping me in her stern way.

As I look back, I see she taught me more about self-discipline than any other teacher I have ever had.

I often wondered why I had started studying Russian. Why hadn't I picked something easier? I remembered it was mostly because of my best friend, Masha. Masha's family was from Russia. She had long blond hair, a silvery laugh, and a manner that spoke "Russian princess" to me. I wanted to be like her. So I signed up for Russian classes when I was in the eighth grade in my New York school, even though I had no particular talent for the language. I thought my burning desire to be a Russian princess and be able to converse with Masha and her family when I went there for dinner, or at least my strong feeling for Russia and the Russian culture, would be enough.

The next year my father was transferred from New York to Maryland, and my teary good-bye to Masha and her family was punctuated by excitement over living in a new city and making new friends. The new school had an even stronger language program, and I signed up for both Russian and French. I dreamed of writing Masha letters in Russian someday, although our teenage lives pulled us in different directions and the letters dwindled to nothing after a few months.

Besides, I had my plate full in the new school. Those next four years were grueling, to say the least. Claire was renowned for her teaching expertise and her toughness.

I drilled verbs, vocabulary, idioms, and pronunciation until I dreamed in Russian, but it still didn't come easy. Claire wanted to turn me from a casual student into one who excelled, and the missing ingredient was self-discipline. She made sure I developed plenty.

I graduated and was grateful to finally be rid of Claire's assignments, but life brought us together again within six years.

Strangely enough, it was through the vitamin business that I had. Claire was given some vitamins by a friend but hadn't known where she could buy more. The company gave her my address. Meeting Claire again as an adult was an entirely new experience. She still had the same exacting manner, but beneath it I could now see a warm heart and a deep love for teaching. We began corresponding each time I sent her a box

Everywhere, we learn only from those whom we love.

—Johann Wolfgang von Goethe

of vitamins. Soon our letters took on a spiritual tone, as she began to tell me of her studies in Theosophy.

I had studied many spiritual paths and had just become a member of Eckankar. So I sent her a book, which she read. Questions started. Although Theosophy remained her primary spiritual interest, Claire was always curious about Eckankar, and we shared many deep discussions about Soul, reincarnation, and other spiritual matters.

Looking back on this unusual friendship, I realize that as the circle was completed I was able to share something of myself with my mentor, just as she had when she taught me self-discipline via the Russian language. Like my grandmother, Claire was a believer in the higher disciplines of life, like doing your best and carrying through. And in those years of language classes and our spiritual discussions, some of this rubbed off on me.

Unexpected Gifts of Love

Sometimes our teachers appear unexpectedly, and they teach us in unexpected ways.

Love is a growing, or full constant light.

—John Donne

Bonnie and Lee weren't planning to have a baby. They had just moved from Oregon to the Midwest and begun new jobs. Comfortably settled into new routines, Bonnie had finally begun to make some progress in her career. But Bonnie's ten-year-old daughter, Julia, kept pestering them to provide her with a sister or brother.

"When are you going to have a baby so my kids will have an aunt or uncle?" she asked over and over.

Bonnie began telling her, "You'll have a sister or brother when God gives you one."

Julia went off that summer to visit family in Oregon. When she returned she told her mother of a dream where Bonnie had had a baby girl. Within three weeks, Bonnie found out she was pregnant. When Debby arrived, it was clear that she was here to teach the whole family more about love.

Love knows hidden paths.

—German proverb

From four to six weeks, Debby "spoke" to them constantly, Bonnie remembers. She was very serious about it and by her facial expressions was obviously trying to say something very important, as if she were telling them the secrets of the universe. When Bonnie held Debby in her arms, she felt as if her heart would burst. "A small stream of love inside began to open my heart wider and wider," Bonnie said, "until it became a rushing torrent."

An unexpected arrival but efficient teacher, Debby changed the life of this small family. "To me she is a gift from God, one that has opened my heart wider than I could have ever imagined," Bonnie said.

Love Softens Rough Edges

We may meet people because of ties from the past, mistakes to be resolved, or love to exchange. This is the pull of karma, the universe's spiritual payment system.

But we also meet people because we have something to teach and something to learn. I found keeping this viewpoint puts me in the higher consciousness of Soul, rather than in the push and pull of karma. Viewing each relationship as an opportunity to learn about myself helps me become more aware of the next lesson I have coming.

Often, a trait I see in the other person will be exactly what I need to learn about. Or maybe I need to review some spiritual law or life skill that this person has mastered.

My close friend Joan, whom I introduced in chapter 1, taught me a very valuable lesson about speaking up. It wasn't easy, but it shored up a weak spot in me that needed attention.

Suffering could build strength, but only if a person acknowledges his or her responsibility for whatever went wrong.

—Harold Klemp

For years before we met, mutual friends would tell me, "Oh, you have to meet Joan. She's just like you in so many ways." Eventually I got curious about this woman, and we got together at a church conference one spring. As our friends had predicted, we hit it off immediately—so much in common. Our love of books and letters, our Martha Stewart jokes, our craft projects, our relationship struggles. But we lived 1500 miles from each other and although letters were fun, they weren't enough. A few summers ago we began spending a week together at a mountain retreat with two other women. My family owns the camp, but I had rarely used it before. It's on a beautiful lake in the middle of the Adirondacks, a perfect place for busy women to enjoy a refreshing and relaxing time.

One summer Joan was very sick and asked if she could visit the camp a week early, to be alone before we arrived. When I came later with Becky, Joan had cleaned and organized the camp and had hot soup and bread waiting for us.

As the week wore on, I wore out. Joan was really not well, and I worried about her constantly. Her migraine headaches would be so severe she'd have to give herself medication via shots in the thigh to offset the blinding pain. True to her kind nature, she kept a cheerful facade. But I could see things were wearing on her dreadfully.

Little did I know how bad it actually was.

Joan is like me, reluctant to show the really bad stuff. Yet it took things getting really bad for our friendship to take a leap forward.

One night, I realized I had been silent too long. I had to speak about the problem that her sickness was creating for all of us during this vacation. She was trying to be so upbeat but inside she was hurting, and the incongruity made me very confused and upset. I didn't even know if she realized how hard it was to be around her. How could I tell her? I loved this friend, and I didn't want to express myself in my usual way—a huge blowup of anger with recriminations, tears, and hurt feelings to be mended later. I wanted to be able to speak and be heard but not hurt her.

That night we made dinner on the porch overlooking the lake. I remember my silence through the first part of the meal as Joan and Becky chatted about the day. I had been looking through some of my grandmother's old letters from camp days and was feeling a little sad. There were so many things I had never told my grandmother, and now she was dead. So I began to talk about the heartache of loving someone and not being able to share your heart with them.

In the conversation that followed, I began to tell Joan what it had been like that week for me. And in laying my feelings out, she was able to relax, open up, and share more of her own struggle. She hadn't wanted to ruin our vacation, but she hadn't realized we could tell what was happening inside of her. We both walked away from the meal with considerably lighter hearts.

After we closed camp that year and went home, I noticed a new level of sharing in our letters to each other. Less and less time passed before she would tell

The only way to have a friend is to be one.

—Ralph Waldo Emerson

me about the bad periods in her life, and I was more open with my frustrations and challenges.

RESPONSIBILITY — THE GREATEST TEACHER

I wondered why this friendship was so different for me. Why was I able to communicate with Joan about tough issues, even about arguments between us, without the traditional blowups I'd used in the past?

One day she sent me a fax. It was a page from her journal on the topic of blame and responsibility.

Our privileges can be no greater than our obligations.

—John F. Kennedy

She had written that blame has a sense of punishment to it; it's about wrongdoing or faultfinding, but nothing to do with lessons learned. Responsibility is about acknowledgment and learning. It's when we ask, What am I to learn from this? This is a higher viewpoint, one I now strive for. Responsibility doesn't give in to anger. It accepts that I may have a part in this situation. It's the great teacher. Only through taking responsibility can love be brought into the situation.

I realized I had been careful and clear about my responsibility in the situations that came up between us, rather than blaming her for it all. Because of this, even when I was very direct with her about a hurt feeling, she had never felt blamed. Our friendship was growing because of this level of mutual responsibility.

CAN SUFFERING BE A TEACHER?

There's a popular belief that suffering builds character. When I look back on times in my life when I suffered greatly, I see that sometimes I learned, sometimes I didn't. What made the difference?

When I brought responsibility into the situation, when I acknowledged my part in it, when I asked what I could learn—I learned. When I refused to take responsibility, I didn't. God does not love me more if I suffer. Life only uses suffering to point out something, to catch my attention. When I am able to accept responsibility in an experience and learn, I can move on.

I heard of a woman who went to the doctor one morning with severe pain between her shoulder blades. She was in agony. The pain had come on very suddenly and was so bad that she couldn't twist or bend.

"How did this start?" asked the doctor.

"I don't know," the woman mumbled.

The doctor persisted, "Did you lift something?" No. "Did you bend over?" No. "Did anything happen differently in your life when the pain began?"

The woman thought for a moment. "I got really angry with my husband about noon yesterday. We had the worst fight in our ten years of marriage. Right after that, the pain began."

Suddenly the woman knew that her pain had started because of the fight with her husband. *Would it go away if we straightened out our argument?* she wondered. *Was my anger actually responsible for this pain?*

That night the woman and her husband decided to sit down and discuss their situation without fighting, without anger.

Two days later, the woman's pain went away.

Finding the Blessing in Painful Lessons

We get stronger from experiences like this, but they are often painful. The easing of heart comes as we slowly see purpose and blessing.

Sally had been seeking a new love relationship for months, something that would make her stronger and more loving. One day she woke up with the inner knowingness that today something would happen toward her goal. When she asked God what steps to take, the answer was different than she expected.

"You have to stay completely centered all day. Remain completely neutral in your attitude toward everything you encounter," said the small voice inside.

God enters by a private door into every individual.

—Ralph Waldo Emerson

Later that day Sally was invited to a potluck supper at a friend's house. When she walked into the room, she immediately saw a tall man who attracted her. He came over and started talking to her. Sally had uncertain feelings about this person, but eventually they sat together and ate supper. He asked her to go on a date soon after.

They dated for several months. There were good times and bad times. Sally began to see that the man was very kind but had a lot of hidden anger inside him that would burst out unexpectedly. She broke off the relationship several times, but they'd get back together again.

What am I learning from this? Sally would ask herself, as they battled yet again.

Not long after, the answer came. The man developed a severe illness which needed extra care and nursing. Sally worked in the health field. She realized she had kept going ahead with the relationship so she could be there to help him through the illness. He had surgery, and for a while the anger surfaced in a big way. Then suddenly he was better. And just as suddenly the relationship ended.

Months later Sally had a sudden traumatic experience come into her personal life. It was a hard time, but she was amazed at how smoothly she got through it. Later she realized that the difficult love relationship months before had given her a new reserve of strength she hadn't had before. It had indeed answered her request to God: it had made her very strong.

SPIRITUAL TRAINERS

If we believe that life is essentially for our spiritual benefit, then it will not be surprising to learn that masters of life are available to help us with our journey through it.

You've probably heard of physical trainers, who come to your house and lead you through a specially tailored workout session. When I am going through a particularly rough change, I like to use the exercise on page 265 to set up an inner relationship with a personal spiritual trainer. I usually focus on my spiritual teacher, Harold Klemp. You can choose any spiritual mentor or teacher you look up to.

Spiritual trainers are helping us work our spiritual muscles every moment of our lives; often we are just not aware of the help we're being given.

When you try this exercise, be sure to keep a record of anything that happens in your dreams. Again, it might surprise you who you meet. Don't disregard the help if it comes in the guise of a friend or someone close to you.

A true spiritual trainer will not try to do our work with turning points for us. Rather he or she will lend a helping hand, give inner and outer guidance, and be a beacon in the night—someone always there to remind us of the purpose of our journey when the signs get

The true laws of God are the laws of our own well-being.

—Samuel Butler

subtle or there is trouble.

My inner guide appears in my dreams about every six weeks or so, more often if crises are big in my life. Sometimes he appears in the guise of a person I feel close to at the time, and the help comes via this person.

In my journal in the past months, I wrote about some great changes I've been going through in writing this book. God sent me the following dreams with masters of life, which helped me tremendously.

Earth is a classroom. Its purpose is to help people develop (usually after many lifetimes) a godlike character.

—Harold Klemp

In one dream, I met a man named Paul Twitchell who has written many books and articles. He is a great spiritual teacher in Eckankar. I was helping him board a train, and I carried his very large, very heavy suitcase for him. At one point I said, "I'd like to know the future sometimes." This dream came when I was very uncertain about my next step. Paul smiled at me very lovingly.

"That's because you're so efficient," he said, and waved good-bye as his train left.

As I thought about the dream, I saw how he was gently advising me to let life take its course, not try to wrap and package it like a parcel for mailing. Life can be messy, but it always proves educational. He was telling me, "Enjoy the surprises, the unexpected gifts."

Another dream was with a very tall man who looked like Jesus. His name is Gopal Das. He told me he had been a spiritual teacher in ancient Egypt. In the dream, he just picked me up and hugged me. I felt enveloped in his huge arms, my feet dangling off the ground, and a feeling of great peace came over me that lasted for days after the dream.

How do you have experiences with masters of life? A friend told me, "The most important thing I've found is that you have to have great enthusiasm, like a child who can't wait for a wonderful treat. Have no fear. Be focused in your attention. Focus on the details of what you're doing, one thing at a time, and that's practice for moving in the inner consciousness to higher places where you can meet these spiritual beings.

"But above all," she added, "have love for God."

Exercise:
Meeting Your Spiritual Trainer

1. Close your eyes, relax, and quietly sing the word *HU* or another sacred word. Feel the love of God enter your heart; put your attention on whatever image will bring you more of this love.

2. Now say to yourself inwardly, "I am Soul. As Soul I am here to learn _____ right now," and fill in the blank.

3. Immediately open your eyes, and write down whatever you got. The answer might surprise you. Realize that your mind might try to cancel out this message, so be prepared to accept the first thing that appears when you say the word *learn*.

4. Now close your eyes again. Inwardly say to your spiritual trainer, "I would like to learn more about this. Please let's meet tonight in my dreams, and you can take me to whomever and whichever place is right for my spiritual development in this area."

There are many paths to the center, but the signposts are all the same — passion, peace, love, and a reverence for life.

—Jennifer
   James, Ph.D.

LOVE IS THE SIMPLEST LESSON OF ALL

A wonderful storyteller, Mike Avery, told me this fable. It shows that no matter how wise we are, we are always learning from true masters of life who appear in many forms.

One day a muskrat who lived on the shores of the North Umpqua river read the long work of a renowned prophet. Not understanding the prophet's treatise, the muskrat undertook a long journey by foot to speak to the man.

Weary and bedraggled, the muskrat arrived on the prophet's doorstep.

"Oh, noble prophet," the muskrat said. "I would like to further understand your magnificent work. I read it, but it was way over the head of a humble one such as myself. But since I am a devotee of truth, I came to learn from you." He bowed low.

"Well," said the prophet kindly, "let's start with my book. Did you understand anything you read?"

"Only this," said the muskrat, "that to know truth you must love something with your whole being."

The prophet stood dumbfounded. "I can teach you nothing," he said humbly, and turning, walked back inside. The muskrat, disappointed, turned to go back home. The prophet watching the muskrat leave said to himself, "What a wise and noble muskrat. He said in one sentence what it took me volumes to say."

Love is often all we have to sustain us in the darker times of change. In chapter 10 we'll look at God's design within the dark night of Soul, the profound crisis of faith.

Ask Yourself:
Who Are the Teachers in Your Life?

Write the answers to these questions. They may help you see more of the spiritual lessons you've learned in the past and present from all the teachers in your life.

1. Who was a mentor in your childhood, and what did you love about this person? What strengths did he or she give you? How have these strengths helped you handle change as an adult?

2. Who is a current teacher or mentor in your life? What aspect of yourself does this person support or spiritually strengthen?

3. As a child or adult, have you had experience with a guardian angel, master of life, or spiritual trainer?

4. If you could have it, would you like a guardian angel or spiritual trainer in your life now?

5. How do you suppose you'd attain this?

10

Crises of Faith

Spiritual Lessons from the Dark Night of Soul

*Tomorrow's joy is possible
only if today's makes way for it.*

—André Gide

10. CRISES OF FAITH

*C*hange brings us a bad day, a difficult year. We get stuck. We struggle to learn something, to move ahead, to acquire new spiritual skills.

Most changes we face affect our belief in ourselves but don't affect our belief in God. Occasionally, though, a person reaches a place of testing which St. John of the Cross called the dark night of the Soul.

Author Robert Marsh describes his experience with the dark night of Soul in his book, *We Are Not Alone: How ECK Masters Guide Our Spiritual Lives Today*. "*Oubliette* is a colorful term for a dungeon with neither a door nor windows. The victim is simply dropped down through a hole in the ceiling. The opening is sealed, and the incarcerated victim is simply forgotten (*oublier* in French means 'to forget'). In the dark night of Soul one feels totally forgotten, as if one has slipped inadvertently from God's sight."

In my life, there have been relatively few times when I felt God had completely deserted me. But when I was in my late thirties, I fell through such a trapdoor and into a severe crisis of faith.

The element of fear is a natural piece of the mosaic of change.

—Christina Grof and Stanislav Grof, M.D.

I stayed in this inner dungeon, this void, for many months, and my lifelong inner companionship with the Divine completely disappeared from my view. I felt nothing. No love, no beauty. No link with God.

Life seemed completely empty to me. Purposeless.

As Marsh says, "My appetite for living drained away. Until then an unquestioned source of life had always nourished my subconscious. But suddenly I could no longer perceive it. . . . It was as if a Technicolor movie had suddenly switched to black and white, and the lovely theme music in the background had simply stopped. Everybody on the screen looked and sounded exactly the same, but there was a vast difference."

Writer Joan Borysenko calls these dark times "extended periods of dwelling at the threshold when it seems as if we can no longer trust the very ground we stand on, when there is nothing familiar left to hold onto that can give us comfort."

There is usually pain in freeing ourselves from this feeling of being forgotten by God. If we pursue the dark night of Soul with the belief that the pain will open a doorway to more beauty and light, then it all seems worthwhile. But it can be hard to hold that belief through the empty times.

Because of the particulars of my personal crisis, God sent me help in the guise of my grandmother, the same person who had been my mentor from early childhood in all things practical or spiritual. She came to me for several months in my dreams and taught me how to find a new footing in life.

To understand how my grandmother could help me in this way, you need to know a little more about her.

She was a prominent Presbyterian at Brown Memorial Church in Baltimore, and to me she had a unique understanding about God. She combined faith healing, bake sales, homemade sermons, and weather predictions. Her faith made her a rock in the church community and the strongest person I knew.

As I mentioned in chapter 5, I began spending weekdays with my grandmother when I was four. Mom would drop me off on the way to work each morning. I would tiptoe into the apartment because Hartzie would be having her quiet time, getting her inner guidance.

Hartzie's business and life's mission was a summer hiking-and-canoeing camp for children. She never advertised; she had faith that word of mouth and God's will would bring the right children to her door. She was right too. The camp was rarely lacking for applicants, and many came back every summer of their childhood. Although we made fun of her all-purpose connection with God, we only half-scoffed when Hartzie's faith appeared to bring sunny weather and a good wind right before a sailing race.

Hartzie guided me through my growing-up years. Although she was a strict disciplinarian and had strong opinions about how things should be done, she loved me dearly. I never doubted that love.

That's why when I reached a crisis in my life, she was the one who rescued me. But the help came after she died.

CHILD IN THE WILDERNESS

It was my grandmother's own crisis of faith, which came about a year before she died, that started me moving closer to God.

A year before Hartzie died, Mom called cross-country one evening to tell me someone had mugged my grandmother. They had knocked her down and stolen her purse. She had lain there in the cold, hurt and frail, waiting for God to help her.

But it was an hour before anyone came.

Later she was angry. Angry that someone in her safe section of town should be prey to such activity. Angry that her husband sat alone upstairs awaiting her return instead of being at her side, sheltering and protecting her. Angry, most of all, that the God she talked to each day during her quiet time had let her lie helpless on the pavement.

When I saw her about a month later, her appearance shocked me deeply. The robust woman was shrunken and pale. She sat, unmoving, in a corner of her living room. Her eyes, which had always been beacons of light and steadiness, now shone with deep fear.

Anger at God had closed the door to her heart, and she could no longer hear God's voice because that inner door was shut. Fear had then replaced the anger and left her empty. Her faith in God had been shaken, and she was simply waiting to die.

At the first serious doubt her faith, a faith based on physical strength and mental ability, had shattered around her like brittle glass. Now she wondered if God really could protect her; she had nowhere else to turn. She didn't see the beauty of life which had always sustained her. It was painful for me to look at the emptiness in her eyes.

In my youth and inexperience, I didn't know how

There is no failure except in no longer trying.

—Elbert Hubbard

to help her. All I could do was sit and hold her hand. That was the last time I saw Hartzie alive.

ENTERING THE DARK NIGHT OF SOUL

I was to face the same emptiness and doubt ten years later. Like my grandmother, I had always depended on a special connection with God. Hartzie's faith had rested on outer proof, like good weather and a full camp roster. Mine had been shored up by brilliant inner experiences and a strong sense of knowing what to do next.

My experience started with anger too. A close friend told me a story of betrayal of trust, and the story stuck in my heart. For some reason I was unable to detach myself from the anger that poured from my friend. She raged, and I, unknowingly, absorbed much of it.

I began to find my days full of anger. Anger at small things, but mostly anger at God. How could God let this happen to my friend? I thought it must be a real injustice since I felt she was such a spiritually advanced person. I didn't stop to consider there might be other sides to the story. I just fumed on her behalf.

The more anger I felt, the deeper I fell.

It's simple in the telling, but the process took months. Slowly I began to doubt that God existed. I looked up and saw empty sky; I looked inside and felt no love. I asked for guidance, and none came. It was as if a big door to all the light and love that guided my life had suddenly shut.

I couldn't see that I was the one who had shut it.

As the door shut tighter, the tests of my dark night of Soul began. At first, it was simply a feeling of losing my spiritual anchor points. I stopped remembering my dreams. I lost my inner guidance, and I felt doubly

A man consists of the faith that is in him. Whatever his faith is, he is.

—Bhagavad Gita

betrayed. I would ask God what to do and end up in a mess when I followed any inner nudges.

For an entire year, I watched my world change. Outwardly all was normal. Inwardly, I walked in a place totally unfamiliar to me.

Like my grandmother before her death, I struggled with the same fear that God had left me high and dry.

The care of God for us is a great thing.

— Hippolytus

CUSTOM-DESIGNED LESSON

God had custom-designed this turning point for me. First, I was given a test of anger—I got too involved in something that was none of my business. Second, I took this anger and shut my heart to love. Third, I bought the illusion that the anger and fear were the reality.

God had sent this lesson to let me make the natural transition away from human faith to a more profound connection with the Divine—spiritual knowing. All my life, my faith in God had been little different from my grandmother's. I loved God as a child loves a benevolent father, a father who would help the child out of every scrape. And now it was time for the child to grow up. It was time to see God in my life in every moment—even without the brilliant inner experiences or the outer verification.

The anger eventually died, but the door was still shut tightly. It was then that I began to realize this situation could be permanent. I was aghast at the thought of going through the rest of my life without the beauty and love I lived by. What could I do? What would propel me out of this emptiness?

Inwardly I asked Harold Klemp, my inner and outer spiritual guide, for help. I had received so much assistance from him, through dreams and outer circumstances, in my years studying the spiritual teachings of Eckankar with him. Maybe he would send someone to help guide me through this void.

And he did.

Suddenly, after months of blackness, I began to remember a recurring dream.. I would be with my grandmother, setting up for a dinner party in her apartment in some beautiful inner place.

As we placed the china and silverware along the table's edge, Hartzie would be discoursing on some lesson she had taught me as a child, like carrying through. "To carry through, dear, just concentrate. You know you can do it. Pay attention to how you're placing that dinner plate, how you put the forks on the table. Put all of yourself there, and God will be there too."

Night after night, my spiritual guide sent me in my sleep to her apartment for instruction, inspiration, and hope—all the things she had given me as a child. She soothed my troubled spirit in the mundane activities that accompanied the dream—brownie-making, dusting the piano, transplanting an African violet.

The dreams and assistance from my grandmother lasted less than a year, and so did my doubts about God. One day the doubts were gone.

During the year I realized I had not recognized God in small things. I could find joy in setting the table or reading a poem—the joy that had been missing. I no longer desperately sought evidence that God loved me in brilliant inner experiences. Now I knew God was indeed in all of life, especially in the most subtle things.

Faith is a living and unshakeable confidence, a belief in the grace of God.

—Martin Luther

About that time, I stopped seeing my grandmother in my dreams. Instead, one night a brief picture of her hallway appeared, accompanied by her voice from the kitchen: "This is the past. I've moved on now."

My spiritual guide knew that, since I was far from God in my heart, the best person to get me back on my feet spiritually and through the next turning point was my grandmother. Only she could remind me of where God truly was—in the small things in life.

Letting Go

Anyone who loves God is a channel for God. Most people who love God, however, are unaware of being channels.

—Harold Klemp

Often during a spiritual crisis, our biggest challenge is in letting go of something we hold dear. Our beliefs about God, as in my case. Our beliefs about ourselves. Or our beliefs about someone else and their influence over our lives.

When Beverly's mother died several years ago, the hardest thing the family had to do was let go of her. Her mother had loved her family more than anything else in the world, and she had controlled the family with an iron hand through this love. When she died, it left a tremendous void.

"The moment Mother died," Beverly said, "I remember feeling very close to her. Suddenly I felt I had to find my brother. I thought my mother was looking for him, and I ran outside. It was one of those southern spring mornings where the air was alive and the sky an incredible blue. The light hurt my eyes. I realized it was a spiritual light and that I had somehow helped Mother leave the dimly lit bedroom and enter a brighter, larger space. And I felt peaceful and happy."

The matriarch of the family for so many years,

Beverly's mother continued to influence it even after her death. Beverly began having dreams in which her mother would be trying to run the family business but having a very hard time of it. There was a strong feeling that her mother was straddling two worlds, trapped in some awful place. She could not let go of her earthly life, and the family couldn't let go of her either.

One day a very strange thing occurred which helped resolve the family's spiritual crisis. Beverly went with her son, Thomas, to an Asian grocery store. Her son picked out what he thought was play money and asked if he could have it. Beverly said he could.

At the register, the clerk looked at the boy in a funny way. "Do you know what these are?"

"No," said Thomas.

"These are hell bank notes," the clerk told them. "These are how you buy your loved ones out of hell. We have a ceremony where we burn them to free our trapped ancestors."

Thomas turned to Beverly suddenly and said, "Grandma."

Beverly was a bit shocked. Even though she had not mentioned her dreams, Thomas seemed quite sure he could help Grandma. Then she realized that somehow he knew his dead grandmother was in trouble. "Fine," she said, "we'll take them home and burn them." That night Thomas had a dream where he entered a big bank and handed the hell bank notes to a banker. "This is for my grandmother. Is she here?" he asked the banker. "Yes, she's here," said the banker.

Beverly's dreams with her mother ended shortly after that.

The final resolution occurred when Beverly visited the family home that Christmas. She found that every decision being made in the family business was based on how their mother would've handled it. And the business was dying. She decided to make one last attempt to help her mother—and the rest of the family—let go.

One day she was alone in the office at lunchtime, and she said out loud, "Mother, you're dead. You can go now, you don't have to run this place, we can handle it." Immediately the lights went out. They stayed out for a long pause, then went back on.

Light will fall on something, say, a pink peony petal in an otherwise shaded garden, and it will capture me and deliver me from myself.

—Adair Lara

Later that day Beverly and her sister talked for a long time about how to move forward. The family was finally ready to let go of the woman who had run their lives for so long.

Throughout the experience, Beverly learned how hard it is to let go, how this inner surrender can be the most difficult part of change. "But I learned that God guides us through the most painful separations," she says, "through each step, in the most loving way."

Asking for Help to Let Go

Diane also experienced something like this during her divorce. It was difficult to sever ties with someone she had been with for twelve years. Finally she had a dream which helped her resolve some of the pain and begin to let go.

In the dream she was led by her spiritual guide down a set of dark stairs to a beautiful park. There were rolling hills, green meadows, beautiful lakes. Her guide was working with her, helping her relax because she was so tense from the traumatic experience of the divorce. Diane looked over to her left, and there was her ex-husband. He was also being helped to heal.

She felt great relief at this and realized that the dream showed her she could let go her concern and attachment to him. He was being helped too.

"I was sad he wasn't speaking to me," Diane said, "but the dream set my mind at ease—that this is what was best for us, that we would heal the best and the most quickly separately." Friends had been coming up to her and telling her she would soon become friends with him. But Diane felt strongly that they needed to heal separately. The dream confirmed it. No matter what happened outwardly, she could remember the dream.

During a spiritual crisis there is often a period of waiting, when everything we knew or believed in has been swept away and nothing new has yet filled the empty place inside. During this transistion time, often the best action is a closer listening to the still small voice inside yourself. Listen and improvise. The new direction will come.

My friend Fran, a jazz musician, told me that jazz musicians have a saying, "When in doubt, lay out." Every song has transitions from one part to the next. When you are improvising one step, the next step in the song shows itself. "When I am unsure of the next step in a situation, I'll ask Divine Spirit, 'Show me what I don't know about this' or 'What do I need to learn here,'" she told me. "And these kind of questions require patience, the 'laying out,' when you improvise while you wait for an answer." Sometimes the answer may come in a waking experience as it did for Beverly or in a dream as it did for Diane.

Exercise:
Laying Out

When you feel stuck with a change, practice laying out.

Ask your inner guide or God, "Please show me what I don't know about this" or ask, "What do I need to learn here?"

Watch for the answer in waking life and in your dreams. While you're waiting, improvise.

Everything comes if man will only wait.

—Benjamin Disraeli

WHEN WE'RE READY FOR A CHANGE

A spiritual crisis can even occur around smaller events, like changing a longtime residence. When we, as Soul, are ready for a change, the mind may not be aware of it. Fear surfaces, and we struggle—until we decide to surrender and receive the gift of the change.

In a writing workshop I led, a woman read a beautiful story about how she encountered such a crisis when moving from an apartment to her first home.

The apartment had been an upper story, back-alley location; brick walls were all she saw from her windows. She had felt a deep longing for greenery and open spaces, and she set a goal to someday live surrounded by trees and flowers.

She had noticed for some time that she was not happy with her life, but she didn't connect it to where she was living and her longing for country spaces. Still the signs were there in little things.

Finally one night she asked God for some help. What was wrong with her life?

She didn't recall much from her dreams that night, but she woke with a wonderfully peaceful feeling, as if everything was going to be all right. Change was coming; she was sure.

That morning two things happened: Her husband said he'd like to begin looking for a place in the country, and the landlord announced he was selling the apartment building to a land developer. The couple would have to find a new place to live.

Suddenly the woman was frightened. Now that it was a reality, she wasn't sure that such a change would be good for her. But remembering the peaceful feeling from her dream, she began inwardly turning her problem over to God.

All is change; all yields its place and goes.

—Euripides

And it was only a few days later that they found their new home through an ad in the newspaper. Only fifteen minutes farther into the country, the house sat on a small lot surrounded by trees. After a few days of unpacking and settling in, the woman felt her life had become a wonderful thing. She realized that the move—despite her fears—was a gift.

She now looks forward to coming home, making dinner in their tiny kitchen, and looking at the shade trees around their home. A big step for her—and a very positive one.

When she told me about the experience, the woman said she was now aware of the subtle help she had received in her dream.

For her, the house was a spiritual metaphor.

As Soul, she was ready to make an inner as well as outer change, and the new home gave her "more freedom inside," she said. Her living quarters paralleled the new freedom she felt in her life. Just being in an open space with lawn and trees—away from the cramped quarters and brick walls—allowed her heart to open. This letting go is the key to getting spiritual assistance during times of crisis.

Exercise:
Playing the Sound of Change

A friend says, "I'm not an accomplished pianist, but I made up an exercise to practice letting go and letting God work through me. The results were amazing. When I can let go, it allows me to play music I find extremely uplifting."

Sit down at the piano. Imagine you are observing yourself. Maybe you are sitting in a chair next to the piano, watching yourself play.

Now put your hands on the keys, still watching yourself. And begin playing. You can close your eyes. Imagine playing the sound of the wind blowing through the trees, then the sound of a cold winter day.

Finally, imagine playing the sound of your change. Play the sound of help coming to you during this change and how it feels to be completely assisted by God and life in every way.

The key to this exercise is the observer viewpoint. You can also do this exercise with singing. Start by singing a line from a favorite song, then make up a line about your change and the help you're getting.

Seize the moment, seize the day— and embrace life with joy and wonder.

—Harold Klemp

How to Keep Getting Assistance

Bryan Mattimore, a good friend and talented creativity expert, writes about the hidden benefits of creative dreaming in his book *99% Inspiration*. Dreams become a valuable resource for spiritual assistance—and anyone can tap into this resource. Bryan gives many examples of how dreams are used by inventors and creative people to solve problems they can't solve in the daytime.

The key to keeping this inner resource available, says Bryan, is to use the dreams you're given to make way for more.

"To keep your dreaming subconscious mind functioning at its highest efficiency (so that you can rely on it when you need it most to solve a real-world problem)," Bryan writes, "you must continually give it problems to solve. If need be, set daily or weekly idea goals for yourself when you're just starting out. . . . Ultimately, with time and a few successes, you won't even question it. You'll just come to expect success."

When we're in the midst of major changes, dreams can be a major lifeline.

Destiny grants us our wishes, but in its own way, in order to give us something beyond our wishes.

—Johann Wolfgang von Goethe

Places for Spiritual Healing

God gives sincere seekers all the tools they need to take themselves through a difficult turning point. But sometimes the pain of letting go requires a spiritual healing. Where do such healings come from? How can we get them?

A friend who had recently lost her husband told me about an exercise she had received inwardly from her spiritual guide. She called it the Emerald City exercise because it reminded her of a scene in the movie version of *The Wizard of Oz*. And this exercise became her way of receiving healing during her spiritual crisis.

Darlene had always understood that she could help herself through depression or other emotional downs by using the creative power of imagination. She could imagine herself in a situation or a place that would act as an antidote to the problem. She'd used this technique before, and it always worked. So why not this time?

So she imagined herself in heaven, entering the Emerald City.

Remember in *The Wizard of Oz* when Dorothy and her little band of friends go into the city? They are greeted by wonderful beings who take them to a place where all their needs are taken care of. The scarecrow gets new straw, the tinman is polished, Dorothy gets her hair done. They are restored inside and out from this marvelous love and pampering.

Darlene's Emerald City was much the same. The first time she went, someone sat her down in an extremely comfortable chair, leaned her back, and started brushing her hair very slowly. There were lovely coral-colored lights and soft music—just the kind Darlene loved. Then the caretakers gave her a massage.

"Each time I went, it was different," Darlene said, "and I knew it was real because there were details I wouldn't have thought of. One time I was in a huge dark warehouse, and someone flipped a light switch. In front of me was a white alabaster ballroom floor. And I could dance! I could dance like I was on ice skates training for the Olympics! I could go as fast as I wanted, leaping into the air, carried by the wind.

"The lightness of myself as Soul, the freedom of

The wish for healing has ever been the half of health.

—Seneca

creativity to dance and leap, was exhilarating. It filled me, completely saturated my emotional body. It brought me peace and release from pain. And every time I'd go to this city, I'd have an experience like this. The people there had complete unconditional acceptance of me."

One day Darlene thought she needed more emotional rehabilitation, so she did her exercise and went to the Emerald City. She'd been going for about six months, now less frequently. The caretakers greeted her and said, "We have a room ready for you with a milk bath, but we wanted to tell you first that there's a new arrival who needs some comfort. We wondered if you'd like to help care for her."

It was completely Darlene's choice. She said yes, she'd like to help someone else. She was honored that they would ask her to do something like this. That she'd healed this much! So she went over to the woman.

"I knew exactly what to do for her, what to ask her, how to soothe her ragged, aching heart," Darlene said. "It was a miracle."

The unconditional love she had received in this place of healing flowed through her to another Soul in need. She saw how this experience had helped her gather another tool necessary to continue her journey home.

Before trying this exercise make an inner appointment to go to the Emerald City.

It can be any sort of place you can imagine—but it must have the ability to polish everything about you. A fabulous health spa that tones every part of your body. You will come back from your trip to the Emerald City with all of you—inside and out—in tip-top shape.

Exercise:
Going to the Emerald City

Before going to sleep or doing a spiritual exercise, write down an image of what you think your Emerald City might be. You might see beautiful beings combing your hair, mending your clothes, massaging your tired muscles, polishing your shoes. You may want to play a grand piano, dance in a beautiful ballroom, or paint sunrises. Whatever would bring your bodies into health and wellness is possible here.

In the morning or after the exercise, make note in your journal about how you feel.

When I tried Darlene's technique, I got great results. After I was massaged, pampered, and bathed in healing light, I was taken to a room. It looked familiar. In fact it looked like the Fear Room in the exercise I created on page 76.

Sometimes even to live is an act of courage.

—Seneca

I had recently gone through some trauma over a television show for my book. Showing the videotape of the show to some close family produced a strange reaction and quite a bit of criticism. I was hurt by the lack of support. Slowly resentment and anger had built up inside me.

When I looked inside the room, instead of fog I saw again that thick layer of molasses-like gunk on the floors, walls, and ceiling.

"What is that stuff?" I wondered aloud. The technician answered, "This time it's your anger."

I knew that to thoroughly clean my inner emotional

state, I would need to tackle the room. What a messy job! But the caretaker made a phone call, and within minutes help had arrived in the form of ten neatly attired cleaning ladies with vacuum cleaners. They each took a portion of the room. I watched those super-powerful vacuums suck up all the molasses from the floors, even cleaning deep into the carpet where the stuff had oozed. They scrubbed the walls and ceiling with a wonderfully fragrant soap. By the time they finished, the room was spotless.

Then my inner guide appeared. He took me to a separate room, and we sat down to watch a movie. On the screen appeared the scene I had so dreaded reliving—my family watching my television interview. He stopped the film, and we stepped into the movie. As I walked around, touching each person in the room, I forgave them and myself for the hurts of that day.

I felt wonderfully light after this exercise, not having realized how the anger had weighed down my heart.

The greater perfection a soul aspires after, the more dependent it is upon divine grace.

—Brother Lawrence

HOPE

In the television series *I'll Fly Away,* heroine Lily Harper said, "With change often comes fear of the future, the unknown. But also hope."

I wrote this down one evening when we were watching the show. Hope to me is ever-present, because I am convinced of the constant help I am given by God. Even in times of great crisis, God is always there.

Ray Bradbury, the famous science-fiction writer, said, "Living at risk is jumping off the cliff and building your wings on the way down." That's where God helps me most: giving step-by-step instruction on building wings. Life often feels like a continuous out-of-control free fall, until we begin trusting that we do indeed receive the help we need. When we begin to notice that a superior consciousness is guiding our lives, we know that what is good now can only become better in the future.

But when we dive headfirst into a spiritual crisis, hope and trust often vanish—because we can't see where we're going. Sometimes we ache inside for a change, but we don't know we've been living inside a room filled with stale air until we allow ourselves to step outside and take a deep breath of fresh air. Luckily life always brings us what we need—despite our fears and doubts.

This has happened to me often enough. I fought change, kicking and screaming. Until I realized that good was indeed becoming better, change just meant fear to me.

How do we keep reminding ourselves of the ever-expanding property of life? How do we let hope and love replace fear?

During a time of great change in my life many years ago, I did the exercise below. I wrote myself two lists: (1) everything that I was afraid could happen in my life, and (2) everything I was grateful for having now. The "afraid of" list included fears both great and trivial, such as my cats being poisoned by an irate bird-loving neighbor. The "grateful" list included those who loved me, those I loved, and the bounteous aspects of my life. I put both lists away in my journal, making a note to review them in a year.

The loftiest towers rise from the ground.

—Chinese proverb

Exercise:
A List of Fears and Blessings

1. Take a sheet of paper, and on one side list everything you are afraid might happen in your life. Let yourself go—list even the silliest of things. Whatever makes you uneasy goes on the list.

2. Turn the paper over, and list all the things you are grateful for in your life right now. Include things you take for granted, like shelter, food, clothing, your family.

3. Fold the paper. Put it in an envelope, and mark a date one year from now on the outside. Put a reminder in your calendar to look at the paper then and see what has changed.

When the year was up, I read both lists. The "afraid" list made me laugh: nothing on it had happened except one item, and that change was definitely for the best. The "grateful" list had only expanded, grown more wonderful.

And many points on my "grateful" list were gifts from my spiritual master.

THE GARDEN OF THE HEART

In times of great darkness and crisis, the last thing we usually feel like doing is embracing life and opening our heart to God. But that is exactly what allows our heart to expand, to blossom like a flower in a garden. It's exactly the key that can turn things around the fastest and easiest.

This attitude of gratitude will bring us many rewards. It gently encourages us to give our all to everything we do.

Stan, an artist friend, designed the following exercise to bring gratitude and joy into his life. He says it always brings changes, and with the changes, healing.

A rising sun had always been an important symbol for him. It was his logo for many years when he had his own graphics design business. It symbolized new beginnings, hope, and the gratitude he had for life. So he created this exercise. Like Darleen's Emerald City exercise, Stan's technique of watching the sunrise brings powerful results each time I try it.

If we could
count the stars,
we should not
weep before
them.

—George
Santayana

Exercise:
Watching the Sunrise

Go outdoors early enough one morning to see the sun just peeking over the horizon. As the sun rises, imagine your life rising with it. Imagine a feeling of love for your life expanding in your heart, and open yourself to the blessings of God.

COLOR RETURNING TO LIFE

Just like the dawning sun brings color back to the world in the form of light, so love expanding in the heart brings joy to our vision of what is possible in our lives. Expanding our vision can be a slow process for some of us. One example is a friend I'll call Anna. Anna is a beautiful, talented woman in her midthirties who experienced this after a series of unsuccessful relationships and marriages left her feeling unsatisfied and stuck.

Unhappy relationships followed one another in a

very predictable pattern for years, resulting in a spiral of crises for Anna. She knew things weren't working, that she'd lost touch with what she really wanted in a love relationship, but she didn't know how to stop the downward spiral in her life. It wasn't until Anna met her present husband, Jake, that the pattern was broken, allowing her to gain a greater vision about herself and what she could have in her life: a lasting and successful marriage that would keep growing.

Anna's pattern went like this: Each time she met someone who attracted her, she sparkled and shone. The man was usually dazzled and led her in a whirlwind courtship, showering her with gifts and promises of happiness. But as the golden days of romance passed and the relationship began to demand commitment and compromise, Anna would lose interest. She would feel a deep restlessness, and unconsciously her eye would begin to rove, seeking the next encounter, the next relationship. The next bout of depression.

Soon after her second marriage ended, Anna met Jake. Jake was older; he had also been through two marriages before he met Anna. He recognized her restlessness as something he had also experienced, and he was aware of what it did to relationships, since it had broken up several of his. But Jake and Anna were strongly drawn to each other, and the challenge began for both of them—to make this one last. Both Anna and Jake were tired of the merry-go-round of romance. Also, Jake was willing to work at their relationship. He made Anna look at herself and her beliefs, and challenge them.

Anna's new perspective allowed her to move forward and change her approach to life.

The first test of a truly great man is his humility.

—John Ruskin

Not long after this Anna had a dream that showed her how far she had come. In the dream she stood in front of a full-length mirror. Jake stood beside her.

"You're not wearing black and white anymore," Jake said.

"No," said Anna, fanning out the skirt of her bright orange-red dress. "I am wearing all colors now."

Anna realized the dream meant she had moved from a state of black and white—or narrow viewpoints about life and relationships—to one of many colors, a wider vision.

WAYS LIFE TEACHES US

As you've seen in the stories in this chapter, life continually guides us, even in moments of darkness. It teaches us through dreams and also through messages in the waking state. It will often send me a glimmer of hope or light via a not-so-subtle outer sign called a waking dream. It can be a series of unusual events: three wrong-number phone calls received in a day, seeing a series of red cars near my house, finding the same song on the radio each time I turn it on. They catch my attention, shake me loose from my apathy. Over the years of studying change I've come to understand that these are often important messages to me from the Divine. And these waking dreams can be deciphered in the same ways as my nightly dreams. Here are some examples.

Once when I was discouraged about my spiritual progress, I began to see yellow school buses everywhere I went. If I was on the freeway, a school bus would pull in front of me. If I was stopped at a traffic light, two or three school buses would be turning in the cross traffic. I puzzled about this message for days. Then it hit me. A school bus means school. School is for learning, and I was a student of life. To me the color yellow on the bus was a symbol for Soul, myself in my highest state. The message was, "Soul is still learning."

Another time I had a terrible pain in my shoulder, in the trapezius muscle. I went to doctors and masseuses, but I couldn't seem to shake the pain. Finally I began to see it as an extraordinary event—a waking dream. I began to decipher it. When I thought of the word *trapezius* I immediately saw a trapeze. It was locked up and not swinging freely, as it should. I realized the tight muscle might represent an area of my life that was also locked up. When I identified the real problem and dealt with it, my shoulder stopped hurting.

Each person will have his or her own ideas as to what a message means for them. For each, it may be different. These messages are very personalized to the listener.

These small "coincidences" sound meaningless to some people, but to me they are veritable lifelines during moments of spiritual crisis. They make me laugh at myself, they make me look again. They make me welcome love into my closed-up heart.

SPIRITUAL TRANSFORMATION

Through each painful experience of losing touch with the flow of life, I discovered something new about myself. A new level of inner strength. Sometimes the trauma of the dark night of Soul teaches us this kind of priceless lesson that we can't get in any other way. It takes letting go of all our preconceived ideas about ourselves, our life, God. We must lose what we think we know before we become softer, more receptive to listening, more grateful for the inner guidance.

Life becomes our best teacher. We learn more about the spiritual laws of life. How we may have been out of sync with them. How the pain, discomfort, negative emotions, crises, and lack of love came from working against one or more spiritual laws. Through dreams and waking messages, life points out the law that needs to be followed. If we are paying attention, we can adjust ourselves accordingly.

Get ready for a surprising chapter: a discussion of how we have all lived before, and how these past lives are influencing us right now, every day.

Look around yourself for help in everyday life, because an answer will come as surely as a flower in spring to an alpine meadow.

—Harold Klemp

Ask Yourself: What Are Your Dark Nights of Soul?

Write your answers to these questions. They may give you clues as to how you handle dark times in your life.

1. What's the worst experience you've ever had in your life in terms of its negative effect on your belief in God or the order and beauty of the universe?
2. How long did it take you to move through this? What skills did you use? Did anyone help you?
3. Do you have any friends or family members who have been through this? Have you talked to them about it?
4. Why do you think God or life gives us these dark times?
5. What spiritual strength did you gain from yours?

11

Past Lives and Present Turning Points

Lessons from Past Times Bring You Changes Today

While we cannot change the past, with the wisdom of Spirit we can change what it means to us and to our future.

—Susan Taylor

11. PAST LIVES AND PRESENT TURNING POINTS

I began to have memories of past lives in 1974. They came in dribs and drabs. Often I'd have a strong feeling for a place or person—without a clue as to why.

A turning point for me was realizing just how these lives were affecting me today, in subtle—and not so subtle—ways.

Reincarnation and past lives have slowly become accepted topics in Western culture. I remember when movies like *Heaven Can Wait* appeared in the eighties. The idea of reincarnation intrigued many people, and there was a flood of books, TV shows, and films with views about the afterlife that were different from those of typical Western culture.

In the past five years, three strong incidents have come to the fore for me, all past-life experiences that influenced the present. All showed me more about myself as a person today. And I came to know this as the real spiritual purpose for our memories of past lives.

I faced these memories at first without many skills or tools. Each experience was a turning point, but none

What remains of a story after it is finished? Another story.

—Elie Wiesel

manifested as great outer changes; they were inner realizations. They required me to take inner action. By the time the third incident emerged, I had begun to suspect just how much the past was affecting the present.

I was better prepared to read the signs.

The first story involves what was planned to be a pleasant camping trip my husband and I took one summer. The second started in Paris, France, on a short journey one summer with my younger sister. The third is about repeated visits to the Black Hills of South Dakota and what I discovered there.

HIDDEN INFLUENCES OF THE PAST

Several summers ago my husband and I started packing for our first canoe trip. I had always been uneasy about being alone in the wilderness, even though it pulls me with its intense beauty. My childhood summers were spent canoeing lakes in the Adirondacks of upstate New York near my grandmother's summer camp. Now living only a six-hour drive from the remote Boundary Waters wilderness area of northern Minnesota, I imagined, with pleasure, paddling remote lakes under cloudless skies.

As we packed, I was blissfully unaware of how my underlying unease had taken hold of the planning, but it began to show in the heaps of food I wanted to bring.

Nothing seemed enough. Every trip to the store brought home more freeze-dried packages, another bag of fruit or candy bars, a couple more boxes of emergency rations.

The pile grew in a corner of the living room—more than a week's worth of rations for a family of five.

Driving north that weekend was a gentle process of shedding familiar cities and sights. We passed patchwork fields and neat farmlands, going deeper into the unknown territory of the wilderness. We stopped to visit farm stands and a roadside restaurant.

The day was warm and pleasant, and the bright blue canoe on the roof rack shone in the sunlight.

As we neared the wilderness area that afternoon, I grew drowsy and lethargic, lulled by the gentle sounds of the car. In my half-sleep, the scent of the pine woods filled the air, and a strange dream crossed my vision.

* * *

I stood in a sunlit forest clearing, dressed in greasy buckskin, the tight loop of a beaded band on my upper arm. I knew I was alone, and it frightened me very much. A tight band also gripped my heart; for some reason I knew I must be very quiet. The name Monegwa came to mind.

* * *

The car jolted, and I woke suddenly, a cold, constricted feeling in my chest.

I didn't mention the experience to my husband, not wanting to disturb his long-awaited vacation. But information was coming fast, in vivid inner visions, and I wondered what I had naively set in motion with this trip.

PARENT LAKE

We arrived at Snowbank, the first lake, toward evening. Our plan was to paddle across the lake and spend the night at a shoreside campsite, then portage the canoe to a second, more remote lake the next morning. But I convinced my husband to push on, in

An occasional change of scenery makes the show come alive!

—Sherry Suib Cohen

the few hours of light left in the summer evening.

I made it sound easy: a relaxed paddle to the portage trail, maybe a mile to carry our gear and canoe, then another lake to cross as the sun set behind the trees.

The remote lake is Parent, isolated and accessible only by air, paddle, or foot.

As we loaded the canoe, I joked about the abundant food supplies, then silently added more packages to the space beneath my canoe seat, not sure why it was so important but wishing I'd brought even more. We set off across Snowbank, enjoying the slanting rays of evening light and the sound of other canoeists in the distance. When we reached the portage trail on the far side, we discovered the canoe was too heavy with supplies to lift out of the water, so we unloaded it and began carrying the first of many boxes and bags up the root-strewn dirt trail that led to Parent Lake.

My first glimpse of Parent Lake gave me an unexplained shock. It looked eerie in the setting sun, a bank of dark clouds casting an almost greenish light over the surface.

Much rougher than Snowbank, the water was thrashed by a sharp wind that caused waves to lap aggressively against the rocky shoreline. Our paddles pushing through the water like heavy spoons in molasses, we slowly worked our way across the rough lake. The shoreline, studded with deformed pines and ravaged by the wind, hung dark shadows over the lake's surface in the twilight.

It seemed to take forever to reach our campsite, and as we pulled the canoe onto a rocky beach, I was again overcome by an almost incapacitating drowsiness and great sadness.

There are times to go back and there are times not to go back.

—Gina Cerminara

What was going on?

The uncomfortable feelings paralyzed me until I was unable to perform the simplest task, even unpacking a pot to boil water for tea. The sun was setting rapidly now, and I sat hunched on a fallen log while my husband set up the tent and started the cooking fire. The feeling that overcame me, shutting out all others, was that I would die soon, in this place, and no one would know.

The stupor continued through the evening. That night, before I fell into a light sleep, I listened for a long time to a pair of loons calling, laughing, across the lake. The comforting sound counteracted the deep sadness I felt and relaxed my heart. I seemed to remember someone I loved telling me a story about loons—God's gentlest birds—protecting the frail beings in this world. I drifted to sleep listening to their almost-human cries and smelling the strong piney scent of the trees that encircled the clearing.

Just before birth, the soul allegedly pictures what it hopes to accomplish on earth in a particular lifetime.

—John Konner

* * *

In my dream I am again Monegwa, and I am sitting on a fallen log, stiff with misery. I have walked all day to this remote clearing on the shore of a small lake. I am very far from my home territory, which is good because my parents want to kill me. I have observed them commit a heinous crime against the tribe. They have lied to the elders, and I am blamed. My grandmother has secreted me out of the camp at night, taking me to a trail that stretched in the distance.

Seven years old, hardly a man, I must go into the wilderness alone and try to survive.

Sitting in the clearing surrounded by pines, I remember my grandmother's parting words. She has told me to listen for the loon, the bird of laughter and joy, my protector in this life. The loon, she says, will remind me that there are those in the tribe who still love me. Leaving her I feel great sadness, and fear pulls at my heart. The harsh beauty of the wilderness offers me little comfort.

Because I am weak with sadness and unable to stir myself to find food or make a fire, I die in the clearing a few days later.

Here, *of course, is all that you love, all that you expect, all that you are.*

—Henry David Thoreau

* * *

The dream was only a faint memory as we packed up early the next morning and paddled away from the pine clearing on the shore of Parent Lake.

The farther we went, the better I felt. Our canoe glided swiftly over the now-glassy water, and the portage trail was sunlit and mostly downhill. The first thing I heard when we arrived back at Snowbank was the clear, happy sounds of children's laughter echoing from a nearby cove.

The window that opened on Monegwa's life and death at Parent Lake dramatically brought to the fore my unease with being alone in the wilderness. But it didn't fully erase it, because at first I had almost no memory of the two visions and the dream. Pieces to the puzzle of what had happened that night came to my awareness very slowly over the next few months.

Because I wanted to solve the mystery of that lifetime and ease the strong feelings of fear in this one, I paid close attention to the road map God gave me to uncover the memories I had buried.

Slowly I was able to see that I needed to resolve a problem from a past life that was still affecting my present life. That resolution was a major turning point for me.

Feelings like these are often clues. They intrude into the present when it is time for Soul to face something from the past, reconcile or understand it, and move on. I had a chance to gain a broader perspective, but the information I received about my life as an Indian boy came in fits and starts.

Eventually there was a healing, and I made peace with that life.

It was the process of writing about the feelings and images that allowed me to see that wilderness experience as a spiritual turning point. It was a big release of past debt, or karma, allowing me to forgive myself and others in that life. It moved me into a new level of trust that life could and would take care of me, as Soul—as it hadn't taken care of a small Indian boy alone on the shores of Parent Lake.

PAST TO PRESENT—BOTH TURNING POINTS

Reliving this experience was not easy. I was puzzled as to why I loved the woods, lakes, and mountains as a child, but this particular place triggered such a sense of terror. Since then I've not been very comfortable with this northern wilderness, although I love its beauty and long to spend time there. I've tried, but even traveling down the road toward the Boundary Waters wilderness area causes cold sweats and great angst. If I stay to the lakeshore of Superior, out of the pine trees and away from the deep forests, I am fine.

My memories of that lifetime involved turning points about trust and about truth.

I had told what I knew as the truth, was cast out, and died horribly. In this life, I have been very outspoken but it has always been tempered with a sense of reserve.

I know that truth is more relative, less black and white, than I knew it as a young Indian boy.

Memory is a tricky thing. It all has to do with our own point of view, which always puts us at center stage.

—Carol Burnett

The turning point came about when I visited Parent Lake and experienced the fear and sadness of Monegwa's life. But most important was my spiritual assignment: to figure out a lesson from that life, the telling of truth, and begin to understand where it fit in the present.

Exercise:
To Imagine the Past

1. List ten imaginary lives you'd like to have had.

2. Spend twenty minutes looking through five magazines to find pictures that tell about these lives.

3. Paste one picture for each life in your journal.

4. Next to the picture, write a story about that life.

5. Read the stories, circling any information that might give you a clue to yourself today.

DISCOVERING THE STORY

One Saturday afternoon, my husband and I were having a late lunch at a restaurant in Minneapolis. I was feeling balanced and good, usually the state of mind I have to have to get clear on a past-life puzzle, so I began talking about how strange our camping trip to Parent Lake had been. I told him about the extremely strong emotions I still felt were associated with the place, a clue that there was something worth looking at, something I was not remembering.

He suggested I begin jotting down images and feelings I remembered from the trip.

I had a small notebook in my purse. So I took it out and wrote down several phrases that came to mind: "blue sky," "bright blue canoe on car roof," "gray waters of Parent Lake, waves crashing, feeling so tired and lonesome, hopeless," "sounds of children calling across Snowbank Lake when we turned back for home." I didn't have much of a clue as to how these images would add up as I was writing. But because I had taken that first step forward—because I wanted to see what the experience held for me—I began learning more.

That week, memories of the dreams and vision about Monegwa began to return. I didn't recall his name right away; one morning I had an image in contemplation of an Indian boy, and I silently wondered what his name was. It popped into my head.

I tried a writing exercise. I began creating a "fictional" story based on a camping trip and past-life recall. Like an unfolding dream, the pieces came. I knew they were not fiction; they were mine. I collected parts in my journal from dreams, a passing remark I overheard, a sentence I read in a book.

And so I discovered my own story.

The last function of reason is to recognize that there are an infinity of things which surpass it.

—Blaise Pascal

Exercise:
Writing Your Own Story

If you are drawn to a particular time or place, write a short story about it with yourself as the main character. Let any ideas come to mind and put them on paper, no matter how silly they might sound. Let your imagination roam freely.

Keep this story in your journal.

When you feel a sincere desire to learn something about yourself, ask God, "Please show me what I need to know about this time."

Memories may escape the action of the will, may sleep a long time, but when stirred by the right influence, . . . they flash into full stature and life with everything in place.

— John Muir

TREASURE HUNT

Strong feelings, good or bad, that seem out of place for the situation often signal the influences of a past life.

My friend Robin told me about a situation like this in her life. She did some freelance graphics work for a young man several years ago in Portland, when she was just getting started in graphics. After a week or so, she said, it became apparent that she had a deep loathing for this man, for which there was no obvious reason. Although he was mild-mannered, she felt a kind of evil.

The longer she worked for him, the more upset she felt. She didn't want to have such a closed heart for someone.

One night, after a particularly unsettling encounter with her employer, Robin was sitting with her family in a pizza parlor. Suddenly she had a vision. She saw that this young man had been one of the attackers on

Pythagoras's mystery school in ancient Greece. Robin had been an initiate there. In the raid, this young man had deliberately shot her through the heart with an arrow.

Robin realized that the reason for her present association with this man was simply to be able to forgive. She was able to do this while doing a spiritual exercise, and soon the business association ended.

Like items in a treasure hunt, the clues to past life influences are often hidden in unexpected places. Like my friend Robin, I had to want to find them. I have a good imagination, and I've practiced letting it bring me unusual ideas to consider, things that don't fit a logical framework. I work with hunches, nudges, and brain-storming often in my work, which has trained me to more easily accept stray images that floated in as I pieced together the reason behind my unreasonable terror of Parent Lake.

"There are techniques to see past lives, but the real reason to do it at all is for healing rather than just curiosity," my friend Robin said. "I had to have a sincere desire to move beyond a certain condition in my life which was holding me back. For me, just wanting to know out of curiosity is not enough to bring forth a past-life memory.

"As I look at my own patterns, I see that past-life memories have always come spontaneously when I needed to release an attachment which was blocking me from taking my next step spiritually."

A TRIP BACK TO MEDIEVAL FRANCE

My next experience connected with the lesson of Monegwa's lifetime in a very neat and efficient way. It

Showers of love rain down upon us simply because we are Soul, a divine spark of God.

—Harold Klemp

also became a turning point about speaking the truth, but in a different way.

After years in Christianity, yoga, Zen Buddhism, and other spiritual studies, I became a member of Eckankar in 1975. It wasn't until 1993 that I began to realize I had a deep fear of telling others about my religion. From my own extensive searching, I believed wholeheartedly in individual freedom to choose a spiritual path, so I tried not to push my beliefs on another.

But my reluctance went beyond that.

I was actually afraid of talking to people who asked me, even begged me, for information. All too well I remembered the horror of "saved" friends or door-to-door preachers who cornered me to proselytize about their new religion. I wanted to give people their space and never be seen as preachy or pushy. I also hesitated to reveal some of the more mystical experiences I had had with dreams and past lives, not sure if anyone would understand them or, worse, make fun of me. I told myself this reluctance to share was a good thing: I was just being respectful. But actually it was born of fear, not love.

So God gave me a window into the past to look through and let go of this fear.

I was to go to Paris one July for an annual Eckankar seminar in Europe. Thousands of Eckankar students from all over the world would attend the three-day event.

Unexpectedly, a month before I left, my younger sister called from Baltimore. She had had a brilliant idea: Since she was due a vacation away from kids and husband, could she join me in Paris for a week of sightseeing?

When men are ruled by fear, they strive to prevent the very changes that will abate it.

—Alan Paton

Ann knew very little about my spiritual beliefs. We didn't have a particularly strong religious background in our family, although the children attended a Quaker school until college. Both my grandmothers had been intensely religious Christians, and although I tried to follow their footsteps, I had too many unanswered questions. Following my own heart meant choosing a path away from the family's beliefs.

My family also prized tradition and intellectual pursuits. Although as children we were encouraged to be creative and innovative, we were also urged to excel academically. Logic was important. And I was afraid of ridicule if I shared my illogical, heart-driven searching with them. I was afraid of the scorn and joking, so rather than risk that I kept my beliefs largely to myself for almost twenty years.

I knew that if my sister joined me in Paris, it would be inevitable that she would ask about Eckankar. I would be meeting her between seminar activities; there was no way to avoid it.

To get spiritual freedom, one must first give it.

—Harold Klemp

A deep-seated fear was beginning to surface, but over it was a love for my sister and a delight in the thought of spending a week vacationing with her.

So I said yes.

Ann was coming from Baltimore, I from Minneapolis, but we were to meet in Boston for the flight to France. Her connecting flight came in after mine, and I waited at the gate, checking my watch to make sure we'd still make the Paris plane. With twenty minutes to spare, we ran for the international terminal, lugging Ann's carry-on baggage. By the time we boarded, most of the passengers were already seated.

As Ann and I, out of breath, made our way down the

aisle to our midplane seats, I happened to notice Harold Klemp, the spiritual leader of Eckankar. He was seated with his wife, Joan, on the right side of the plane.

Operating from a point much higher than my previous fears about Ann and Eckankar, I reached down to tap Joan on the shoulder. "I'd like you to meet my sister," I said. Harold cordially shook Ann's hand, and we made small talk for a few seconds before the steward swept us into our seats.

Ann had questions. Who was that man? Was he the head of Eckankar? And would I please tell her — finally — exactly what this religion was?

During the week in Paris, Ann had a lot of opportunity to hear about Eckankar. Everywhere we went, friends from past seminars greeted me and were introduced to her. "Isn't the seminar wonderful?" they'd exclaim, and I'd agree. Ann and I had discussions about my reluctance to share Eckankar with my family, and I got up the courage to ask her to attend the Sunday talks and creative arts performances, which she did.

When I got back to the States, I realized I had opened an inner floodgate.

The fear of sharing my personal religious beliefs became more intense for a few months, and yet it seemed everyone was asking. Women in my Saturday group, my cooking assistant in classes I taught, our neighbor down the street — all wanted to know. There was no avoiding it, without seeming rude.

Each time I spoke to someone about my belief in past lives or inner guidance or dream study, I found myself reacting very severely afterward. I would literally be in a cold sweat, my stomach in knots, trembling inside.

The past-life connection was made when a friend

Man is a history-making creature who can neither repeat his past nor leave it behind.

—W. H. Auden

at work passed on a novel she had finished, *By All That Is Sacred,* by Laura Gilmour Bennett.

The story took place in France, mostly the Languedoc region in the south. The main characters, a British man and an American woman, had begun having unexplained dreams and visions of another time in the south of France, so many that they were eventually compelled to drive there. The visions were about the Cathars, members of a small religious band who broke away from the Catholic Church. Cathars were considered heretics but flourished in that area of France for many years before being wiped out by the church and nobles. As many as two hundred were massacred in a single incident, sent to a fiery death.

As I read this fascinating story, I felt without a doubt that I had been in the Cathar movement, perhaps not in the massacre but certainly persecuted for my beliefs.

The Cathar beliefs seemed very primitive to me, compared to my present-life understanding of God, but I felt a strong connection with the Cathar people. Without knowing why, I felt they were good people, dedicated to their understanding of God, right and wrong, and a simple desire to live within their beliefs. Because they were seen as a threat to the church in that region of France, they had been exterminated.

Like poison purged from the body, the fear of talking about my religion has slowly left me.

Now I feel less of a sudden clench in my gut when someone asks me to share my beliefs. I now know where the fear came from. I understand that once it was a survival tool for me, and I also know I have reached a turning point—I can let it go.

Harold Klemp writes, "When we can fill ourselves

The Past is such a curious Creature.

—Emily Dickinson

with this love of God more and more, finally there is no room in our heart for the darkness of fear." The idea behind learning about the past is simply this: to fill ourselves with so much love that there is no room for fear.

Exercise:
Letting Go of Past Fear

Close your eyes, relax, and ask this simple question: *What can I do to get rid of fear and have more love?*

Accept whatever comes. Take a minute afterward to write down your answer or image. Reflect on it as you read the next story in this chapter.

We have to do with the past only as we can make it useful to the present and the future.

—Frederick Douglass

TIME AS A TEACHER

Like Robin in the earlier example, I have found that awareness of past lives only comes when we sincerely desire to change something in ourselves—and when we are ready to receive the information.

It's not useful to Soul's journey to have a lot of extra information about the past or future—unless it is helpful to our growth in the present moment. I receive my information only as I can make use of it and grow. Mostly I get glimpses of lifetimes when I was helpful, stood true to my values, or was a heroine who died courageously. I've been spared many of the lives when I was on the wrong side of truth, when I did dastardly deeds or hurt others.

This next story is a recent gift from God. Apparently I could use the less-than-complimentary information about myself in order to wrap up another turning point.

Ever since I moved to Minnesota, I've wanted to spend time in South Dakota and Wyoming. The rugged, arid land draws me strongly. Others remark on its dullness; to me it is beautiful in its subtle colors and harsh landscape. I convinced my husband one summer to take a driving trip for ten days that would include the two states; we would make up our itinerary as we drove.

Everything went fine until we reached Rapid City, South Dakota, on the edge of the Black Hills.

We took a motel room there for the night. I remember a detective movie being on television and watching until I fell into an uneasy sleep. My dreams were about Native Americans, the 1800s, and scenes right out of the movie *Dances with Wolves.*

I woke in the night with an incredible feeling of regret—horrible regret. But I had no idea where it came from.

The feeling cleared as we left the Black Hills and did not resurface until we tried another trip the next year. The same thing happened. As soon as we passed the Badlands and saw the forest-covered mountains at the edge of the state, I'd experience it again: deep regret. Once I got hysterical, crying that I'd lost something I could never get back and that I hadn't meant to do it.

Light didn't dawn on this experience until our fourth trip.

My husband and I were standing at an overlook along one of the roads through the Badlands, when I saw a vision of him falling slowly over the side. It came with an incredible urge to push him over the cliff.

Repect the past in the full measure of its deserts, but do not make the mistake of confusing it with the present.

—José Ingenieros

I was shocked, disgusted, and afraid. We have a loving relationship, and I'd never want to see him hurt. But there it was — and with it came the familiar Black-Hills-vacation feeling of deep regret.

"Step back, Tony," I cried, my mind filled with images of his body hurtling to the rocks below us.

He looked at me strangely. "Are you all right?"

I could hardly speak, overcome with a sense of protectiveness and aghast at these black feelings within myself. It took days and weeks for the feelings to sort out. I realized that again it was a past life coming up to be accepted, dealt with — a negative side of my character and a black deed I had committed against my brother in a past lifetime as a Native American in the Black Hills.

The lesson from that experience was to be able to accept myself as a person who had done good things and bad things, who had been the victim and the perpetrator.

Past lives are rarely rosy things. We don't especially need to remember the bright spots; more often it's the darker ones that are the best teachers.

THE PAST SOLVES A MYSTERY

In a Turning Points workshop I told this story of the Black Hills and of the accompanying horror and personal shame that came with the memory. I spoke about how I had come to forgive myself and how humble I felt learning that not only do we have glorious lives, we have plenty of self-serving ones too. I ended with the comment that this Black Hills lifetime, with all its pain and self-imposed misery, had taught me a lot more than the prettier ones.

One woman immediately raised her hand. She was

Each little thing that we do passes into the great machine of life.

— Oscar Wilde

a little skeptical about the usefulness of such a memory. She basically didn't understand why I hadn't gotten more information.

Didn't I want to know more about why I pushed my brother off the cliff?

What was the use, she argued, of even getting any past-life recall if you didn't get the whole picture?

Some people get past-life memories in complete stories, full of details, like a well-edited novel. I don't. Past-life memories don't come to me in pretty packages, neatly tied with bows. Because I am naturally skeptical, I have to hunt for clues, follow inner treasure maps, and accept that life is essentially quite messy. I wish for complete and well-tested recipes for living, but usually end up with improvisation and nonlinear trails.

What is the usefulness of sometimes jumbled, sometimes logical memories of other times we acted on the stage of life as Soul?

For me, it may solve the mystery of an unexplained terror.

It may tell me a little about why I love one person, one place. Why I am repelled by another. It may clue me in to my never-ending desire to spend time in Paris but my unexplained unease with the southern coast of France.

From this spotty information, I get some peace of mind that I am not crazy: these feelings are real.

I believe that whatever information I get from past lives is monitored by God. God knows what I need and how much. Some people write about famous lifetimes— they were Marie Antoinette or Einstein. I have never had such recall. My lifetimes have been humble, but educational to me as Soul. I have always grown in my

To excel the past we must not allow ourselves to lose contact with it.

—José Ortega y Gasset

understanding with each experience of a past life. And I learned how to live more fully in the present, knowing what I know about the past.

God knows that the information I get with these occasional memories will make me a more compassionate person today. I feel that is the only spiritually valid reason for remembering a past life.

Journey of Three Thousand Years

My friend Linda Anderson, in her book *35 Golden Keys to Who You Are & Why You're Here,* tells a fascinating story of a trip to Singapore that unexpectedly brought back memories of a life three thousand years ago as a Chinese woman.

Linda had been invited by a good friend to speak at a religious seminar in Singapore. It was her first trip to Southeast Asia, and she was very excited about exploring a culture she knew little about.

A month before the trip, she had an unusual dream. In the dream she was a young Chinese peasant woman, married into a family where her mother-in-law despised her. In the dream scene, the elderly woman was ridiculing the food Linda had cooked for dinner. It was a hard and miserable life.

Those who do not remember the past are condemned to relive it.

—George Santayana

Later that week Linda had another Chinese experience, this time during her daily spiritual exercise. It began an unusual series of inner visions and dreams with a woman named So Jahn.

Linda realized that the upcoming trip to Singapore was triggering past-life memories and unveiling an important story that had bearing in her life today.

In this experience, Linda met So Jahn and learned that this woman serves as a guardian angel working with people in Asia in dreams and other inner experiences to help them learn more about themselves as Soul and how to serve God better. In ancient China So Jahn started her spiritual mission by studying with a great teacher named Lai Tsi. Linda was startled when she heard this name, because Lai Tsi is a well-known teacher in Eckankar, Linda's religion.

The experience was so real, and Linda felt huge waves of love pouring from So Jahn's tiny body as she told her story. Appearing to be about fifty years old, So Jahn was dressed in traditional Chinese dress; her feet were bound in the custom of wealthy women in ancient China. So Jahn described her teacher Lai Tsi arriving at her wealthy father's home in a horse-drawn carriage to teach So Jahn the mysteries of God. Although it was traditional to marry, So Jahn's father let her stay home and learn from this ancient sage.

We live in reference to past experience.

—H. G. Wells

Linda was fascinated by this inner experience and wrote it down in detail in her journal, describing So Jahn's appearance and costume, the horse-drawn carriage—all the while, wondering how it would affect her upcoming trip to Singapore.

When she arrived in Singapore, Linda told her Chinese friend, C., about So Jahn's appearance and related the details of the inner conversation. C. was not surprised that Linda had had such a vivid experience, since reincarnation is a common belief in the East. But she was amazed that a Westerner would know so much about ancient Chinese customs, especially never having studied the culture or visited Asia.

They decided to visit a nearby museum to learn more about that era. Could Linda arrange another visit from So Jahn, to find out which province of China she was from? C. asked.

As soon as Linda asked inwardly, So Jahn appeared again with her teacher, Lai Tsi. She said she was Cantonese. Her name *Jahn* meant "pearl" in the Cantonese dialect. In ancient China, fathers often named their daughters after precious jewels. Linda recorded the details in her journal.

Later that day, Linda and C. visited a wax museum to see figures of peasant people in that era. Outside the museum is an exact replica of the horse-drawn carriage that carried Lai Tsi to So Jahn's home. Linda stood and stared at it. It was a strong confirmation that her inner experiences had been more than just fantasy.

While she was in Singapore, Linda had several more dreams and visions with So Jahn.

The most important happened right before the seminar. In this experience, So Jahn took Linda to a field where a peasant girl was working. Linda immediately recognized the girl from her dream—it was herself in that past life! So Jahn smiled at her kindly as they watched the girl labor. "You were very shy in that life," So Jahn told Linda, "but you had the Light of God in your eyes, even though you were filled with fear and loathing from your mother-in-law's cruel treatment of you. Some days I would come to the field where you were working, and we'd quietly speak about God."

One momentous day, the peasant girl met So Jahn's teacher, Lai Tsi, and recognized him as the Master she had been meeting and learning from in her dreams. After that day she talked with So Jahn about the meeting and about her dreams. So Jahn helped her interpret them spiritually.

While this experience was happening Linda again

The supreme happiness of life is the conviction that we are loved.

—Victor Hugo

felt huge waves of love. She realized it was the immense love she had for So Jahn from this past life. As So Jahn concluded her story, Linda sat with tears streaming down her face.

"I didn't tell you everything about myself when we first met inwardly," So Jahn said, "because I wanted you to learn Chinese history and rediscover for yourself details about our past life together and why you are here in the East again today."

When Linda returned to the United States after the seminar, she had strong memories of her experiences with So Jahn and Lai Tsi and even a dream where she was speaking fluent Chinese.

It is love, not reason, that is stronger than death.

—Thomas Mann

WHAT DID YOU LEARN?

I asked Linda what she learned from these dramatic experiences. How did it help her life today to see a life three thousand years in the past?

"It was an experience of two Souls whose lives were rejoined in love," she told me. "We simply found each other again. It explained for me the affinity I have for that part of the world and the Chinese people, even though I am a Westerner this lifetime. It also reminded me that women can become guardian angels and work toward spiritual mastery, as So Jahn did and as I am working toward in my present lifetime."

This past-life experience showed her more about her spiritual connection with the ECK teachings, that they reached back thousands of years.

HOW TO REMEMBER YOUR OWN PAST LIVES

Do you want to learn how to remember your past lives? You may already have the ability. Here's how I learned how easy it is to remember more about our past lives.

Several years ago I took a creative writing class, and my instructor asked us to bring in old photographs for a class exercise. We passed them around the circle, each person choosing one unfamiliar photo that struck a chord. I decided this would be a great way to practice inner guidance. I had a nudge to choose a tiny black-and-white picture of a solitary woman in front of a whitewashed one-room house, the prairie in the background. We were then asked to sit quietly with the picture and begin writing whatever came to mind—whatever thoughts or images struck our fancy.

I began to write a story of an elderly woman standing in front of her house in the last summer of her life. She had been a creative person but hampered by convention in the city. Her mother had wanted her to be a doctor, which was fairly radical in those days, but the thought of being around all that sickness repulsed her. She had been a brooding, serious girl, stiff in the company of others but joyous and carefree off by herself. Her mother had seen life in neat boxes, but as a young girl this woman had seen it in fragrant waves of color, like the autumn-tipped trees blowing wildly in the wind or the expanse of prairie she imagined was west of her coastal home.

She had found the house in the aged photograph when she ran away from home. She had traveled west and lived there for the last fifty years of her life. She saw the house as a stray puppy looking for someone to care for it, and she had plenty of time, generosity, and patience.

I was silent for a long time after reading my story

We are as high on the path of spiritual consciousness as we've ever been. Everything that we've been in the past has been put together, as Soul gaining the greater experience.

—Harold Klemp

to the group. Emotion had crept into my voice, and I almost began to cry. The lifetime was so real. And I keenly remembered the feeling of being strong, alone, and in love with that part of the country. It also explained how I happened to now be living on the Minnesota prairie and why I used every chance I got to drive into the country.

The group marveled at how alive the woman had become for me. I realized that years of developing my inner perceptions had allowed me a peek into a past life of my own, through the aged photo. I may not have been the woman in the picture, but through the exercise, I understood more about why I loved the prairie, solitude, and having my own house.

Exercise:
Time Travel

Borrow five old photographs from friends or relatives, preferably of people you never met or don't know too much about. Arrange them before you on a table. Get your journal and a pen; sit down before the photos, and relax by closing your eyes and breathing deeply for a few minutes.

Now look at the photos. Choose one that lights up for you, that speaks to you in some way. Put away the other photos, and set this one in front of you.

Imagine you are writing a fictional story about this person. Ask inwardly to meet this person and know something about his or her life. When you have finished writing, see if the story sounds like something you may have experienced yourself in a past life.

Happiness comes to us in many forms.

—Terah Kathryn Collins

Understandings like this have helped me meet turning points and handle them better. Memories of other times that have come into the present to be resolved have enriched my life beyond measure.

In the final chapter, we'll bring together the various threads of mastering change and look at an ultimate goal: Working with God and life in complete harmony during all our turning points.

Ask Yourself:
Have I Lived Before?

Write your answers to these questions. You may learn something about yourself.

1. What did you like best about your childhood? What were your favorite places, and why? Who were your favorite people?

2. What are three places anywhere in the world that fascinate you? What aspects do you love about these places? When you went there the first time, did you feel as if you'd been there before?

3. Who are three people in your life that you are strongly drawn to? When you met these people, did you have a sense that you'd known each other all your life?

4. Have you ever had any dreams about these places or these people in other times?

5. Do you believe you've lived before? Why or why not? If you do, what spiritual lessons are repeating for you from past times?

12

Our Song within the Great Song

Blending Spirituality and Everyday Changes

We are not the victims of luck or anything else. What we are today is the result of our own actions and thoughts.

—Harold Klemp

12. Our Song within the Great Song

Several years ago my husband, Tony, decided to have routine surgery on his foot to repair a bone chip. He had fallen off a ladder that summer, and the bone chip in his toe caused a little discomfort every now and then. The surgery was on a Friday in February, one of the coldest days of that winter. The temperature was minus 24 degrees.

I dropped Tony off at the outpatient surgery desk and went home to warm up.

At noon, his surgery successful, Tony called me to pick him up and bring his crutches. The temperature was only a few degrees warmer. As I hurried across the street to the hospital entrance, crutches in hand, I didn't see the thin patch of ice.

Down I went, hitting my head—hard. A cracking sound echoed in my ears. A flash of pain streaked across my eyes. I lay there, not moving, trying to regain my senses.

The first thing that crossed my mind, as I lay there in the middle of that frozen street, was, *Why this? Why now?* I slowly pulled myself to my hands and knees, gathered the crutches under one arm, and crawled to

The universe is change; our life is what our thoughts make it.

—Marcus Aurelius Antoninus

the emergency room entrance.

"I think I need help," I told the startled nurse. "I just fell on the ice outside." *There's no better place to do this than in front of a hospital,* I thought, as a three-alarm headache began to pound my temples. Tony was still upstairs in the outpatient surgery ward. "I don't mean to one-up you," I told him when I called. "But I'm downstairs in the emergency room."

I must not be for myself, but God's work, and that is always good.

—Henry David Thoreau

Hours later, as we drove home—me with a lump on my head and Tony with his bandaged foot—I stewed over the bad timing and unfairness of life letting me fall. And today of all days! Why hadn't the hospital salted the road in front of their emergency entrance? What if the doctor's warnings came true, and the fall caused a real head injury? Coma? A cracked skull? My mind wound around this track of negativity, getting deeper and deeper into the victim's mire.

Suddenly, I had to laugh at myself. At home, my desk was piled with the final draft of this book—about spirituality and change. And here I was, whining mightily about this unexpected inconvenience that had come into my Friday morning.

Could I put my own beliefs into practice? Could I find the hidden benefit in this change? So over the next few days, I looked hard for the blessings. And there were quite a few.

Sunday I noticed the longtime stiffness had gone from my neck. A car accident many years ago had left the muscles tight and my flexibility limited. Now it felt as if some burden had been lifted; I could move my neck much more freely. By the following week, I noticed a real change in my writing: the editing for each chapter of this book I worked on after my fall went much more smoothly. I had better ideas, stories to fill any remaining gaps had poured in from friends and people I had interviewed, and the chapters were easier to wrap up. I remembered the doctor pointing to where my head had hit the pavement, calling it the part of the brain that processes light.

Some strange symbology, I thought at the time. But it looked indeed as if this book was bringing some light to my own understanding about change. It was as if the fall opened up some locked area inside, changing my own ability to process the inner light.

I realized that, strangely, the slip on the ice had been a spiritual wake-up call and an important turning point to be embraced.

EMBRACING CHANGE

Through my own and others' stories, I've been trying to illustrate an important principle: change is to be embraced rather than avoided.

Change is a gift from God, a doorway to the next spiritual level, and we are a creative force in our own lives. To no longer be the victim of change is to master change. This mastery allows you to see the hand of God at work in your life and create a future that reflects confidence in a divine plan and a higher purpose.

Most of us manage this every now and then. Maybe you can remember times in your own life when it seemed as if you stood in the calm eye of the hurricane. Events whirled around you, yet you felt accepting and at peace.

You felt a certainty that a higher power was in charge.

We can relax in that state. While we know we are the creative force behind our changes, we also know

In the time of trouble avert not thy face from hope, for the soft marrow abideth in the hard bone.

—Hāfiz

God is in control of those events. This brings us protection through the currents of change.

Each time I can see this divine hand working in any area of my life—my writing career, my friendships, my living situation, my businesses—I begin to witness the miracles that come to me. And I surrender to the higher force in my life that brings these miracles. I realize how rarely do I actually know what's best for me in the largest sense. I stop trying to manipulate my life based on what I know, from my limited, human perspective. I state my preferences but let God bring me gifts beyond my imagining. It leaves me living in a state of joy.

When I can do this, I also begin to see how carefully I am watched over and protected as I move through my turning points. The following story illustrates the depth of that protection—and the always-perfect timing.

The spiritual purpose of life is to learn to give and to receive love.

—Harold Klemp

Perfect Timing

When my husband and I decided to sell our home and move into my dream house, the prospective buyer had to have the property appraised for their loan. An appraiser would come to check the home and verify that the house was worth the loan amount being requested.

One of the ongoing problems we had dealt with during our years in that house was a stucco-covered chimney.

It sat on the south wall of the home, and long cracks ran across it. Each summer, we would patch the cracks, and the chimney would be fine until the next freeze. We had had the chimney checked the first winter. A sweep came to clean the flue, and I asked him to check for any chimney damage. There was none.

So my husband and I kept patching the stucco each

summer, confident that cosmetic damage was our only problem.

The morning the appraiser was scheduled, my husband took a walk around the house to see that everything was in order. When he rounded the south corner of the house, he saw a table-sized chunk of stucco lying on the ground, surrounded by pieces of what looked like cement.

In the night a hard freeze had caused the stucco to peel off the chimney face, exposing a totally disintegrated layer of brick underneath. The timing couldn't have been worse.

Now what we had always considered a minor repair in our preparation to move had become a major expense.

The appraiser simply wrote on his form that day, "Repair chimney stucco," but when we sought estimates from several repairmen, they told us the problem was much worse than that. No one would repair the stucco; the brick underneath wouldn't support it. A far worse hazard had been exposed just before our move—the chimney itself was unstable and could collapse.

I calculated we would still break even on the sale of the house if the chimney rebuilding didn't go higher than $800. That seemed awfully high at the time, but my heart really sank when I heard the estimates.

The last contractor that came out gave us the lowest bid—$3000.

Your Bigger Story

My husband and I talked it over. Our guiding principle thus far had always been: Do it right.

If we did our best at each decision point, working economically and fairly, then things would work out. We

Hope is a risk that must be run.

—George Bernanos

trusted this totally and hadn't been disappointed thus far, but it seemed now the principle was no longer working.

For a few days, as we read the estimates and analyzed our financial situation, we toyed with the thought of asking the new owners to pay part of the bill. After all, we would be out of the house in a few weeks, and they would have years of enjoying the new chimney. Wouldn't it be fair and economical to present this cost as an added-in condition of the sale?

The more we tossed around this idea, the worse I felt.

My stomach had been an indicator throughout the process of selling our house—if I felt the least bit queasy about an option, there was something spiritually not right about it. Other people might get a headache, have a minor accident, or hear an inner voice. I got an upset stomach. And my stomach was really acting up now.

There is a Power whose care / Teaches thy way along that pathless coast.

—William Cullen Bryant

Following the spiritual principle of Do what you have agreed to do, I realized that the cleanest action spiritually was to accept the chimney as our responsibility and take care of it.

We had the money, although it would wipe out much of our savings. So the next week we hired a contractor, and the work began. He agreed to our conditions: the new chimney had to be finished within seven days so we could close on the house.

UNEXPECTED PROTECTION

About that time, there was a streak of below-zero weather, but the contractor kept to his word, and the work continued under a tent of plastic wrapped around the scaffolding. They had to tear into the chimney foundation and pull away all the layers of brick.

By Monday, they were finished, and the appraiser signed off on our repairs.

The incident passed, swept away by new decisions and events that cropped up each day with the new house we were buying. I didn't think much about the chimney. The amount of $3000 only popped into my mind whenever I reviewed our depleted savings account.

The day we signed the final papers for the purchase of our new house, we stopped by the post office to pick up some mail. There was an envelope from my literary agent.

Inside was a check for just under $3000 made out to me!

I was flabbergasted. A royalty payment for my third book usually arrived every four or five months, but I'd forgotten that one was due. Not only that, but the two previous payments had been very small: $79 and $400, respectively. Nothing like $3000.

Suddenly the image of the $3000 chimney came into my mind. I began laughing out loud right there in the post office, then I ran out to the car to show my husband the good news.

God gives, but man must open his hand.

—German proverb

Our Lives as Works of Art

We took this as proof positive that God was protecting us as long as we were willing to work cleanly and honorably with life. We had also benefited from a great lesson here. Because we had done what we agreed to do with no expectation of being bailed out, God had brought us the means to rebalance our life and take care of the unexpected problem.

Key to this experience for me was (1) doing what I had agreed to do, and (2) having no expectations of being bailed out at the eleventh hour.

To be full participants with God as agents of change, to work in harmony with life as coworkers, we must be fully aware of our place in the order of life. As this awareness grows, we actually have fewer desires concerning the outcome of situations. And when we let go of desire, divine protection is given.

I had to give up my desire to "get back the money we were losing" paying for the chimney. Working from the highest state, we no longer want more money, more love, more this, more that.

 We begin to have total trust in God that the correct outcome will be provided.

Whoever falls from God's right hand / Is caught into his left.

—Edwin Markham

Exercise:
What's the Highest in Your Life?

Take a minute, and ask yourself about any experience in your life: What can this experience teach me about myself and life? What is the highest state I can hold within this experience?

My husband's and my highest state during our chimney story was: We want to do what is fair, economical, and spiritually clean.

Whatever your highest state, if you can hold it during challenging times, God will provide the best possible outcome.

A VIEW FROM LOVE

Ultimately, lessons like these are designed to teach us more about love rather than the use of power. Sometimes they are hardships of money, sometimes family, other times they pinpoint a next step we can take toward being more of who we really are. And they are created to match our exact areas of strength and weakness.

Ilona and Jon were driving home one evening when suddenly Ilona had a vision of herself at her mother's funeral. She felt a strong pull toward Norway, where her parents lived and where she had been raised.

Ilona had always had a strong inner link with her mother because of their shared beliefs in God. They had always been able to hear each other across the miles that separated them. Occasionally Ilona would call to ask if Mom was preparing a dish of one kind or another; Ilona had smelled it, and yes, her mother was just that minute cooking. Or Ilona would call and say, "It's me," and her mother would answer, "I know, I've been sitting here by the phone waiting for you to call."

But her mother was a perfectly healthy sixty-year-old woman. So this sudden inner vision troubled Ilona. Why would she think of her mother dying?

Not long afterward a dream came. In the dream, Ilona met a family friend who had died of cancer many years ago. The friend brought Ilona a message about a parent dying of cancer and the daughter traveling by air to go to the parent's bedside.

Ilona woke from the dream greatly concerned. She felt a strange urgency that she couldn't shake. She knew something was very wrong.

She tried calling her parents several times that day but was not able to get through.

Finally her stepfather called. Ilona's mother had been rushed to the hospital the night before. She had

I know not where His islands lift / Their fronded palms in air; / I only know I cannot drift / Beyond His love and care.

—John Greenleaf
    Whittier

been in great pain, and the doctors had found a tumor. It was cancer.

Ilona immediately left for a two-week visit to Norway. She found her mother in waning health and the family in turmoil. The visit required all the inner and outer strength Ilona could muster. Not only did she have to keep herself together, she felt a strong spiritual purpose in being with her mother in these last weeks of her life: to help her mother loosen the final ties that held her here and prepare to make the inner journey of death.

During the visit Ilona had a striking dream that showed her how close the end was. In the dream she went to buy train tickets for her parents, her husband, and herself, but Ilona's mother's personal ID card was missing and the ticket agent wouldn't give her a ticket without it. Ilona tried to come up with a solution. Her mother calmly accepted it and trailed behind in the crowd as the others boarded and the train began to roll out of the station. Ilona knew this dream was significant: her mother's departure from this life was coming soon.

Prosperity is a great teacher; adversity is a greater.

—William Hazlitt

Eventually Ilona had to return to the States, even though she wanted to stay. On her last night in Norway, as she and her mother sat talking in the kitchen around midnight, Ilona noticed the digital stove clock read 00:00. Everything has been resolved, she realized. It was time to leave.

After Ilona left, her mother's strength faded quickly, until she could barely move from the bed. Ilona kept in contact by phone; although her mother couldn't talk at this point, their inner communication was strong. Ilona had many dreams and inner experiences with her mother during those last days. In one, the family was walking single file down a steep hill to a pier where a ferry waited to take Mom to the other side, then they all watched as Mom spread her wings like an eagle and soared into a bright flash of golden-white light.

After her mother died, Ilona remained in a cocoon of grief for days. The pain was acute. She'd often ask God, "How much longer will this go on?" Her close friend had died, and she felt her whole world was atilt.

She finally did a spiritual exercise that gave her the peace and freedom from grief she much needed and brought back the love.

In the exercise, she acknowledged her myriad of feelings about her mother's death. The feelings ranged from grief to joy to regret, and deep gratitude for the final moments they had shared. Then Ilona walked back in her imagination through her life and other lives, remembering the moments she had shared with her mother, as far back as she could recall. All this she filled with love, as if she were filling an empty glass with water. Returning to the present, she then imagined every moment in the future filled with this same divine love from God.

Suddenly, she saw her mother. They stood side by side at a ceremony attended by many spiritual masters. When they turned to face each other, they looked deeply into each other's eyes, spiritual beings both, without the limits that had been present in their human life together.

Ilona felt great peace, a realization that all life flows back from whence it came, into the heart of God. She saw her lives and her mother's as a string of experiences, like connecting diamonds, sparkling with love. And working in harmony with life meant being part of this love.

The great and glorious master-piece of man is to know how to live to purpose.

—Montaigne

"I knew we would never be apart because we were united in God's love," Ilona said. "Nor would we ever again need to be together, since our bond was beyond personality and time."

After a debauch of thunder-shower, the weather takes the pledge and signs it with a rainbow.

—Thomas Bailey Aldrich

Exercise: Connecting Diamonds

1. Acknowledge all your feelings about a change, both the negative and the positive ones. Review them in your mind like a series of short movies.

2. Trace back in time through the change, from present to past, reviewing the experiences you had, still looking at them from this level, as an observer watching a movie. See how all the experiences connect like diamonds on a necklace.

3. Those experiences that appear highlighted to you are key lessons or turning points. Bring them into the present moment, and imagine all the wisdom, strength, and love for life that came out of those experiences extending into the future, like a beam of light you can travel on. Imagine these experiences are clear like glass. See love pouring into them, washing them clean.

4. Visualize the love moving into your future, cleaning out your obstacles and replacing them with peace and freedom.

SMALL MIRACLES

A friend who manages international spiritual conferences told me a fascinating story about a problem that taught her a pointed lesson about the interworkings of life and how to stay in harmony with it. It all centered around a search for a cello player.

The conference was to begin in Minneapolis on a Friday morning. It would feature inspirational speakers, workshops, and a relaxing program of music. Thursday, the lead cello player called long-distance. She had thrown her back out and would be staying at home in bed instead of playing in the ensemble. It appeared impossible to find a last-minute replacement for the difficult pieces to be played on Sunday. Here's how the story worked out, in my friend's words.

"Just before the seminar, I had asked what I could do to be the best vehicle for God. The answer I got was deceptively simple: Just do all the things that you are asked to do. I mulled over this insight and decided I could commit to it.

"I would do everything that was asked of me during the next four days.

"Thursday afternoon I was standing in the central office where we coordinate all the functions of the conference. A staff member came up to me and asked, 'Do you have a refrigerator in your room?'

"Most of the hotel rooms had no refrigerators. But my room happened to have one. I said, 'Well, actually, yes.'

"She then handed me a paper bag. 'Would you take my lunch for tomorrow over to your hotel and put it in the refrigerator?' she asked.

"I was nonplussed. There was so much to do, and the hotel was a good ten-minute walk. The errand would take a costly half hour. Not to mention that I'd have to turn over my room key so she could fetch the bag early next morning. The whole thing felt uncomfortable, and I was about to refuse.

There is no reality except the one contained within us.

—Hermann Hesse

"But something made me hesitate for a moment. And in that moment, I remembered my promise. Do everything I was asked to do.

"So I took the bag and headed for the skyway to the hotel. I was grumbling to myself a little as I walked.

"Once at the hotel I ran into the composer of one of the ensemble pieces. Face aglow, he said, 'I'm so happy to have that incredibly skilled cello player coming. My whole piece really depends on the cello melody.'

"I didn't have the heart to tell him that the player had just canceled. I shifted back and forth on my feet and smiled weakly.

"He continued, 'Of course there's a woman here all the way from Brisbane, Australia, who's also incredible on cello. She plays in the symphony. Her name is Kaja.' At that moment my walkie-talkie crackled. It was a coworker with a message for the bookroom manager. 'We have a volunteer here who would like to work in the bookroom,' he announced. 'Her name is Kaja, and she's from Australia.'

"I couldn't believe the timing. I immediately got on the air and had my coworker detain Kaja for a few minutes, explaining our dilemma.

"She said she would be happy to help, but she had no cello with her.

"I put the lunch in the refrigerator, wondering at the divine timing involved in meeting the composer and hearing about Kaja—all over a lunch bag.

"The miracle continued from there. 'Well, we've just found a cello player,' I announced to general cheers back at the central office. 'Now we just have to get on the phone and call every music store to find her a cello.'

"The news was not good. Minimum rental was $225

Evidence of trust begets trust, and love is reciprocated by love.

—Plutarch

for a student-grade cello—basically a cardboard box with strings to a skilled player.

"We told Kaja of our problem, and she decided to call the Minnesota Orchestra. Amazingly enough, she connected with the lead cellist, who was interested in her situation. He agreed to meet her outside Orchestra Hall, convenient to the seminar location.

"Kaja went to a meeting at a local hotel and sat down to enjoy the speakers. After a while she heard someone say, 'Just two more minutes,' and thinking the meeting was over, got up to leave. She was out the door by the time she figured out that the two-minute warning was for one of the speakers. But she went outside anyway.

"There she ran into a Japanese fellow. It was the cellist from the Minnesota Orchestra.

"They walked back to her seminar together, and he asked her about the activities. By the time they arrived, he was fascinated with what she was telling him and happy to loan Kaja a priceless German cello.

"For me the gift of this entire experience was in being able to perform the small, menial task of taking someone's lunch over to the hotel—and seeing God use it and me for a much greater purpose."

Being a participant in miracles like this one means you are naturally in the right place at the right time. My friend was in the right place to meet the composer and find the cellist. In the story I told in chapter 6 about finding my dream house, I just happened to be passing it when the real estate agent was putting on the lock box.

Five minutes earlier or later wouldn't have worked for either of us.

The great end of being is to harmonize man with the order of things.

— Oliver Wendell Holmes, Sr.

Walking in Rhythm

In a 1988 article in *Writer's Digest* magazine, author Natalie Goldberg talks about how paying slow and careful attention to life is essential to becoming a good writer. That there is a feeling of harmony, or being part of a natural rhythm, that comes when you do this.

"In slowing down," she says, "you can experience the space in every situation and the opportunity inherent there." Slowing down and paying attention allows each person to walk in rhythm with life.

Instead of complaining that God had hidden Himself, you will give Him thanks for having revealed so much of Himself.

—Blaise Pascal

When I get out of step, when I move through life carelessly, not heeding the natural rhythm, turning points speed by in a blur — and life catches me unaware when the cumulative price of change hits. I've seen this in others as the much-discussed midlife crisis, where someone shucks stability to ride their motorcycle down a deserted highway.

Like a well-edited film unfolding on the screen, the turning points follow each other in a certain order that is beautiful to see. Goldberg is talking about the reminder we can use when we lose the fluidity and pace of life: focusing on the smaller turning points that flow within the larger ones. This is a real key to training ourselves to live in harmony with life.

Bettine Clemen, a world-renowned flutist, said once that when she's preparing to practice or perform, she'll first try to bring as much love into her heart as possible. She does this through a simple exercise of playing one note. As she plays the note, she really concentrates on the sound, the feeling behind it, until she gets to the point where she can feel love. When she feels she's being as clear a vehicle for love as possible, she starts playing.

This technique works well in most arenas of life to help us walk in rhythm, as Goldberg says.

The Disciplines of Change

I'm intrigued that so many authors who write about the mythic basis of our lives also talk about major change encompassing smaller stages. Joseph Campbell's hero's journey includes a call to adventure and vision quest, tests and trials, the return of the hero, and the integration of lessons learned into daily life. Gloria Karpinski calls it the dance of transformation.

These specific stages, as I spoke about in chapter 1, follow a definite pattern.

There's the step of facing the change, which essentially means overcoming the wall of inner resistance to find a new understanding. At some point, you begin to investigate the change and gradually remove any inner obstacles to the change. Not unlike the hero's journey, this is usually a time of testing by some ordeal or severe lesson. Can we let go of fear and replace it with love? This is the most difficult part, but it leads to personal transformation. Then we accept the change and begin to integrate the new person we have become and move on from there.

Remember my turning point in chapter 1, where I was learning to slow down with my work? I went through very specific steps in realizing what was happening and navigating the turning point. First came my old belief that I was valuable to the job only as a producer of materials, and an efficient one at that. Then I encountered the problem with my arm—I could no longer work fast and furiously. I knew a turning point was coming, but I resisted it mightily because I couldn't see how I could be valued if I didn't produce.

Next came a new understanding: my coeditor telling me it really was OK to slow down; in fact it was preferable because she could no longer keep up with me.

What a revelation! Maybe I could be a valued worker without being a production machine. This brought a sense of commitment. I was now eager to see how to fully wear this new role at work. I was alert for a clue, which was happily provided by my friend at lunch that week.

For two years I worked on the next stage of this turning point, acceptance of a new way of being. Now I am integrating my new understanding: that I am valued as a person not just for the quantity I produce. I believe this will last a lifetime, as I translate my new knowledge into working every day.

God speaks through the voice of conscience, holy scriptures, feelings. . . . human love, intuition, dreams.

—Harold Klemp

This change has been life transforming for me because I followed these four stages carefully. Each time I cycled through them—and they repeat over and over as we encounter varied aspects of our change—I looked at how I could take one small step to the next level. I believe the change kneaded out the tight knots of my spiritual center and had a transforming effect because of these small steps.

In *The Artist's Way,* Julia Cameron talks about the trap of making sweeping changes all at once, rather than one small change each day. We like the dramatic side of change. We like to rush to the edge of the cliff and say frantically, "I can't leap! I can't!" Well, you don't have to.

If you listen carefully, each change in your life will present itself in a careful sequence of steps to follow.

Exercise:
Mapping Your Own Steps to Change

Using the steps below, chart your own journey through a change.

1. Facing or realizing the change
2. Removing inner obstacles, exploring the change
3. Assessing current skills, where you are now and how to get where you want to go
4. Envisioning the qualities of your change
5. Setting a goal
6. Taking a step forward
7. Gathering skills to live in the new change

Analyze a recent turning point, whether large or small, inner or outer, using these steps. Can you find the steps within the turning point?

This is especially helpful when you meet a difficult turning point or one that you don't understand. Look to the past, and try this exercise on any change that still puzzles you.

Nothing is to be had for nothing.

—Epictetus

TAKE TIME TO SMELL THE FLOWERS

Midway through my experience with learning to slow down at work, an unexpected gift appeared on my desk one morning.

It was a potted plant of freesias. I had admired them in my coworker's office the day before. They were fragrant, pale-lilac flowers with golden centers.

Surely a sign, I thought at the time, *but of what?*

The freesias lasted ten days. Each morning I enjoyed their heavenly fragrance and color, and as I clipped the spent blossoms I realized a major change had come to me, marked by the life of the plant. I had turned a corner.

I was feeling a lot better about myself at work. The days no longer went by in a blur of machinelike production, and I still had a stack of edited books to show I'd been busy.

I realized with a smile that the freesias had been my own private symbol for the past week or so, reminding me to "stop and smell the flowers."

Who says God doesn't have a sense of humor?

*To see things
as they are,
the eyes must
be open.*

—Antonio
Machado

LESSONS OF LOVE

Over and over in this book, we've talked about how to build, as one workshop participant phrased it, your "loving relationship with change."

There's a secret behind this.

The main key to spiritually successful change is the ability to listen to God. When we listen to God, or life's plan, we gather love into us. And that love chases out fear, stinginess, anger, and concern about change. Love smoothes the uneven currents in change as we listen more closely to God.

The two aspects work in tandem. You become closer to God through love. And, as you grow closer to God, or life's plan, you gather more love to you.

If God feels far away, as happens for me when I am in the testing stage of change, I concentrate on love. I've found that giving—to my husband, my dog, my plants—will soften my heart and bring in a little love. And a little grows until it becomes more.

Slowly there is grace. It comes as a relaxed feeling,

almost like a big sigh, where I give up my tightly held will and start to listen to God.

WE CAN'T DO IT WITHOUT GRACE

We're raised in our modern society to be independent and self-sufficient, a good thing. But there comes a point in changes, especially big ones, where we have to lean on God's grace. We do everything we can ourselves, then we have to let go and let God take over.

Cary had a dramatic experience with this when she spent three months working on a fishing boat in Alaska. She was away from everything and everyone familiar, among strangers who didn't know her.

She had a goal of being a good worker, but things kept unexpectedly going very wrong. She couldn't keep it together. The strain of the incredibly hard physical labor caused her to constantly lose her temper and cry. Spiritual techniques for balance that worked beautifully back home didn't work here.

One night Cary was very discouraged; she saw all the tools she had to handle life and knew that they had proven useless in this totally new situation.

After the three months had passed and she was back home, she reflected on her experience. *What did I learn?* she wondered. And after a while it came: She had learned her own limits. She had seen that her will and her skills could work up to a point, but there would always be tough times in her life when she faced the unexpected and had to lean on God.

"Now I know," Cary told me, "how much I can do and how much is grace, or divine power assisting me. I had to go through this horrible experience, try everything I knew to keep my balance and fail, before I

*Active contemplation . . .
is to awaken
and prepare the
mind, to turn
the heart
towards God, to
arouse a desire
to know God
better.*

—Thomas
   Merton

realized how much God works in my life every day."

I had a similar experience one summer at a lake. We had always anchored a wooden raft several hundred yards offshore to swim to and lie on in the sun. Each summer the raft had stayed anchored, tied to a heavy block of cement sunk to the bottom. But this summer, no matter if the lake was calm or stormy, the raft would loosen itself and by morning be lodged down the lake against someone else's dock.

Not a having and a resting, but a growing and a becoming.

—Matthew Arnold

By the third time I had swum, canoed, or waded to retrieve the raft and reanchor it, I knew something odd was going on. It was a time in my life of great changes, and I felt the raft was a message about them.

What did it mean to me? Well, having a raft to swim out to was an important physical marker for us on the lake. I didn't want to venture far out from the dock without it. And it was familiar; it had been there every summer.

That night I dreamed that something I loved dearly, a beautiful vase, had broken in my home, cracked irreparably, and pieces were all over. The incident upset me terribly. "I'll never get the pieces back together," I kept saying. My inner guide came and held me. "It doesn't matter if things change," he said. In the dream he showed me how my anchor points, the familiar things in my life like the vase or the raft, would break and become dislodged, but I would remain secure if I stayed close to God's love.

Ellen Cotton, granddaughter to Ralph Waldo Emerson, was talking about the difficulties of ranching alone northeast of Wyoming's Big Horn mountains, where she was often snowed in for days or weeks at a time in winter. Gretel Ehrlich, writing in her book *The*

Solace of Open Spaces, asked Ellen how she managed the isolation. Did she possess special qualities of strength? Ellen pulled out an old kaleidoscope. When things got really bad, she gave it a whirl. "See," she told Ehrlich, "it's impossible to keep just one thing in view. It gives way to other things and they're all beautiful."

What happens when we look at things in a new way? When we lose our trusted anchor points? Or our belief that we can handle things just fine with our willpower or our skills?

We grow.

WHAT IS YOUR NORTH STAR?

Friend and writer Jamie Davis wrote me from Oregon, "Several years ago I had an experience where my inner guide said to me, 'Anchor yourself to the North Star.' Have you ever seen one of those long-exposure pictures of the North Star at night? The photographer leaves the shutter of the camera open all night, and you can see all the stars appearing to trace circles around the hub of the North Star as the earth rotates." The North Star is Jamie's symbol of an ultimate anchor point.

It gave Jamie a new dimension to the phrase *turning point* as the hub, the point that changes swirl around. If you can find your own North Star, turning points can become a natural process of life, not something foreign at all.

Later that month, Jamie was given an unexpected gift by his in-laws, who were visiting from abroad. They had recently been on a trip to Alaska and handed him a baseball cap souvenir from that state. On it was the North Star.

Few have greater riches than the joy / That comes to us in visions, / In dreams which nobody can take away.

—Euripedes

As you finish reading this book, do you find you've changed your image of what your own North Star is? Look back in your life or in your journal. How have you altered your idea of turning points and their impact on your life?

Our truest life is when we are in dreams awake.

—Henry David Thoreau

Is your own North Star more clear in your sky now?

It has helped me in the past when grappling with a particularly difficult change to make myself a contract to master change as Soul. It's a powerful reminder that I am not a victim but that I am an agent of change, working with God in my life each moment.

Here's an example of a contract if you'd like to try this exercise.

Exercise:
Writing Your Contract with Yourself about a Change

1. On a blank 5"x7" index card write the following contract to yourself to help you master change:

   Dear _____ (your name):

   I agree to learn as much from _____ (name the change) as possible.

   I agree to pay attention to life as it guides me through this change, because I know I work in partnership with change.

   I acknowledge myself as a cocreator of my life.

   Signed _____

   Date _____

2. Carry this card in your wallet or purse for six months as a reminder.

A NEW ROAD

I loved *The Secret Garden*. It's a book about a child who discovers a hidden walled garden and uses it to heal herself in an unexpected way, through love and compassion for someone else. We each have a secret garden inside ourselves when there is stillness and we can hear the whisperings of God, telling us how to direct our lives.

God makes the divine plan known to us in ways we can handle at any one time—sometimes in humorous ways like my freesias, other times in more serious ways. Each time we are ready for a new and finer level of awareness about our lives and how to welcome the next turning points, the details of that level emerge. Like climbing a ladder, each step offers a new view-point, as well as new spiritual laws to learn.

Moving up spiritually is a process of learning how to see and be at each new level. And each time we move up, we drop old habits that are no longer needed.

This is the essence of a turning point. And it is not an easy process.

The key is staying tuned to God's guidance, and to the rhythm of life. This brings true spiritual freedom—a level beyond coping, beyond getting through each day.

It brings us the ability to relax as God carries us safely home.

Whenever I doubt the presence of God in turning points, I remember that evening at nineteen, when I was crossing the lake in the Ozarks. I remember my feelings of uncertainty—how the ferry carrying my car looked too small, too unsteady, without any security in railings on the sides.

The water looked choppy at first, but I remember

You could not step twice into the same rivers; for other waters are ever flowing on to you.

—Heraclitus

how it smoothed out as we passed the islands in the middle of the lake.

It may look safer to stay onshore or find a longer, harder way around each turning point that comes. But the view from the middle of the lake is much better than the one from shore. And the more times I travel across, the more I trust that I will reach the other side.

The horizon always looks different from there, but there is also an exciting new road to travel.

On all the peaks lies peace.

—Goethe

Ask Yourself:
How Can I Bring More Meaning into My Everyday Changes?

Write the answers to these questions. They may help remind you of your spiritual purpose during change.

1. In what ways has your outlook on change improved as you read this book and practiced the exercises? Write a short description of how you handle change now.

2. In what ways do you still hinder your mastery of change? How can you make best use of and benefit from a present problem or change?

3. In what ways do you trust your heart in change? How can you do this more?

4. How can you begin to work more closely with life, or God, in future changes?

EXERCISES

BIBLIOGRAPHY

With gratitude for the opportunity
to use excerpts from the following works:

Anderson, Linda C. *35 Golden Keys to Who You Are & Why You're Here*. Minneapolis: ECKANKAR, 1997.

Archer Butcher, Ann. "The Power of 'HU,'" *Earth to God, Come In Please* . . . Minneapolis: ECKANKAR, 1991.

Bailey, Joseph V. *The Serenity Principle: Finding Inner Peace in Recovery*. San Francisco: Harper & Row, 1990.

Bass, Rick. *Winter: Notes from Montana*. Boston: Houghton Mifflin, 1991. Reprinted by permission of Houghton Mifflin Company/ Seymour Lawrence. All rights reserved.

Bender, Sue. *Plain and Simple: A Woman's Journey to the Amish*. San Francisco: HarperSanFrancisco, 1989.

Bennett, Laura Gilmour. *By All That Is Sacred*. New York: Avon Books, 1991.

Blackwell, Frances. "Love Never Dies," *ECKANKAR Journal* 18 (1994): 29–31.

Borysenko, Joan. *Fire in the Soul: A New Psychology of Spiritual Optimism*. New York: Warner Books, 1993.

Brown, Les. *Live Your Dreams*. New York: William Morrow and Company, Inc., 1992.

Bryan, Mark, and Julia Cameron. *The Money Drunk: 90 Days to Financial Freedom*. New York: Ballantine Books, 1992.

Burnett, Carol. *One More Time*. New York: Avon Books, 1987.

Burns, David D. *Ten Days to Self-Esteem*. New York: William Morrow, 1993.

359

Cameron, Julia, with Mark Bryan. *The Artist's Way: A Spiritual Path to Higher Creativity.* New York: G. P. Putnam's Sons, 1992.

Cerminara, Gina. *Many Lives, Many Loves.* New York: William Sloane Associates, 1963.

Chapman, Joyce. *Journaling for Joy: Writing Your Way to Personal Growth and Freedom: The Workbook.* Van Nuys, Calif.: Newcastle Publishing, 1995.

Chopra, Deepak, and Judith Sills. "How to Be Your Best in '94." *McCall's,* January 1994, 105–6.

Cohen, Sherry Suib. *Secrets of a Very Good Marriage: Lessons from the Sea.* New York: Carol Southern Books, 1993.

Collins, Terah Kathryn. *The Western Guide to Feng Shui: Creating Balance, Harmony, and Prosperity in Your Environment.* Carlsbad, Calif.: Hay House, 1996.

Cook, Marshall J. *Slow Down . . . and Get More Done.* Cincinnati: Betterway Books, 1993.

Cousineau, Phil, ed. *The Hero's Journey: The World of Joseph Campbell.* San Francisco: Harper & Row, 1990.

Davidson, Jeff. *Breathing Space: Living and Working at a Comfortable Pace in a Sped-Up Society.* New York: MasterMedia Limited, 1991.

Ehrlich, Gretel. *The Solace of Open Spaces.* New York: Penguin Books, 1985.

Elgin, Duane. "Discovering Simplicity," *Simple Living,* Vol. 1, No. 1, 1. Excerpted by permission of *Simple Living,* 2319 N. 45th St., P.O. Box 149, Seattle, WA 98130, 206-464-4300.

Epel, Naomi. *Writers Dreaming.* New York: Carol Southern Books, 1993.

Fahden, Allen. *Innovation on Demand: How to benefit from the coming deluge of change: make creativity work for you and your company.* Minneapolis: The Illiterati, 1993.

Fields, Rick, with Peggy Taylor, Rex Weyler, and Rick Ingrasci. *Chop Wood, Carry Water.* Los Angeles: Jeremy P. Tarcher, 1984.

Fisher, Mary Pat. *Heart of Gold: The Light Within Life.* Storrs, Conn.: Fenton Valley Press, 1985.

Fontana, David. *The Secret Language of Dreams: A Visual Key to Dreams and Their Meanings.* San Francisco: Chronicle Books, 1994.

Glaser, Elizabeth, and Laura Palmer. *In the Absence of Angels: A Hollywood Family's Courageous Story.* New York: G. P. Putnam's Sons, 1991.

Goldberg, Natalie. "Slowing Down." *Writer's Digest,* August 1988, 39–40.

Grof, Christina, and Stanislav Grof. *The Stormy Search for the Self: A Guide to Personal Growth through Transformational Crisis.* Los Angeles: Jeremy P. Tarcher, 1990.

Hay, Louise L. *You Can Heal Your Life.* Carlsbad, Calif.: Hay House, 1984, 1987.

Hey, Barbara. "Changing Times." *SELF,* August 1989, 150–55.

Houston, Pam. "The Meaning of Success (revised)," *ELLE,* January 1996, 91–92.

Hugo, Richard. *The Triggering Town: Lectures and Essays on Poetry and Writers.* New York: W. W. Norton, 1979.

Hunt, Lynn. "Six Steps to Use Writing to Understand a Dream," *The ECK Writers Update,* January 1996, 6–7.

James, Jennifer. *Success Is the Quality of Your Journey.* New York: Newmarket Press, 1986.

Johnson, Debbie. *How to Think Yourself Thin.* Portland: Deborah Johnson Publishing, 1994.

Karpinski, Gloria D. *Where Two Worlds Touch: Spiritual Rites of Passage.* New York: Ballantine Books, 1990.

Kelly, Marjorie. "Breakup, resurgence of AT&T offer a lesson about change," *Minneapolis Star Tribune,* March 4, 1996, D3.

Keyes, Ralph. *Chancing It.* New York: Little, Brown, 1985.

Klemp, Harold. "Turning Points," The *Mystic World,* Spring 1992.

——————, *Ask the Master,* Book 2. Minneapolis: ECKANKAR, 1994.

——————, *The Dream Master,* Mahanta Transcripts, Book 8. Minneapolis: ECKANKAR, 1993.

——————, *The Drumbeat of Time,* Mahanta Transcripts, Book 10. Minneapolis: ECKANKAR, 1995.

——————, *The Golden Heart,* Mahanta Transcripts, Book 4. Minneapolis: ECKANKAR, 1990.

——————, *The Living Word,* Book 2. Minneapolis: ECKANKAR, 1996.

——————, *The Spiritual Exercises of ECK.* Minneapolis: ECKANKAR, 1993.

——————, *What Is Spiritual Freedom?* Mahanta Transcripts, Book 11. Minneapolis: ECKANKAR, 1995.

Krantz, Judith. "Tips on a Happy Marriage," *New Woman,* February 1996, 72–73.

Lara, Adair. *Slowing Down in a Speeded Up World.* Berkeley: Conari Press, 1994. Excerpted by permission from Conari Press, 800-685-9595.

Lawrence, Brother. *The Practice of the Presence of God.* White Plains, N.Y.: Peter Pauper Press, 1963.

Layard, John. *The Lady of the Hare: A Study in the Healing Power of Dreams.* Boston: Shambhala, 1988.

Levine, Judith. "Reconciliation: A Daughter Finds an Unexpected Blessing in the Tragedy of Her Father's Illness," *New Woman,* November 1995, 61.

Lewis, C. S. *The Seeing Eye and Other Selected Essays from Christian Reflections.* Ed. Walter Hooper. New York: Ballantine Books, 1967.

Lindbergh, Anne Morrow. *Gift from the Sea.* New York: Vintage Books, 1978.

Marsh, Robert. *We Are Not Alone: How ECK Masters Guide Our Spiritual Lives Today.* Minneapolis: ECKANKAR, 1994.

Mattimore, Bryan W. *99% Inspiration: Tips, Tales & Techniques for Liberating Your Business Creativity.* New York: Amacom, 1994.

Mead, Nathaniel. "Breakthroughs in Cancer Research," *Natural Health,* January/February 1996, 82–85, 135.

Merton, Thomas. *What Is Contemplation?* Springfield, Ill.: Templegate Publishers, 1978.

Millman, Dan. *Way of the Peaceful Warrior: A Book that Changes Lives.* Tiburon, Calif.: H J Kramer, 1984. Reprinted by permission of H J Kramer, P.O. Box 1082, Tiburon, CA 94920. All rights reserved.

Moore, Mary Carroll. *Turning Points: How to Handle Change in Your Life.* Minneapolis: ECKANKAR, 1995.

Murphy, Francis, ed. *Walt Whitman, The Complete Poems.* Middlesex, Eng.: Penguin Education, 1975.

Nelsen, Jane. *Understanding: Eliminating Stress and Finding Serenity in Life and Relationships.* Rocklin, Calif.: Prima Publishing & Communications, 1988, 800-632-8676.

Pilgrim, Susan. *Living InSync: Creating Your Life with Balance and Purpose.* Deerfield Beach, Fla.: Health Communications, 1995.

Progoff, Ira. *At a Journal Workshop: The Basic Text and Guide for Using the Intensive Journal Process.* New York: Dialogue House Library, 1975.

Redford, Robert. "Family Values." *Vogue,* November 1992, 149–52.

Reynolds, David K. *A Thousand Waves: A Sensible Life Style for Sensible People.* New York: William Morrow, 1990.

Rico, Gabriele Lusser. *Writing the Natural Way: Using Right-Brain Techniques to Release Your Expressive Powers.* Los Angeles: J. P. Tarcher, 1983.

—————, *Pain and Possibility: Writing Your Way Through Personal Crisis.* Los Angeles: Jeremy P. Tarcher, Inc., 1991.

Robbins, John, and Ann Mortifee. *In Search of Balance: Discovering Harmony in a Changing World.* Tiburon, Calif.: H J Kramer, 1991. Reprinted by permission of H J Kramer, P.O. Box 1082, Tiburon, CA 94920. All rights reserved.

Ronner, John. *Do You Have a Guardian Angel? and Other Questions Answered about Angels.* Murfreesboro, Tenn.: Mamre Press, 1985.

Ross, Ruth. *Prospering Woman: A Complete Guide to Achieving the Full, Abundant Life.* Mill Valley, Calif.: Whatever Publishing, 1982. Reprinted with permission of New World Library, Novato, CA 94949.

Ryan, Micheal "Why People Fail—And Why They Don't Have To," *Parade,* May 22, 1994, 4–5.

Sarback, Susan, with Paula Jones. *Capturing Radiant Color in Oils.* Cincinnati: North Light Books, 1994.

Sarton, May. *Journal of a Solitude.* Copyright © 1973 by May Sarton. New York: W. W. Norton, 1973.

—————, *Plant Dreaming Deep.* Copyright © 1968 by May Sarton. New York: W. W. Norton & Company, 1968.

Sessums, Kevin. "Never Look Back," *Vanity Fair,* February 1996, 80.

Sinetar, Marsha. *Elegant Choices, Healing Choices.* New York: Paulist Press, 1988.

Spencer, Sabina A., and John D. Adams. *Life Changes: Growing through Personal Transitions,* © 1990 by Sabina A. Spencer and John D. Adams. Reproduced for Mary Carroll Moore by permission of Impact Publishers, P.O. Box 1094, San Luis Obispo, CA 93406. Further reproduction prohibited.

Stoddard, Alexandra. *Making Choices: The Joy of a Courageous Life.* New York: William Morrow, 1994.

Taylor, Susan L. *In the Spirit: The Inspirational Writings of Susan L. Taylor.* New York: Armistad Press, 1993.

Tieger, Paul D., and Barbara Barron-Tieger. *Do What You Are: Discover the Perfect Career for You Through the Secrets of Personality Type.* Boston: Little, Brown, 1992.

Volkman, Arthur G., comp. *Thoreau on Man and Nature.* Mount Vernon, N.Y.: Peter Pauper Press, 1960.

Ware, James, trans. *The Sayings of Confucius.* New York: The New American Library of World Literature, 1955.

Watson, Catherine. "In Borneo, a Blessing Disguised as a Curse." *Minneapolis Star Tribune,* 26 September 1993, 1G, 3G.

Welwood, John. *Journey of the Heart: Intimate Relationships and the Path of Love.* New York: HarperPerennial, 1990.

Wiesel, Elie. *Sages and Dreamers: Biblical, Talmudic, and Hasidic Portraits and Legends.* New York: Simon & Schuster, 1991. Reprinted with the permission of Rawson/Scribner, a Division of Simon & Schuster.

Williams, Becky. "How God Answered Me," *ECKANKAR Journal,* 1996, 65–67.

FOR FURTHER READING AND STUDY*

35 Golden Keys to Who You Are & Why You're Here

By Linda C. Anderson

Discover thirty-five golden keys to mastering your spiritual destiny through the ancient teachings of Eckankar, Religion of the Light and Sound of God. The dramatic, true stories in this book equal anything found in the spiritual literature of today. Learn ways to immediately bring more love, peace, and purpose to your life.

The Spiritual Exercises of ECK

Harold Klemp

This book is a staircase with 131 steps. It's a special staircase, because you don't have to climb all the steps to get to the top. Each step is a spiritual exercise, a way to help you explore your inner worlds. And what awaits you at the top? The doorway to spiritual freedom, self-mastery, wisdom, and love.

Journey of Soul

Mahanta Transcripts, Book 1

Harold Klemp

This collection of talks by Eckankar's spiritual leader shows how to apply the unique Spiritual Exercises of ECK—dream exercises, visualizations, and Soul Travel methods—to unlock your natural abilities as Soul. Learn how to hear the little-known Sounds of God and follow Its Light for practical daily guidance and upliftment.

The Dream Master

Mahanta Transcripts, Book 8

Harold Klemp

If you don't believe dreams are important, you're missing out on more than half your life. Harold Klemp, the Dream Master, can show you how to become more aware of your dreams so you can enjoy a better life. But *The Dream Master* is not just about dreams. It gives you the keys to spiritual survival, and is about living life to the fullest on your way home to God.

*Available at your local bookstore. If unavailable, call (612) 544-0066. Or write: ECKANKAR Books, P.O. Box 27300, Minneapolis, MN 55427 U.S.A.

ABOUT THE AUTHOR

Mary Carroll Moore is an award-winning author and national columnist with the *Los Angeles Times* syndicate. Her books have been feature selections of *Prevention* magazine and Homestyle book clubs. Her columns and articles have appeared in eighty-six newspapers and magazines in the U.S. and Canada.

Mary has faced and survived cancer, bankruptcy, and the dissolution of a marriage. In this book, she candidly, sometimes humorously, discusses the most devastating moments in her life. Mary shows how she overcame the fear of change with insights gained through Eckankar, Religion of the Light and Sound of God. Today she is a successful author, editor, and columnist. She lives a healthy, love-filled life in the marriage and home of her dreams.

During her twenty-five years as a specialist in the food, health, and self-help fields, Mary has been a guest on over thirty-five television and radio talk shows, including *Evening Magazine;* "All Things Considered," Minnesota Public Radio; and Lifetime Cable Network.

As an ordained minister in Eckankar, Mary has led workshops around the world on how to deal with change through heightened spiritual awareness. Her educational background, including a master's degree from San Diego State University, also helped her design practical tools to use life's turning points as catalysts for finding deeper spiritual meaning.

In her book *How to Master Change in Your Life,* she gives sixty-seven specific exercises for handling change successfully—

368

whether in home life, business, career, marriage, parenting, friendships, or health.

"People want more than emotional and psychological methods for dealing with change," she explains. "They're hungry for the spiritual wisdom and love that are the gifts found in every turning point of life."

For information about Eckankar workshops on change and spirituality or to share stories about your own spiritual journey, write to:

Eckankar
Att: Public Information
P.O. Box 27300
Minneapolis, MN 55427 U.S.A.
FAX: 612-474-1127